1980s Project Studies/Council on Foreign Relations

STUDIES FORTHCOMING

Some 20 additional volumes of the 1980s Project work will be appearing in the course of the next year or two. Most will contain independent but related studies concerning issues of potentially great importance in the next decade and beyond, such as resource management, human rights, food policy, population studies, and relations between the developing and developed societies, among many others. Additionally, a number of volumes will be devoted to particular regions of the world, concentrating especially on political and economic development trends outside the industrialized West.

Rich and Poor Nations in the World Economy

Rich and Poor Nations in the World Economy

ALBERT FISHLOW

CARLOS F. DÍAZ-ALEJANDRO

RICHARD R. FAGEN

ROGER D. HANSEN

1980s Project/Council on Foreign Relations

McGRAW-HILL BOOK COMPANY
New York   St. Louis   San Francisco
Auckland   Bogotá   Düsseldorf   Johannesburg   London   Madrid
Mexico   Montreal   New Delhi   Panama   Paris   São Paulo
Singapore   Sydney   Tokyo   Toronto

The Council on Foreign Relations, Inc., is a nonprofit and nonpartisan organization devoted to promoting improved understanding of international affairs through the free exchange of ideas. Its membership of about 1,700 persons throughout the United States is made up of individuals with special interest and experience in international affairs. The Council has no affiliation with and receives no funding from the United States government.

The Council publishes the quarterly journal *Foreign Affairs* and, from time to time, books and monographs which in the judgment of the Council's Committee on Studies are responsible treatments of significant international topics worthy of presentation to the public. The 1980s Project is a research effort of the Council; as such, 1980s Project Studies have been similarly reviewed through procedures of the Committee on Studies. As in the case of all Council publications, statements of fact and expressions of opinion contained in 1980s Project Studies are the sole responsibility of their authors.

The editor of this book was Abe Goldman for the Council on Foreign Relations. Thomas Quinn and Michael Hennelly were the editors for McGraw-Hill Book Company. Christopher Simon was the designer. Teresa Leaden supervised the production. This book was set in Times Roman by Creative Book Services, Inc.

Printed and bound by R. R. Donnelley & Sons.

Library of Congress Cataloging in Publication Data

Main entry under title:

Rich and poor nations in the world economy.

(1980s project/Council on Foreign Relations)
Includes bibliographical references and index.
1. International economic relations—Addresses,
essays, lectures.   2.   Underdeveloped areas—Foreign
economic relations—Addresses, essays, lectures.
I. Fishlow, Albert. II. Series: Council on Foreign
Relations.   1980s project/Council on Foreign Relations.
HF1411.R49   338.91   77-14319
ISBN 0-07-021114-0
ISBN 0-07-021115-9 pbk.

1 2 3 4 5 6 7 8 9 R R D R R D 7 8 3 2 1 0 9 8

Contents

THE POLITICAL ECONOMY OF NORTH-SOUTH RELATIONS: AN OVERVIEW AND AN ALTERNATIVE APPROACH

Roger D. Hansen

Foreword: The 1980s Project

No issues have generated more international controversy in recent years than those surrounding economic relations between rich and poor nations. Those relations have been a major focus of the work of the 1980s Project of the Council on Foreign Relations. The studies in this volume and those in a companion volume, *Reducing Global Inequities,* by Howard Wriggins and Gunnar Adler-Karlsson, arise from that work. Separately and jointly, they convey a sense of the diversity of the interests and goals of what have come to be called Northern and Southern states. And they prescribe ways in which often-conflicting interests may be harmonized and goals brought nearer achievement. They are all part of a stream of studies to be produced in the course of the 1980s Project, each one dealing with an issue likely to be of international concern during the next 10 to 20 years.

The ambitious purpose of the 1980s Project is to examine important political and economic problems not only individually but in relationship to one another. Some studies or books produced by the Project will primarily emphasize the interrelationship of issues. In the case of other, more specifically focused studies, a considerable effort has been made to write, review, and criticize them in the context of more general Project work. Each Project study is thus capable of standing on its own; at the same time it has been shaped by a broader perspective.

The 1980s Project had its origins in the widely held recognition that many of the assumptions, policies, and institutions that have characterized international relations during the past 30 years are inadequate to the demands of today and the foreseeable demands of the period between now and 1990 or so. Over the course of the next decade, substantial adaptation of institutions and behavior will be needed to respond to the changed circumstances of the 1980s and beyond. The Project seeks to identify those future conditions and the kinds of adaptation they might require. It is not the Project's purpose to arrive at a single or exclusive set of goals. Nor does it focus upon the foreign policy or national interests of the United States alone. Instead, it seeks to identify goals that are compatible with the perceived interests of most states, despite differences in ideology and in level of economic development.

The published products of the Project are aimed at a broad readership, including policy makers and potential policy makers and those who would influence the policy-making process, but are confined to no single nation or region. The authors of Project studies were therefore asked to remain mindful of interests broader than those of any one society and to take fully into account the likely realities of domestic politics in the principal societies involved. All those who have worked on the Project, however, have tried not to be captives of the status quo; they have sought to question the inevitability of existing patterns of thought and behavior that restrain desirable change and to look for ways in which those patterns might in time be altered or their consequences mitigated.

The 1980s Project is at once a series of separate attacks upon a number of urgent and potentially urgent international problems and also a collective effort, involving a substantial number of persons in the United States and abroad, to bring those separate approaches to bear upon one another and to suggest the kinds of choices that might be made among them. The Project involves more than 300 participants. A small central staff and a steering Coordinating Group have worked to define the questions and to assess the compatibility of policy prescriptions. Nearly 100 authors, from more than a dozen countries, have been at work on separate studies. Ten working groups of specialists and generalists have been convened to subject the Project's studies to

critical scrutiny and to help in the process of identifying interrelationships among them.

The 1980s Project is the largest single research and studies effort the Council on Foreign Relations has undertaken in its 55-
year history, comparable in conception only to a major study of
the postwar world, the War and Peace Studies, undertaken by the
Council during the Second World War. At that time, the impetus
to the effort was the discontinuity caused by worldwide conflict
and the visible and inescapable need to rethink, replace, and supplement many of the features of the international system that had
prevailed before the war. The discontinuities in today's world are
less obvious and, even when occasionally quite visible—as in the
abandonment of gold convertibility and fixed monetary
parities—only briefly command the spotlight of public attention.
That new institutions and patterns of behavior are needed in many
areas is widely acknowledged, but the sense of need is less
urgent—existing institutions have not for the most part dramatically failed and collapsed. The tendency, therefore, is to make do
with outmoded arrangements and to improvise rather than to undertake a basic analysis of the problems that lie before us and of
the demands that those problems will place upon all nations.

The 1980s Project is based upon the belief that serious effort
and integrated forethought can contribute—indeed, are indispensable—to progress in the next decade toward a more humane,
peaceful, productive, and just world. And it rests upon the hope
that participants in its deliberations and readers of Project
publications—whether or not they agree with an author's point of
view—may be helped to think more informedly about the opportunities and the dangers that lie ahead and the consequences of
various possible courses of future action.

The 1980s Project has been made possible by generous grants
from the Ford Foundation, the Lilly Endowment, the Andrew W.
Mellon Foundation, the Rockefeller Foundation, and the German Marshall Fund of the United States. Neither the Council on
Foreign Relations nor any of those foundations is responsible for
statements of fact and expressions of opinion contained in publications of the 1980s Project; they are the sole responsibility of the

individual authors under whose names they appear. But the Council on Foreign Relations and the staff of the 1980s Project take great pleasure in placing those publications before a wide readership both in the United States and abroad.

Edward L. Morse and Richard H. Ullman

1980s PROJECT WORKING GROUPS

During 1975 and 1976, ten Working Groups met to explore major international issues and to subject initial drafts of 1980s Project studies to critical review. Those who chaired Project Working Groups were:

Cyrus R. Vance, Working Group on Nuclear Weapons and Other Weapons of Mass Destruction

Leslie H. Gelb, Working Group on Armed Conflict

Roger Fisher, Working Group on Transnational Violence and Subversion

Rev. Theodore M. Hesburgh, Working Group on Human Rights

Joseph S. Nye, Jr., Working Group on the Political Economy of North-South Relations

Harold Van B. Cleveland, Working Group on Macroeconomic Policies and International Monetary Relations

Lawrence C. McQuade, Working Group on Principles of International Trade

William Diebold, Jr., Working Group on Multinational Enterprises

Eugene B. Skolnikoff, Working Group on the Environment, the Global Commons, and Economic Growth

Miriam Camps, Working Group on Industrial Policy

1980s PROJECT STAFF

Persons who have held senior professional positions on the staff of the 1980s Project for all or part of its duration are:

Miriam Camps	*Catherine Gwin*
William Diebold, Jr.	*Roger D. Hansen*
Tom J. Farer	*Edward L. Morse*
David C. Gompert	*Richard H. Ullman*

Richard H. Ullman was Director of the 1980s Project from its inception in 1974 until July 1977, when he became Chairman of the Project Coordinating Group. At that time, Edward L. Morse became Executive Director of the Project.

PROJECT COORDINATING GROUP

The Coordinating Group of the 1980s Project had a central advisory role in the work of the Project. Its members as of December 31, 1976, were:

COMMITTEE ON STUDIES

The Committee on Studies of the Board of Directors of the Council on Foreign Relations is the governing body of the 1980s Project. The Committee's members as of December 31, 1976, were:

Rich and Poor
Nations in the
World Economy

Introduction

Roger D. Hansen

One of the most publicized issues of international politics in recent years has been the claim of the governments of a large majority of the world's states, inhabited by more than half the world's population, that they are not receiving an "equitable" share of the world's wealth and power. The essays that follow consider various aspects of this issue, and they represent a major part of the 1980s Project's work on what has come to be called, for shorthand purposes, "North-South relations." The countries generally covered by the term *South* range from the oil-rich and rapidly industrializing nations of OPEC through the so-called Third World countries (middle-range developing countries with per capita incomes generally exceeding $900 per year, an expanding modern industrial base, and generally favorable growth prospects) to the so-called Fourth World (the world's poorest countries, concentrated in South Asia, black Africa, and the Caribbean region, in which annual per capita incomes fall below $200, the industrial base is generally very narrow, and growth prospects are, at best, uncertain). The term *North* is generally equated with the richer countries of Western Europe, North America, and Asia (Japan, Australia, and New Zealand).[1]

[1] Other 1980s Project volumes also concerned with North-South issues include the companion volume to this one, *Reducing Global Inequities*, by Howard Wriggins and Gunnar Adler-Karlsson. In addition, there will be a series of 1980s regional volumes, each analyzing and exploring the probable economic and political development of the region in the coming years and the

1

As the following essays amply demonstrate, North-South relations are the subject of considerable dissensus among the community of policy makers and academic specialists for whom they are a central and continuing professional concern, just as they are a source of contention among nations. Within the community of analysts, dissensus can be traced to at least three major sources. First, there is disagreement on the definition of what is at issue in North-South relations. What is the nature of the present developing-country "challenge" to the international system? Does it derive primarily from a growing Southern desire for increased economic benefits from the system? Is it, instead, primarily a drive for enhanced developing-country identity, autonomy, and psychic "status" in the global system? Or is it best understood as part of an endless pattern of realpolitik in the nation-state system whereby "status quo" powers (essentially the developed, Northern countries) are being challenged by a group of "revisionist" states demonstrating a growing desire for their own place in the sun and their feeling that the structure of the present system denies them equal access to that place in a great number of political, economic, technological, and organizational ways?

A second source of dissensus among analysts is rooted in the rank ordering of individual value preferences. As the essays in this volume dramatically illustrate, analysts of North-South relations can share similar values but arrive at very different prescriptive conclusions simply because they order those values differently. To cite but one example, an analyst like Carlos Díaz-Alejandro, who places major emphasis on the goal of *state autonomy* in the international system, will develop a set of prescriptions that differ greatly in their first-order implications from those of other analysts whose personal value preferences give a higher standing to the goal of welfare/equity, particularly if their emphasis is on *interpersonal* equity considerations, which generally imply a much more "interventionist" international system.

---

role it might play in world politics. The volumes will focus on the Middle East and North Africa, Latin America, Africa, and Southeast Asia.

Finally, dissensus is rooted in opposing judgments concerning the linkages between normative policy prescriptions on the one hand and intended results on the other. Here the basis of contention will often be a set of empirical issues, to wit, What would be the actual effect of certain international economic reforms on the prospects for more rapid and equitable economic development in the South? As illustrated in the essays in this volume, Albert Fishlow and Richard Fagen will probably never agree on the same set of policy prescriptions because they disagree on their assessment of the linkage between certain international reforms and the consequences of those reforms for the process of economic development. As their essays also demonstrate, their differences are at least partly rooted in differing value preferences. But a careful reading of Fishlow's essay will establish beyond doubt his concern for the "equity question" that is central to Fagen's analysis; therefore, a good part of the explanation of their divergent views on policy prescriptions lies in judgments about the capacity of certain policies to achieve goals that both authors share.

Of the challenges faced by the authors of the essays in this volume, Albert Fishlow's was perhaps the most difficult. He was invited to produce an essay that would examine the capacity of a reformed international economic system to support the process of rapid and sustainable economic development within the world's developing countries. Implicit in his task were the following constraints: (1) remain within the general framework of a *global* international economic system, not one characterized by regional blocs and preferences; (2) pay attention to the political constraints that would set limits to the *types* and *degrees* of reform considered "feasible" over the relevant time period of interest to the project; and (3) prescribe a set of reforms that, within the constraints introduced by points 1 and 2 above, would have a high probability of increasing the pace of economic development and achieving the general goals of a "moderate international order" implicit in the work of the 1980s Project.

Fishlow met this challenge in an essay that sets forth goals and prescribes policies with considerable precision and yet also makes evident his notion of present-day constraints to the adoption of these policies and the achievement of these goals. Readers should ponder Fishlow's arguments and then ask themselves, Do the goals set forth seem appropriate in the context of the North-South arena over the coming 15–20 years? Can the prescribed policies achieve them? And can the present constraints on the reforms suggested by Fishlow be overcome within a relevant time period? No two readers will respond identically to these three questions. But Fishlow's excellent essay forces one to address them.

The essay consolidates into a very few pages both Northern and Southern misperceptions of empirical issues concerning the functioning of the present international economic system and succinctly analyzes the misperceptions that each side of the North-South debate holds about the desires and the goals of the other. It then anesthetizes the "New International Economic Order" (NIEO), diagnoses its strengths and its ailments, performs some radical surgery on it, and in the process creates a "Fishlow International Economic Order" whose general principles are too compelling to be dismissed without very serious consideration by either radicals or conservatives. In essence, Fishlow has responded to both the *perceived* and the *real* economic needs of the developing countries but in doing so has considerably enhanced the analytical and conceptual validity of their case for reform.

The reader, like Fishlow himself, is left to question the feasibility of his program of reforms. As Fishlow notes in his discussion of policy prescriptions, "Three priority areas in which significant measures can be taken to make market mechanisms operate more effectively are trade, international capital flows, and direct private investment. Each set of transactions occurs under circumstances that often fail to conform to the competitive model."[2] Do Northern governments have either the will or the *political capacity* to remove most of the market imperfections detailed by Fishlow, imperfections that, in his view, constrain both aggregate developing-country growth rates and the possibilities for greater degrees of interpersonal equity *within* developing countries?

[2]See Fishlow's essay in this volume, p. 56.

The reader is also left to consider Fishlow's normative preferences and his analysis of the linkages between his prescribed policies and the goals that he himself seeks to achieve. Fishlow devotes considerable attention to domestic equity questions within developing countries and argues that his prescribed policies can achieve far greater degrees of *internal equity* at the same time that they increase aggregate growth rates. But he would be the first to note that on this crucial issue "domestic policies count," and that there may be a slip between posited policy and achievement of the goal. (As noted below, this *possibility* in Fishlow's view becomes in Fagen's a high *probability*.) That Fishlow has ultimately produced more questions than answers is hardly surprising given the extremely difficult nature of his task. But his essay is a cogent and provocative starting point from which to contemplate the problems, prospects, and possibilities inherent in North-South relations in the 1980s.

While Fishlow was asked what a reformed version of the present international economic system might look like, Carlos Díaz was asked whether a far more radical restructuring might offer greater opportunity for the development prospects of most Southern countries. Specifically, Díaz was asked to examine the degree to which the currently fashionable concepts of "Southern self-reliance" and "delinking" from the present international economic system might contain elements of a strategy that would help to achieve Southern goals in the realms of economic development, domestic equity, and national autonomy. In asking Díaz to analyze and critique the case for *delinking*—in short, a policy of limiting or completely dissolving certain types of international economic ties between developing countries, either singly or as groups, and the present international economic system—the Project was requesting the analysis of a concept that, while fashionable at the rhetorical level, has never been advanced with any conceptual rigor or comprehensiveness. And as Díaz remarked, his "definitive" critique of the strategy will have to await something approaching a "definitive" presentation.

The absence of that presentation has not prevented Díaz from producing a comprehensive work that in one essay (1) explains as well as analyzes the origins of developing-country interest in the concept of delinking, emphasizing the fundamentally political origins of this line of thought; (2) constructs and then critiques the delinking approach in its pure form; (3) presents his own version of a much reformed international economic system that would incorporate the relevant insights rooted in·the delinking concept; and (4) unleashes some parting obiter dicta that, while not of direct relevance to the issue of delinking in either pure or refined form, could hardly be more pertinent—indeed crucial— to a clearer understanding of the political, psychological, and perceptual as well as the economic aspects of the present North-South relationship.

In the course of his essay Díaz persistently draws the reader's attention to the political realities that underlie much of the economic analysis and discussion generally monopolizing today's North-South debate. His critique reveals the weaknesses in the analytical underpinnings for *both* the extreme delinking (Southern) case and the extreme laissez faire (Northern) case. It further emphasizes the political and sociological roots of the decoupling notion, roots that are intimately linked to the goals of national autonomy and domestic equity. Finally, and obviously related to this Southern desire for greater national autonomy, Díaz's examination of the political foundation of the present (as well as past) international system(s) presents a good deal of evidence that international economic structures are inevitably skewed in favor of the nation-states and interests groups that have created and sustained them and that the day-to-day result of these structural underpinnings is an ongoing process producing international economic outcomes biased in favor of the system's creators.

Against this analytical background Díaz tries his own hand at system reform, and the reader will be interested in comparing his prescriptive proposals with those of Fishlow. Indeed, the degree of similarity between Díaz's and Fishlow's reform proposals is both striking and interesting—all the more so given the different tasks, starting points, and modes of analysis that characterize the two essays.

Both Fishlow and Díaz view the present historical moment as somewhat propitious for the introduction of reforms that would strengthen the prospects for movement toward the goals of increased global welfare, domestic equity, and national autonomy.

6

While neither is Panglossian enough to lose sight of the constraints on such a process, Richard Fagen's contribution to this collection of essays balances their general optimism by emphasizing those constraints.

Fagen, a political scientist, was asked to reflect upon the potential of a "reformed" international economic system to enhance Southern developmental goals and the welfare and autonomy goals at the *personal* as well as the *state* level. The profundity of his pessimism, it should be noted, flows to a considerable degree from his *normative* concerns, which focus on the issue of "absolute poverty" in developing countries, and his *analytical* observations, which lead him to believe that even rapid growth rates in developing countries will do little to alleviate the absolute poverty problem (or significantly alter present patterns of highly unequal income distribution). At the very outset, he puts forward the premise that while Southern elites can be expected to win fairer shares of global product and opportunities over the next decade through an essentially political struggle, this North-South "struggle for fairer shares does not promise an improvement in equity in the South."[3]

Fagen thus suggests that even if all the international economic reforms prescribed by Fishlow and Díaz were to overcome Northern constraints to their acceptance and implementation, those one billion people in the South who presently live at the very margin of existence would benefit little—if at all—from the increasing shares of global product that would be gradually shifted to the developing countries.

The pessimism [on this issue] derives from linked hypotheses arguing that (1) normatively defensible equity goals in the South . . . will be extremely hard if not impossible to meet given the kind of economic development that characterizes the majority of Southern nations; (2) Southern elites and Northern societies more generally have few enduring incentives (and limited structural potential) for altering the dominant patterns of economic development; (3) the only *genre* of changes in the South that would enable serious assaults on the equity issue to be made involve socialist forms of economic organization . . . ; (4) from

[3]See below, p. 165.

7

the Northern point of view these have been and are the most difficult kinds of changes to adjust to domestically and internationally; (5) these kinds of changes on a global scale would seriously threaten, both theoretically and in practice, a moderate international order of the sort envisaged by the 1980s Project.[4]

Fortunately for the reader, Fagen's precise and logical presentation literally defies misunderstanding. On the basis of present empirical evidence and theoretical understanding concerning the issues he raises, one can agree with Fagen, take sharp issue with him, or feel that neither theory nor empirical evidence permits much beyond conjecture at this time. But anyone who seriously entertains a discussion of goals, norms, order, welfare, and equity over the coming 10 to 20 years *must* face the issues raised by Fagen and the analysis that leads to his ultimate pessimism. Most Northerners will disagree with Fagen in larger or smaller degree, as does Fishlow in this volume. But all who do so owe it to themselves and to the profound issues at stake to understand quite clearly what parts of his argument they are rejecting, their own empirical and theoretical reasons for such a rejection, and the probability of error weighted by the goals at stake.

The final essay in this volume will consider in more detail some of the main themes in the essays by Fishlow, Díaz, and Fagen and explore a further major issue in North-South relations that is not directly examined in their work.

[4]Ibid., p. 166.

A New International Economic Order: What Kind?

Albert Fishlow

Introduction

The UN General Assembly, in a Sixth Special Session convened in April 1974 in the immediate aftermath of the petroleum
crisis, concluded its deliberations by committing itself

to work urgently for the establishment of a new international economic
order based on equity, sovereign equality, common interest and cooperation among all states, irrespective of their economic and social
systems, which shall correct inequalities and redress existing injustices,
make it possible to eliminate the widening gap between the developed
and the developing countries and ensure steadily accelerating economic
and social development and peace and justice for present and future
generations.[1]

With this declaration a new phase in international relations
has begun. The North-South cleavage, long in evolution, has
been formally elevated to at least equal prominence with the
global East-West division. The structure of the international
economic system has come to be seen as the principal factor
coloring political interactions among most of the nation-states
of the world. This confrontation of the rich and the poor has
been framed in the language not only of economics but also of
ethics: with striking rapidity it has become the classic struggle
between the privileged and the dispossessed, between the ad-

[1]U.N. General Assembly Resolution 3201 (S-VI), May 1, 1974, as reported
in the *U.N. Monthly Chronicle*, vol. XI, no. 5, May 1974, p. 66.

vantaged and the exploited. Thus, Geoffrey Barraclough proclaimed, "it has become obvious—if it was not obvious before—that we stand at a watershed of history."[2]

As time passes, that initial judgment seems somewhat less apt. Indeed, the subject was never broached in the foreign policy debate between American presidential candidates in the fall of 1976. But for all the quietude and the overshadowing of other more immediate political concerns, the fundamental challenge remains, one to which the industrialized nations are yet to define an adequate response. It is not surprising that they have not. The banner of the New International Economic Order (NIEO) is a symbol not only for a specific comprehensive program but also for the very relevance of the problem of global underdevelopment to the prosperity of the developed world.

How can, and should, the North respond? Neither leaders nor foreign policy analysts have reached consensus. After almost full rejection of both the substance and the rhetoric of the NIEO—undoubtedly in part because it seemed to legitimize and validate OPEC policies—the United States subsequently modified its stand. Kissinger's encyclopedic catalog of proposals at the Seventh Special Session and the compromise resolution that emerged initiated a second, more conciliatory phase that some European nations had earlier advocated. Its principal fruit thus far has been the Jamaica reform of the International Monetary Fund (IMF); the Paris Conference on International Economic Cooperation (CIEC) and the UN Conference on Trade and Development (UNCTAD) have seen much more modest progress.

To some conservative critics, this stalemate has been anticipated and welcome. They, on the whole, find the present structure of international economic relations not merely protective of the interests of the North but also equitable. The principle of nondiscriminatory liberal trade is not only appropriate, they feel, but already largely governs economic interactions. Concessions to ill-conceived demands inspired by the South would run the

[2]Geoffrey Barraclough, "The Haves and the Have Nots," *New York Review of Books*, May 13, 1976, p. 31.

risk of arousing expectations that would be insatiable and un-realizable. For this school, the major deficiency in the present international economic system is the nationalist, irrational policies of states that make them inadequate competitors; it is the fault not of the industrial world but of themselves that the developing nations are underlings. "Such an approach does not imply bleak prospects for development in Third World countries. As in the past, Third World countries which maintain growth-oriented investment and exchange rate policies will experience rapid economic development."[3]

Radicals are equally skeptical. Any grand global compromise that promotes interdependence and integration into the world economy is likely to reinforce political dependence and internal income inequality while producing limited, if any, economic advantage. Even those who must be regarded as moderates are candid about the priorities. "[Poor nations] must work to establish or strengthen *domestic* structures in order to increase economic justice. . . . If the international climate is unfavorable to more egalitarian patterns in the international economy, the South may have to reduce its participation. . . . Such links with the North have helped to perpetuate change-resisting forces in developing economies."[4] Self-reliant development—giving precedence to basic structural socialist reformulation and international isolation rather than to appropriate exchange-rate policies—is the real hope.

Reformist accommodation is thus not self-evidently a guarantor of a just and flourishing interdependent order in the 1980s. Short-term compromise, even were it attainable, could prove to be an unstable and unenforceable solution. And agreement itself could be precluded by an unintended and unholy alliance of conservative interests in the industrialized nations and radical forces in the developing countries.

[3]Nathaniel Leff, "The New Economic Order—Bad Economics, Worse Politics," *Foreign Policy*, no. 24, Fall 1976, pp. 216–217.
[4]Samuel L. Parmar, "Self Reliant Development in an 'Interdependent' World," in Guy F. Erb and Valeriana Kallab (eds.), *Beyond Dependency*, Praeger, New York, 1975, p. 25.

A more optimistic assessment is justified. The New International Economic Order, despite occasional rhetorical excesses, does not as formulated hinge upon a fundamentally different conception of international economic relationships. It inherently accepts the mutuality of benefits from trade and foreign investment and rejects the Marxist contentions of inevitable exploitation. What it proposes are structural reforms to underwrite a more favorable division of the gains to the Third World than the marketplace presently affords. There is implicit recognition of a positive sum basis for meaningful negotiation and one in which many developing countries might share, albeit not evenly.

There is, moreover, little danger that the coercive power of the South could transform accommodation into a process of continuing economic appeasement. Even admitting significant control over the supply of some raw materials, monopolists are limited to setting price or quantity but not both. There are inherent market limitations to commodity power without the specter of economic and political retaliation even being raised. The OPEC meeting in December 1976 provided vivid testimony.

In the third instance, despite the overriding importance of domestic policies in determining the internal distribution of income, the external environment can make a difference. Countries faced with rising inflation and slowing growth owing to inadequate foreign-exchange earnings have an even more difficult time of designing adequate distributionist policies. Nor does integration into the world economy require complete abdication of national policies and objectives. It provides opportunities and imposes constraints simultaneously—a bittersweet package that both Manchester liberals and neo-Marxist radicals prefer to view partially.

These circumstances and the potential economic gains to the developed countries, as I shall elaborate in Chapter One, lead me to argue that reformism is not only feasible but desirable. In Chapter Two, I offer the principles and priority components of such a reformed international economic structure. In Chapter Three, I enter briefly into the prospects of bringing it about.

A new economic order will not lead to a radically altered global distribution of income, although the South as a whole, and most certainly its relatively higher-income nations, should benefit. Capitalist institutions will survive, but experimentation to satisfy internal egalitarian objectives could lead to more varied economic models. At best it will be a world in which the North-South dichotomy becomes sufficiently blurred to allow for cooperative resolution of pressing universal problems that threaten the prospects for a just and orderly global community of nations.

ONE

The Feasibility of Reform

THE IDEOLOGICAL FOUNDATIONS OF THE NEW INTER-NATIONAL ECONOMIC ORDER

The agenda of specific reforms of the international economic structure advocated by the developing nations is by now well known. A brief recapitulation will therefore suffice. Of longest standing are initiatives to increase the price and volume of developing-country exports: indexed prices for commodities to guarantee stable and favorable terms of trade and preferential access to markets of developed countries. A second category comprises measures to regulate and enhance the beneficial consequences of inflows of foreign private capital: limitations on the scope of activities of multinational corporations; development of independent sources for the transfer of modern, but appropriate, technology; and improved access to capital markets for development finance on more satisfactory terms. A third set of demands relates to the flow of public resources: at a minimum, fulfillment of the goal agreed to by the developed nations that 0.7 percent of GNP be allocated to aid; and a debt moratorium for hard-pressed developing countries burdened by debt service and amortization payments. A fourth area comprehends new rules for the international monetary system: linkage of IMF special drawing rights to needs for development finance and more abundant compensatory finance from the IMF on more generous and less supervised terms. A last group of reforms call for mod-

17

ification of the very decision-making structure of international economic institutions to enhance the role of the South: revised voting allocations in the IMF, World Bank, and the General Agreement on Tariffs and Trade (GATT) and serious, direct negotiations encompassing the full, interrelated agenda.[5]

Stripped of emotional content and extravagant hortatory demands with limited policy consequence—such as insistence upon reallocation of global industrial production—the agenda is not as revolutionary as many commentators seem to have made out. Both those resistant to the Southern cause and those most eloquent in its behalf share in the guilt of exaggeration. Together they have defined a different, perhaps latent, North-South struggle that could evolve. What is at issue now, however, is decidedly *not* the "validity of the economic system which has dominated the world since the great outward thrust of the industrialized West a century ago."[6] Nor is it the excommunicable anticapitalist heresy: "These governments are ideologically committed to the redistribution of wealth and to the frustration of business enterprise which creates wealth. Since the wealth they wish to distribute does not exist in their own countries, they have decided to redistribute the wealth of the United States and the nations of Western Europe."[7]

This is not to deny that a consistent ideology, and one going to the equity of the international economic system, underlies the New International Economic Order. It is not a random or incoherent package of ad hoc reforms. But the organizing theme is a familiar one and is rooted in conventional economic theory to boot. The ideology sustaining principal Third World demands is nothing more or less than the doctrine first enunciated by Raul Prebisch in the late 1940s when he was Secretary-General of the Economic Commission for Latin America. Its elaboration provided the basis for postwar import substitution policies pursued by many developing countries and inspired the later formation of UNCTAD (appropriately enough under Prebisch's leadership).

[5]For a useful analysis of Third World demands and their status at the beginning of 1976, see Roger D. Hansen et al., *The U.S. and World Development: Agenda for Action, 1976*, Praeger, New York, 1976.

[6]Barraclough, "The Haves and the Have Nots," p. 31.

[7]Irving Kristol, *Wall Street Journal*, July 17, 1975.

The essence of the doctrine is its scientific demonstration of systematic bias in the distribution of benefits from international trade, a bias favoring the powerful industrial exporters of the "center" and disadvantaging the weak producers of raw materials in the "periphery."[8] Few spokesmen for developing countries today doubt that "the great industrial centres not only keep for themselves the benefit of the use of new techniques in their own economy, but are in a favorable position to obtain a share of that deriving from the technical progress of the periphery."[9] The debate at the UN Sixth Special Session is replete with examples of restatement of that central complaint of asymmetry in commercial relations between North and South.[10]

The perception persists despite academic criticism that has decisively circumscribed unconditional assertions of a secular adverse trend in the terms-of-trade of primary commodities and qualified its analytical justification.[11] Self-serving interest is only part of the explanation for the doctrine's survival. Another part derives from the historical circumstances of developing-country integration into the international economy. Most frequently, the significant role in the expansion of the export sector of the South was played by foreigners. Up until the Second World War at

[8]An early statement is to be found in the 1949 Annual Report of the [UN] Economic Commission for Latin America (ECLA), *The Economic Development of Latin America and Its Principal Problems*, United Nations, New York, 1950. A later, condensed and revised version for academic audiences can be found in Raul Prebisch, "Commercial Policy in the Underdeveloped Countries," *American Economic Review*, vol. XLIV, May 1959, pp. 251–273.

[9]ECLA, *The Economic Development of Latin America*, p. 10.

[10]See the Sixth Special Session debate reported in the *U.N. Monthly Chronicle*, vol. XI, no. 5, May 1974, pp. 98–184. Time after time, developing-country delegates spoke of economic dependence, unequal relationships, and, in more extreme versions, exploitation.

[11]See M. June Flanders, "Prebisch on Protectionism: An Evaluation," *Economic Journal*, vol. 74, June 1964, pp. 305–326, and references cited there. For some historical evidence on the terms-of-trade, see Paul Bairoch, *The Economic Development of the Third World since 1900*, University of California Press, Berkeley, 1975, chap. 6. More recently, a group of UN experts have failed to find support for such a universal view of terms-of-trade movements. The record is mixed both for commodities and for time periods. The UNCTAD consultant group findings are reported in the *New York Times*, May 25, 1976, p. 1.

least, foreign capital and technology were directed to ventures that would make available raw materials or other products complementary to the industrialized economies. Bouyant demand and competition among the industrialized countries for reliable sources of supply meant that many national producers of raw materials were brought into the market. Entry was easy, but exit was not. During cyclical downswings in the industrialized countries in which demand and prices fell sharply, a private calculus dictated continuing raw material exports—especially when exchange-rate devaluation offset declining world prices. But from a social standpoint, a more limited development of the export sector might well have been indicated, a conclusion reinforced by the progressive emergence of new suppliers. The dynamics of comparative advantage in the South were principally determined by the benefits to be gained in the North.

Foreign control over the marketing of commodity exports, which was often the case, could compound the disadvantage. Vertical integration might lead to prices for inputs which were unfavorable to the primary producer though consistent with an overall maximization of profit for the foreign firm. And even when marketing alone was involved, profit could be earned on production volume independent of price, and this provided incentives for excess supply.

A large foreign presence thus tended to produce a lower price for primary products than would a world in which peripheral countries actively looked to their own interests. Conversely, one should not dismiss the presence of cartelized and administered industrial prices in international trade, at least from the beginning of the twentieth century on. At this distance it is easy to forget that "between a third and half of world trade was subject to some degree of cartel control during the inter-war period."[12] Both components of the terms-of-trade worked to the disadvantage of developing countries.

These conditioning circumstances—which for some countries were sustained until relatively recently and may even continue—cannot help but influence the present perspectives of the South.

[12]P. T. Ellsworth, *The International Economy*, Macmillan, New York, 1958, p. 129, cites these estimates of Fritz Machlup and Edward Mason.

Few enough Southern countries have been able to build on international trade as a basis for autonomous growth. And even now that the earlier pattern has been largely superseded by one of greater state power, as reflected in nationalization of resources, export taxes, and other governmental controls, there still is cause for concern. The highly individualized trade in sophisticated manufactures and the significant value of transactions that occur within firms—about half of United States–based multinational exports were intracompany in 1970—give rise to suspicion that there may be more competition in the price determination of exports of the developing world than in the price determination of their imports.[13] And specific if still quite limited empirical studies further the impression that however mutual are the gains from trade, the distribution of benefits under contemporary circumstances is not exactly determined by competitive theory.[14] When bargains were struck, the developing countries have not always been in advantageous positions.

This aspect of the Prebisch doctrine does not relate to movements in the actual terms-of-trade but rather speaks to deviations from what they *should* have been. It cannot be refuted or confirmed by data on historical trends in the terms-of-trade, although many observers have sought to do so. While the claim for compensation for an "unfair" distribution of benefits endows developing-country demands with moral fervor, its importance can be exaggerated. Of at least equal significance is a straightforward, non-value-laden statement of the Prebisch thesis that turns on the observed structure of international demand.

Low income and price elasticities of demand for the products of the periphery can cause a chronic deficiency of foreign-exchange earnings even under fully competitive conditions. En-

[13]According to the 1973 U.S. Tariff Commission report, *Implications of Multinational Firms for World Trade and Investment and for U.S. Trade and Labor*, of $72.8 million of United States multinational corporation–related exports to the world, $35.6 million could be identified as between parents and affiliates or to other affiliates. Other studies have estimated, largely on the basis of these data, that between one-quarter and one-third of total world trade in manufactures is intrafirm.

[14]See Constantine Vaitsos, *Intercountry Income Distribution and Transnational Enterprises*, Oxford University Press, New York, 1974.

gel's law, which states that the percentage of expenditures on foodstuffs declines as income rises, has with some validity been generalized to an income-inelastic demand for primary products as a whole; with greater affluence, demand for goods declines relative to that for services, and with material-saving technology, the demand for inputs becomes even less responsive to increased income. Price insensitivity of demand for necessities has, with considerably less validity, been generalized into inevitable unresponsiveness to price for all commodity exports; for individual countries, international demand is always more elastic, and substitution possibilities among materials (or among suppliers) may give rise to rather substantial price responsiveness—at least for individual commodities.

The essence of the Prebisch position is that the growth of world output must progressively increase the ratio of industrial to primary production and thus diminish the opportunity for trade in the latter. Industrial production in fact does seem to have increased much more rapidly than primary production—both historically as well as in the postwar period. And recently, unlike earlier, the growth in the volume of trade in manufactures has also outstripped the exports of commodities.[15] Conversely, industrialization in the periphery is handicapped because the modern inputs necessary to efficient capital formation must be imported. To the degree that the quantity of exports necessary to purchase imports must be increased rapidly, export prices fall, frustrating expectations of larger receipts and directly reducing real income. The transition to a more diversified economic structure is thus slowed by balance-of-payments constraints. In the absence of large capital inflows, potential growth in the periphery may be smaller than that in the center and smaller still than

---

[15] It has been estimated in League of Nations, *Industrialization and Foreign Trade*, Geneva, 1945, that between 1876–1880 and 1926–1929 the volume of primary exports grew at about 2.6 percent annually while industrial trade increased 2.4 percent. In the postwar period, industrial production increased 5.7 percent per year between 1948 and 1973 and primary production 2.7 percent. Trade in primary products (excluding fuel) increased 5.0 percent and that in manufactures 8.9 percent. There is no significant difference if 1958 is used as the base. (All data based upon UN series in the *Statistical Yearbook*, 1974.)

desired. Declining terms-of-trade, in this version of the Prebisch thesis, are symptomatic of a problem of inadequate export demand rather than a deliberately distorted distribution of the potential gains from trade. That the problem does not arise from the intent or malice of the industrialized countries makes a difference, enough so that developing-country spokesmen prefer to stress the implications of monopoly rather than the unfortunate workings of the market in their criticisms.

A fundamental conclusion following from this characterization of international demand was the inadvisability of relying on exports. Many developing countries acted upon this idea. A policy of import substitution was given priority over policies of increase, and even diversification, of export capacity.[16] The accumulating costs of the import-substitution strategy—in productive inefficiency, reliance on foreign investment, and inadequate capacity to import intermediate inputs—eventually gave rise in the early 1960s to a new interest in the external market. But the same pessimism concerning the potentialities of trade led developing countries to focus on the very rules of the game—hence the substantial diplomatic effort expended to institutionalize UNCTAD and to frame new policies favoring exports of the periphery while at the same time minimizing foreign-exchange costs. The recognition that national policies were inadequate and the frustrations engendered by unsuccessful preferential regional trading groups meant an increasing concentration on multilateral solutions.

It is exactly on such a basis that the program for the New International Economic Order is conceived: "To seek sustained and additional benefits for the international trade of developing countries, so as to achieve a substantial increase in their foreign exchange earnings, diversification of their exports and acceleration of the rate of their economic growth."[17] There is explicit recognition not only of the potential gains but also of the *necessity*

[16]Paradoxically, import substitution increased export concentration. Because protective devices meant an overvalued exchange rate and limited incentive to exporters, only those products for which comparative advantage was great could profitably be exported.

[17]*U.N. Monthly Chronicle*, vol. XI, no. 5, May 1974, p. 73.

for integration of the developing countries into the global economic system.

Such a position must be differentiated from that of neo-Marxist dependency theorists. Their world vision is quite different. They emphasize a continuing unequal position of the periphery as an inevitable consequence of global capitalism and its requirements for ever greater exploitation imposed by a falling rate of profit. Cheap raw materials and labor in the developing countries, and consequent profitable opportunities for the placement of foreign investment, underwrite the continuing prosperity of the center but not of the periphery. Even successful economic growth, open to some few developing countries that are able to participate in the global division of labor, does not translate into economic development beneficial to all. Instead the client class whose role is to assure domestic policies favorable to the multinational corporations alone is rewarded (and sustained in power). The inescapable conclusion is that interdependence should be rejected; interdependence among unequals is the very source of dependence. Socialist revolution, not international reform, is the crux of the matter: "Any development policy that accepts the framework of integration into [the world] market must fail."[18] Barraclough essentially argues that such a new strategy of self-reliance and detachment defines the present objectives of the Third World; that is what makes it so radical. I dissent. For most of the countries of the South—a preponderant majority when weighted by income—reform of the present order, not its rejection, is the issue.

It is certainly true that the recent report by the Secretary-General of UNCTAD, in preparation for the 1976 Nairobi meeting, devotes a special chapter to "a strategy for collective self-reliance." But it does so in a special way. The report is careful to qualify the objective as an additive rather than a substitutive relationship. What is recommended is more intensive economic interrelationships among the developing countries to reduce the

---

[18]Samir Amin, *Accumulation on a World Scale; A Critique of the Theory of Underdevelopment*, Monthly Review Press, New York, 1974, p. 32.

concentration of trade and strengthen their capacity for joint action. As important as the desire to diminish dependency is a very practical concern: the lack of a sufficient market in the industrialized countries for all the potential exports of the South, particularly with slowing growth of the former.[19] It is more convergent growth, not a widening gap in incomes, that is a source of the problem.

It will not be easy to implement the concept of collective self-reliance. The dual objectives of a more effective and unified bargaining position and a significant restructuring of trading relationships within the Third World are not fully consistent. Experience with regional trade groupings suggests that economic heterogeneity has hardly contributed to their success. The least industrialized countries within common markets wind up with less protection against the manufactures of the more developed and find their own aspirations for diversification frustrated. As a consequence, few regional associations have progressed beyond agreement in principle. The more intense the pressure for lateral economic interrelationships, the more difficult it likely will be to sustain political unity directed to common external objectives. In Latin America and Africa both, attempts at economic integration have not furthered closer political links.

"Collective self-reliance" as officially promulgated is itself a long way from the radical position, and necessarily so. The range of development models within the Group of 77 negates ideological purity, let alone frank adherence to revolutionary change. Unity, now and for the forseeable future, will dominate any Southern strategy. UNCTAD itself makes quite clear that "collective self-reliance is not inimical to global cooperation."[20] That pallid statement reiterates by indirection the thrust of Third World objectives: reform, not rejection. Jahangir Amuzegur, an Iranian who frequently discusses economic issues, himself uses American and not more ideological European trade union ter-

[19]UNCTAD, *New Directions and New Structures for Trade and Development*, TD/183, April 1976, chap. III, A.

[20]Ibid., p. 68.

minology when he speaks of the North-South conflict as a "bread-and-butter issue."[21]

Such a thrust is based on the objective economic circumstances. It has, after all, been a world market dominated by the industrialized countries that has permitted the dramatic OPEC exploitation of monopoly potential. More significantly, the economic performance of the developing world in more recent years—prior to the recession in the industrialized countries—has on the whole improved. Table 1 sets out the growth rates of income per capita by groups of countries. The entries demonstrate a quickening in the pace of expansion of the developing countries relative to that of the industrialized nations, so that the margin in 1965–1973 was more than halved compared with that in 1960–1965. The acceleration in growth was not uniform, however: exporters of oil experienced very rapid growth, while lower-income countries, with per capita income below $200, actually grew less rapidly.

Improved growth performance in the developing world has been associated with increased participation in international trade. Table 2 presents the record of increase in the quantity of exports and corresponding rise in power to purchase imports. The dramatic gains between the earlier and the later period cannot be missed. Both the volume of exports *and* the terms-of-trade moved favorably, as indicated by even larger increases in purchasing power of exports. This meant that the volume of imports developing-country exports could purchase grew by more than 10 percent a year between 1965 and 1975.[22] It was a performance surpassing that of the developed countries and was more than twice the increase that occurred in the early 1960s.

[21]Jahangir Amuzegur, "The North-South Dialogue," *Foreign Affairs*, vol. 54, no. 3, April 1976, p. 557.

[22]The World Bank figures on growth in export quantity seem to understate the comparable IMF and UN estimates. Thus the UN estimate for average annual export quantum growth between 1965 and 1973, calculated on a trend basis, is 8.6 percent. The *World Tables* (Johns Hopkins University Press, Baltimore, Md., 1976) estimate is 8.0 percent. The data for income groupings are drawn from the latter and are quite probably too pessimistic, and the terms-of-trade for individual countries seem much too variable (cf., Bangladesh).

TABLE 1
Rate of Growth of Gross Domestic Product
Per Capita (Percent Per Year)

	1960–1965	1965–1970	1965–1973
Industrialized countries	3.9	3.6	3.6
Developing countries	2.6	3.2	3.3
Oil exporters	4.2	4.6	5.4
Venezuela	3.9	0.8	0.9
Iran	4.2	7.6	7.9
Nigeria	2.7	1.4	6.0
Indonesia	−0.4	4.1	4.5
Higher-income*	2.1	2.8	3.3
Argentina	2.0	2.8	2.9
Mexico	3.8	3.3	2.9
Brazil	1.2	4.6	6.0
Middle-income	3.1	3.2	3.2
Lower-income	1.8	1.9	0.9
India	1.7	2.3	1.2
Pakistan	4.0	3.9	2.0
Bangladesh	1.9	0.6	−2.3

*Western Hemisphere region only, thereby excluding the southern European countries, which also have been eliminated from the aggregate.

SOURCE: World Bank, *World Tables, 1976*, Table 1, for all entries except developing countries. The World Bank includes the relatively more advanced southern Mediterranean countries, biasing the aggregate. Instead, the less inclusive IMF product estimates are used, *IMF Annual Report*, 1976, p. 5, along with population estimates from *World Tables*, adjusted for exclusion of southern Europe.

The contrast holds for oil-exporter developing countries and non–oil exporters alike, but again with the poorest countries lagging.

Performance of individual countries ranged widely. The real export growth in Brazil and Mexico contrasts with a steady decline in Argentina, salvaged only by improvement in the terms-of-trade at the end of the period; the latter enabled Pakistan to increase its imports in the early 1970s, but benefited India to a much more limited extent. The expansion of the world economy in the late 1960s was especially beneficial to those developing countries whose productive structure was more diversified and whose commercial policies were more aggressively outward-looking. More generally, the impressive change in the composition of developing-country exports in the decade between 1963 and 1973 speaks to that point. Manufactures increased from less than 16 percent to 25 percent of total developing-country exports. Employing a more restricted definition, excluding fuel exports from the denominator and nonferrous metals from the numerator, the share of manufactures in exports in 1972 reached almost a third; and manufactured exports accounted for more than half the total increase in the volume of exports from developing coun-

TABLE 2
Export Growth and Terms-of-Trade Changes
(Average Annual Percentage)

	Rate of Growth of Export Volume[a]			Rate of Growth of Purchasing Power of Exports[b]		
	1960–1965	1965–1970	1965–1973	1960–1965	1965–1970	1965–1973
Industrialized countries	7.2	9.6	9.2	7.3	9.8	9.5
Developing countries	5.6	7.6	8.8	4.7	7.6	10.5
(Excluding oil exporters)[c]	(4.7)	(6.9)	(7.9)	(n.a.)	(n.a.)	(n.a.)
Oil exporters	8.4	8.6	10.8	7.3	8.2	14.9
Venezuela	10.2	2.5	7.1	10.7	−1.1	8.2
Iran	11.8	14.3	14.3[e]	n.a.	13.9	20.4
Nigeria	12.9	6.5	13.2	7.3	7.6	18.8
Indonesia	0.6	8.0	18.1	−3.5	1.2	21.0
Higher-income[d]	5.4	5.2	5.9	4.3	5.9	7.4
Argentina	6.3	5.3	2.0	6.7	3.5	5.3
Mexico	3.2	6.0	6.9	1.6	7.1	7.7
Brazil	2.6	9.3	11.3	−0.8	10.7	13.2

TABLE 2 (continued)
Export Growth and Terms-of-Trade Changes
(Average Annual Percentage)

	Rate of Growth of Export Volume[a]			Rate of Growth of Purchasing Power of Exports[b]		
	1960–1965	1965–1970	1965–1973	1960–1965	1965–1970	1965–1973
Middle-income	8.4	4.6	7.2	8.6	4.9	7.7
Lower income	4.5	4.1	3.7	5.0	4.3	3.6
India	3.5	4.9	4.0	5.9	4.6	4.2
Pakistan	9.5	7.1	5.6	7.2	5.8	6.6
Bangladesh	3.9	2.5	0.9[f]	21.2	−14.5	−2.2[f]

[a]Export volume, except for developing-country aggregate, is trend rate of growth of real exports as given in *World Tables*, Table 2. For developing-country aggregate, it is the trend growth of value of exports deflated by export prices reported by the IMF. Developing-country groups therefore do not add to aggregate and are presented for comparison among themselves.

[b]Rate of growth of purchasing power equals growth in export volume plus growth in terms-of-trade between terminal years. Except for developing-country aggregate, which is based on IMF terms-of-trade, data on terms-of-trade come from *World Tables*, Table 2.

[c]Developing-country export volume exclusive of oil exporters has been estimated by deflating the value series by an export price index from which oil-exporter prices have been removed (using 1970 as the base of the price index).

[d]Higher-income countries are Western Hemisphere only, to eliminate the higher-income Mediterranean countries.

[e]1965–1972.

[f]1965–1971.

SOURCES: *International Financial Statistics*, International Monetary Fund, May 1976; *World Tables*, Johns Hopkins University Press, Baltimore, Md., 1976.

tries in 1973.[23] Many nontraditional agricultural commodities were also favored by increased demand and increased prices.

[23]Inter-American Development Bank, *Latin America in the World Economy*, Washington, 1975, p. 14; UN, *Monthly Bulletin of Statistics*, vol. 28, no. 9, September 1974, pp. xviii–xxxv.

Those countries participating most actively in the unprecedented expansion of world trade that immediately preceded the global recession that began in 1974 experienced more rapid economic growth. There is a significant statistical relationship between increases in the rate of growth of gross product and a higher rate of growth of exports. The correlation coefficient between changes in the growth of export volume and changes in product growth for those 28 developing countries with the requisite information is $+0.62$; for changes in the growth of export value and changes in product growth, $+0.53$. Both confirm the relevance of the international market.

Imports by developing countries were further augmented by impressive increases in capital flows in the later 1960s and early 1970s. Declines in official resource transfers were more than compensated by a rising role for private credits. Net capital flows to developing countries in 1973 were three times greater than those in 1966, an increase much greater than the intervening rise in import prices. As a consequence, the period saw significant accumulation of foreign reserves in developing countries. They were not evenly spread, any more than was the acceleration of exports. Again, the more advanced countries within the South were relatively favored by the larger private flows; geographically, the better-off Latin American and East Asian countries benefited relative to those in Africa and South Asia.[24]

Integration into the world economy was accomplished without wholesale sacrifice of the industrialization objectives of the import-substitution period. For the developing world as a whole, manufacturing growth was somewhat more rapid in the later than the earlier period, contrary to the experience of the industrialized countries.[25] On an efficiency scale, the results would probably be more impressive still, as a more open economy encouraged expansion of more productive activities. The neglect of the agricultural sector, as well as of its potential exports, which had characterized the early import-substitution period, tended to reverse itself. Within industry, too, the external and not merely the internal market favored a more sustainable growth strategy.

[24]*Annual Report of the International Monetary Fund*, 1967 and 1974.
[25]*UN Monthly Bulletin of Statistics*, vol. 29, no. 5, May 1975, pp. xiv–xvi.

Thus the initiative seized by the developing world in 1974 built in good measure on recent evidences of increased economic strength within the context of the old order. The New International Economic Order correspondingly had differential significance to Third World countries depending on how they had fared under the old. For the newly rich oil economies, the objective was a global accommodation that would conserve and legitimize the impressive gains achieved by higher petroleum prices and yet limit the obvious harm to other developing countries. For the higher- and middle-income nations in the South, especially those most benefited by the expansion of the world economy, the motivation was likewise conservative: these were the economies now most vulnerable to the threatening global recession. Only for the lowest-income countries, buffeted by higher oil prices, demographic pressures, and least satisfactory economic performance, could a radical transformation of the global order have significant appeal—and their voice was not the most prominent.

It is not surprising, then, that many, if not all, the elements of the program the South was to advocate under the banner of the New International Economic Order were to be neither novel nor incompatible with a world of growing trade and income. Beneath the rhetoric and the demands for longer-term structural reform, moreover, was a pragmatic concern for accelerating capital flows in the short run to prevent rising balance-of-payments deficits from constraining growth objectives. In that more limited and focused goal, the developing countries have been at least modestly successful. In 1974, growth per capita was sustained in most such countries, and even in 1975 it seems to have remained positive, while it turned negative in both years for the industrial nations. That performance was made possible by capital imports to finance a current account deficit of some $66 billion in the two-year period—about as much as had been available during the entire previous decade.[26] In the process, of course, the South became even more entwined in the international economy, making its reform a vital continuing issue and one on which immediate growth objectives also turn. For the

[26]*Annual Report of the International Monetary Fund*, 1976, pp. 5 and 13.

additional indebtedness only briefly postponed the harsh consequences of greater import requirements which were inadequately offset by modestly increasing foreign-exchange proceeds.

THE THREAT FROM THE THIRD WORLD

The confusion surrounding the objectives of the Third World has frequently been matched by a misperception of the role of commodity power. Initially, the promulgation of the New International Economic Order in the aftermath of the stunning OPEC success in quadrupling prices led to the mistaken assumption that the two were inextricably intertwined. To some countries in the South, the greater attentiveness of their audience was proof of the potential of commodity power; that was heady stuff after a decade of frustration and disappointment in UNCTAD. As Ali Mazrui has written, "And then one day the term 'energy crisis' entered the vocabulary of international affairs. A developing country poet might have written, as William Wordsworth did of the French Revolution: 'Bliss was it in that dawn to be alive; But to be young was very heaven!' "[27] To some countries in the North, strident developing-country demands marked only the beginning of an extortionist plot that had to be resisted. Monopoly threats lurked barely disguised in a self-righteous vocabulary of justice and equity. Claimed reparations for past wrongs seemed to have no well-defined limit save that imposed by relative strength and the will to use it.

Commodity power still insinuates itself more than two years after the event, albeit on a diminished scale, as an important conditioning factor in the consciousness of both sides. There is loose talk in the United States of bringing to bear countervailing "food power" and bold references in the South to use natural resources to overcome "imperialist domination [and] neo-colonialist exploitation."[28] To the extent that significant unilateral commodity power can in fact be mobilized by the South, re-

[27]Ali Mazrui in Erb and Kallab (eds.), *Beyond Dependency*, p. 41.
[28]See Emma Rothschild, "Food Politics," *Foreign Affairs*, vol. 54, no. 1, January 1976, and the Dakar Declaration of the Conference of Developing Countries on Raw Materials, reprinted in Erb and Kallab (eds.), *Beyond Dependency*, pp. 213–219.

formism as a strategy diminishes in attractiveness for both sides and any agreement struck has fewer prospects of stability. Because commodity prices have increasingly become defined as the crucial element in any North-South bargain, moreover, the commodity issue merits a fuller airing.

Continuing access to raw materials became in 1974 a very sensitive concern in the North. The OPEC manipulation of both price and supply occurred against a backdrop of the ominous forecasts by the Club of Rome concerning the global depletion of nonrenewable natural resources. The unprecedented rise in commodity prices during the 1972–1974 boom and its palpable effects upon domestic inflation gave immediacy to the problem. The American trend of declining national self-sufficiency and increasing reliance on imports of key materials took on new significance. In 1950 the United States relied on imports for one-half or more of its supplies only of aluminum, manganese, nickel, and tin. By 1970 zinc and chromium also belonged to that group. And projections indicated that by the end of the century, this country would be similarly dependent on imports of all of the basic industrial raw materials except phosphate.[29] The European and Japanese economies have long been dependent on access to external sources. This did not make for a reassuring picture of the future vulnerability of the industrial countries to collusion on the part of the producers.

Yet the reality, both short and long term, is less threatening. Cartelization, if it is to be successful, requires that rather rigorous economic and institutional conditions be satisfied. In the first place, demand must be fairly insensitive to variations in price. Then, an increase in price will yield an increase in total revenue that is only modestly offset by a reduction in the quantity sold. Second, sources of supply, actual *and* potential, must be controlled to prevent a significantly larger output from emerging in response to higher price. If not, monopoly profits cannot be sustained. Third, the producer members must be able to agree upon the allocation of benefits of the cartel among themselves. That means deciding upon supply quotas and the division of the gains; the market alone cannot be allowed to do it. In turn and

[29]Lester Brown, *World without Borders*, Random House, New York, 1973, p. 194.

fourth, the producer members of the cartel must then each be willing to forego the attractions of benefiting still more at the expense of the others; with a slightly lower price, any individual producer within the cartel could capture a much larger market— at least until the others discovered what was happening—and force an end to the arrangement.

In the special cases of petroleum and bauxite, circumstances have thus far favored cartelization and sustained much higher prices for producers. A price-inelastic demand sensitive to increases in industrial output in the developed countries and cartel control over a high percentage of world production and exports characterize both products. And both cartels have successfully survived far different levels of utilization of capacity among individual participants without disruption. But the declining real price of petroleum since 1974, the discord at the Qatar meeting in December 1976, and the new Jamaican accord with foreign aluminum investors all testify to the economic and institutional tensions inherent in even successful cartel arrangements. Saudi Arabia, with less need for immediate revenues, has shown itself unwilling to raise the price of petroleum in order to maximize the development potential of Iran and Venezuela at the continuing expense of its own potentially larger sales. The two-price system adopted at Qatar is the immediate manifestation, putting in doubt arguments about the inevitability of continuing future real price increases. In turn, the Jamaican settlement with Alcoa, Kaiser, and Reynolds on terms that initially were rejected as inadequate was undoubtedly hastened by a change in objective circumstances.[30] Alternative sources of supply could be exploited, as shown by the considerable reduction of bauxite exports from Jamaica in 1975 in conjunction with a 50 percent increase in those from Guinea; the long-run import of Brazil's emergence as a supplier also had to be weighed.

[30]In June of 1974 Jamaica unilaterally imposed a 700 percent increase in bauxite royalties and taxes after negotiations with the aluminum companies had broken down. Later that year Kaiser agreed to sell Jamaica 51 percent of its Jamaican company's assets and all of its mining land holdings in the country and allowed Jamaican representation on its executive board. After strong initial opposition to both the royalty increase and the sale of assets, the other major aluminum companies have followed suit.

Even in these two cases, therefore, joint maximization of profits has not been an easy task. The first phase, limiting supply, is the easiest. Cartelization is inherently most attractive in the short term because market demands and supplies initially reflect premonopoly prices and take time to adjust. This makes demand more price-inelastic and significant alternative sources of supply nonexistent. As a consequence, monopoly gains are at their peak and the issue of their allocation is diffused by immediate absolute benefits. Later on, already adapted to prosperity and with diminished total profits, the cartel countries find it harder to resist envious comparisons. Yet in view of the short-term attractions, the infrequency of concerted efforts to restrict supply by the numerous producers' associations despite the impetus of the OPEC success can perhaps be taken as corroborating evidence of the limits of commodity power. SELA, a Western Hemisphere association of countries deliberately exclusive of the United States, was originally conceived as a regional producers' association for Latin America, but has now virtually conceded its ineffectiveness in this realm.

Severe recession in the industrialized countries, of course, has confounded matters. The last few years are therefore not a fully adequate test. Demand has been weak, requiring sharp curtailment of production and significant accumulation of stocks to sustain price. If it is difficult to allocate gains within a cartel, it is more difficult still to allocate losses. Particularly at the start, there is no common fund from which to compensate. Some associations that might have been more aggressive and indeed did set out to limit supply have undoubtedly been deterred by unfavorable global conditions.

But closer examination suggests that the danger of artificial supply restraints as recovery gathers strength is not a pressing one. Barraclough's principal candidates for cartelization are copper and tin, on the ground, primarily, that exports were limited to a small group of developing countries. In the case of copper, however, all developing-country exports in the 1970–1972 period amounted to only 54 percent of total exports; of the more relevant variable production, their share was smaller. Peru, Zaire, Zambia, and Chile, the largest developing-country producers, together produce less copper ore than do the United States and

35

Canada; the former countries' share in global output is 30 percent.[31] In tin, the developing-country share in exports and production is much greater: the four principal producers—Malaysia, Bolivia, Thailand, and Indonesia—account for 75 percent of exports and 62 percent of production, with the Soviet Union and China accounting for some 21 percent more of primary ore. Yet the United States already produces a fifth of its consumption from reclaimed scrap, as do other industrialized nations.[32] Nor is tin altogether vital. In recent years, its consumption has registered the lowest rate of increase of any principal mineral product.[33] By contrast, petroleum consumption more than doubled in the decade preceding 1973, and two-thirds of oil production was in the hands of developing countries (15 percent more was produced by the Soviet Union). Bauxite demand, satisfied largely by developing-country production, expanded even more rapidly; further factors increasing cartel profits are the extent of intracompany trade and the specialization of refining equipment to particular characteristics of the ores: both circumstances make it difficult for demand to adjust in the short term.[34]

Observed economic patterns reflect the historical system of relative prices. Alternatives not chosen in the past, such as secondary production based on scrap or significant substitution in response to newly less expensive inputs, need not be significantly inferior to those techniques in use; higher prices help call forth unexploited sources of supply and new technologies. Such demand and supply alternatives ultimately limit the coercive power of monopolists. The Shah of Iran showed a keen grasp of economics when he postulated that the price of OPEC petroleum

[31]The share in exports for 1970–1972 is found in Hansen et al., *The U.S. and World Development*, Table B-16, based on The World Bank, *Commodity Trade and Price Trends*; the output share for 1973 is found in U.S. Bureau of Mines, *Minerals Handbook, 1973*. Barraclough refers to a concentration of exports of 80 percent, citing Fred Bergsten in "Threat from the Third World," *Foreign Policy*, no. 11, summer 1973, who gives no source.

[32]Hansen et al., *U.S. and World Development*, and *Minerals Handbook*.

[33]U.N., *Monthly Bulletin of Statistics*, vol. 29, no. 5, May 1975, p. xxvi.

[34]Edward A. Fried, "International Trade in Raw Materials: Myths and Realities," *Science*, February 20, 1976, p. 644.

should rise until it is equal to that of the next lowest cost energy source. What he may not have taken fully into account are the adjustment dynamics that make the short-term maximum price inconsistent with the greatest long-term gains. Once alternative sources of supply are in place, they dominate the determination of price.

The threat of supply curtailment by developing nations in the future thus has to contend with market forces, if not with the direct intervention suggested by some observers. That does not rule out cartelization as a possibility: long-term economic rationality cannot be assumed. The more widespread and concerted the limitation in commodity supply, the lesser becomes the scope for substitution and the more effective is the monopoly. But the more universal the cartelization, the more would developing countries themselves—producers and consumers alike—be adversely affected—and the more difficult it would become to devise a cohesive policy because of the heterogeneity of membership. There is therefore an inherent check to grandiose schemes of limited supply access even without resort to economic or military retaliation by the North.

Commodity power does exist in the South, but it is largely analogous to the "machinery power" of the North. The international exchange of goods conveys real benefits, and any dramatic reduction in global trade would have measurable costs. The North is far from negotiating at dagger point by reason of special vulnerability to suppliers of raw materials. It is precisely such balance, and the potential gains both to producers and consumers from more orderly commodity markets, that make negotiation of the specific commodity issue as well as other reforms a feasible exercise.

GLOBAL PROSPERITY AND INTERNAL EQUITY

A central concern for many in the North, including those most disposed to the cause of greater international equality, is whether reform of the international order will ameliorate the lot of the world's poor. Stable international relations depends not merely upon grand compacts among nations but also upon the evolving internal characteristics of those nations. Persistent high levels of inequality signal societies with a limited degree of cohesiveness, societies whose change is more likely to have disruptive implications for international interactions. Internal concentration of wealth also weakens the prospects for a significant transfer of resources from the North. There is increasingly less sympathy in the developed countries for economic growth that benefits the elites within poor countries and increasing impatience with economic assistance that indirectly perpetuates their power.

The consequences of a reformist New International Economic Order on the distribution of income within the developing world are not easy to disentangle. The issue can usefully be decomposed into three related questions: Will international reform accelerate economic growth in the South? Does economic growth per se yield higher levels of income for the poor? Will a style of economic growth involving integration in the world market penalize those with the lowest incomes?

The consistency between a reformed international economy and economic growth is an imperative. No reform that fails to sustain high rates of output expansion can begin to cope with the aspirations or even the minimal material requirements of the South. By a crude reckoning, perhaps a third of the world's population, excluding China, fell below a poverty standard of $125 (1975 prices) at the end of the decade of the 1960s; the most recent report of World Bank President McNamara reiterates a similar proportion of the absolute poor. Their share of world product scarcely exceeds 2 percent; by contrast, the proportion commanded by the richest 10 percent of the world's population exceeds 40 percent. A coefficient of income concentration based on persons, rather than countries, comes to .66, a level of global inequality greater than found in even the most unequal societies.[35] For those who prefer to stress the attributes of economic

[35] Montek Ahluwalia estimated from a sample of developing countries representing 60 percent of their total population (excluding China) that about half the individuals fell below an absolute standard of $75 personal income per capita in 1969. H. Chenery et al., *Redistribution with Growth*, Oxford Uni-

development, the statistics of malnutrition, infant mortality, illiteracy, etc., tell an equally stark tale.

These miserably poor are concentrated in the world's poorest countries. The Indian subcontinent alone contributes more than half the global total—despite a pattern of relative income distribution that is among the most egalitarian in the developing world. In these countries, even if the poorest 60 percent received 40 percent of total income, their average receipts would remain less than $100 a person. The solution cannot be limited to redistribution of existing resources. More must be brought into being. It is a wonder of compound interest that it translates a rate of per capita growth of 3 percent per annum into a multiplicative factor of 19 over the course of a century.

More can be brought into being by assuring that capital and technology are effectively combined with the abundant labor in these countries. More can be produced and sold if freer international markets convert cheap labor from a liability to an asset. More can be made available in the short term if external lenders are both generous and patient. And more can be accomplished if the scope for indigenous development models is enlarged and the Western model is less obtrusive. A reformist international economic order can contribute in all these dimensions. It can facilitate, but not substitute for, the required domestic initiatives.

Sheer economic growth will not suffice to deal with the problem of deprivation. Few today partake of the earlier faith that democratic politics and more egalitarian economies are an inevitable and logical consequence of accelerated economic growth. Indeed, the conventional wisdom seems to have come full circle: "Increases in per capita GNP are associated with worsening of the income distribution at low levels of development; only at very high levels for low-income nations is higher per capita GNP associated with a more equal income distribution . . . The ab-

---

versity Press, Oxford, 1974, p. 12. Updated to 1975, an income of $75 in 1969 would translate to $125. Robert McNamara's 1976 *Address to the Board of Governors*, World Bank, Washington, D.C., placed the proportion of absolute poor in the developing countries at .47. The developing countries (excluding China) account for about three-fourths of the world's population.

solute position of the poor tends to deteriorate as a consequence of economic growth."[36] And evidence is casually cited of the rapid, unequalizing growth of authoritarian states in the 1960s: Brazil, Korea, Greece, Indonesia, and other examples.

This pessimistic view has been based in part on accumulating statistical evidence suggesting a U-shaped curve relating income shares and income per capita: the proportion of income going to the poorest initially declines as income rises and reverses only much later.[37] Paradoxically, both radical critics and staunch defenders of conservative, market-oriented development strategies have found vindication in these results. Radicals read into them the inevitability of immiserization of the poor when market processes are relied upon; conservatives find justification for the observed deterioration in income equality in the presumed iron laws of economic development.

The data do not bear such a heavy burden. Indeed, the very existence of a meaningful parabolic relationship may be called into question. Here as almost always, it is useful to separate out different levels of development. The very poorest countries not unnaturally tend to have more equal distributions of income: relative inequality is constrained by the condition that the poorest receive enough income to survive. Once beyond such a low level of income—say, $200 per capita—the relationship between equality and income among developing countries is not very systematic.[38] Nor is there any indication that inequality is greater in countries whose levels of income per capita are similar but whose

[36]Irma Adelman and Cynthia Morris, *Economic Growth and Social Equity in Developing Countries*, Stanford University Press, Stanford, Calif., 1973, pp. 185, 189.

[37]For the latest and most complete statement of results, see Montek S. Ahluwalia, "Inequality, Poverty and Development," *Journal of Development Economics*, vol. 3, no. 4, 1976, pp. 3–37.

[38]Thus, taking the data for Ahluwalia's 41 developing countries and dividing them into two groups—one below $200, the other above—the differences in the mean shares going to the bottom 40 or 20 percent between the two groups explains just about as much of the variance as does his parabolic function. That is, once we eliminate the low-income observations, income level doesn't matter much. Note as well that the considerable variance within each group leads to statistical insignificance for the differences between the means.

growth rates are different. Since there are few cases in which we can follow the transition from very low income levels to greater affluence, it is difficult to define the appropriate dynamic relationship.

These doubts do not mean that the development process has no effect upon income distribution. As growth proceeds and the sectoral composition of the economy alters in favor of manufactures and services, there is reason, a priori, to anticipate an increase in inequality.[39] When, in addition, the demand for labor is biased because of technical change in favor of those few with formal education and skills, the effect of sectoral realignment is compounded. A vicious circle of poverty can become institutionalized as a consequence. Higher initial levels of income provide privileged access to those attributes most needed to benefit from modernization. Level of education, condition of health, ability to mobilize small quantities of capital, number of children in the family all influence responsiveness to new opportunities. Some lose out with change. An economy growing from low levels of income can exhibit increased mobility and greater inequality at the same time. In most instances, however, impoverishment is relative rather than absolute. For the limited set of countries for which we can observe change over time, the reduction in equality has not meant declines in the average income of the poorest.[40]

The very fact that the economic transformation of developing countries imposes such unequalizing tendencies while there is little systematic variation empirically tells us that intervening policies can matter and have mattered. Obvious examples are

[39]This is the original hypothesis offered by Simon Kuznets, "Economic Growth and Income Inequality," *American Economic Review*, vol. 45, no. 1, March 1955, pp. 1–28. When there is outmigration from a lower-income, more homogeneous sector to a higher-income, more heterogeneous sector, the measures of inequality will first increase and then decease as more of the population transfers. For a more formal statement, see Sherman Robinson, "A Note on the U-Hypothesis Relating Income Inequality and Economic Development," *American Economic Review*, vol. 66, no. 3, June 1976, pp. 437–440.

[40]This is true for a sample of 13 countries—including Brazil, Korea, Venezuela, and Taiwan—that are sometimes held up as examples of the opposite. See Chenery et al., *Redistribution with Growth*, p. 42.

Cuba and China. Yet what is equally striking is that these socialist experiments do not *end* with the confiscation of physical capital, the planning of output, and the establishment of sometimes arbitrary wages and prices. They also emphasize improvements in the extent and quality of education, wider access to health care, greater concern with nutrition and family planning, and, more generally, policies whose impact is to reduce differences in qualifications among individuals. Far less radical policies of agrarian reform and widespread provision of public goods have a similar impact. It is no accident that universality of primary education is a good index for differentiating countries with higher shares of income for the poorest.

Contrariwise, where relative deterioration of income distribution has occurred, it has frequently been accompanied by policies that have deliberately reinforced inequality beyond the operation of pure market forces. Special advantages have been granted to entice private capital accumulation, while wages for the unskilled have been restrained. Economic policies that are advocated for their contributions to growth have not always been distributionally symmetric.

The correct conclusion to be drawn from research to date therefore would seem to be that the *style* of development is a much more critical determinant of internal equity than the level of income or its rate of change.[41] Sheer increases in income per capita will not guarantee higher standards of living for the poor, but neither will they inevitably deteriorate their standard of living.

That makes important an assessment of how a reformed international economic order might influence internal policy as

[41] In a recent statistical study using data from 25 countries, the role of policy and development styles turned out to be statistically more significant than that of income level in explaining income inequality within the country. In the study, I used the typology developed by H. Chenery and M. Syrquin in their *Patterns of Development, 1950–1970*, Oxford University Press, Oxford, 1975, which differentiates four patterns: primary specialization, balanced growth, import substitution, and industrial specialization. Countries pursuing industrial specialization—with emphasis on industrial production *and* exports—have the most equitable distribution. Interestingly, primary specialization is next, and concentration in export of primary products was found to be irrelevant when included as a variable.

well as the internal economic structure. There do not seem to be unequivocal answers. Radicals fear that the intensification and ratification of global interdependence would only inhibit solution of the poverty problem, both among and within nations. That belief largely motivates the search by radicals for self-reliance. Export-led development in the South is seen to benefit the richer nations who can buy cheaply and to reward foreign and domestic capital disproportionately. Less directly economic, but no less important on that account, integration into the world economy is argued to erode the possibility of indigenous, revolutionary solutions that adequately respond to the aspirations of the poor. The web of trade, and even more the interlacing of propertied interests through extensive capital flows, inhibits change. Whether under the guise of international law, covertly as in Chile, or overtly as in the Dominican Republic, the left is persuaded that the North will defend its advantage to the last.

The purely economic considerations are most easily dealt with. Participation in an expanding world market will be directly equalizing to the degree that export production is labor-intensive. When exports require scarce resources that are highly concentrated in their ownership—land, technology, mineral rights, skills—the access to the world market will increase their relative value. Trade therefore can be, and has been, unequalizing. But even when foreign-exchange earnings are acquired through production processes that contribute to income concentration, their ultimate consequences can be quite different. How large a proportion of the profits is retained domestically, how much goes to the government, and how the foreign exchange is spent also have a considerable impact. Expenditure of oil revenues for agrarian reform by the government of Venezuela influenced income distribution in the opposite direction from that of the direct effect of petroleum exploitation.

Contemporary circumstances probably warrant more attention to such government intervention than to the technology of export production. The past decade has seen a proliferation of export levies, taxes on profits of foreign enterprises, nationalization of mineral resources, and other deliberate measures that affect the international distribution of the benefits of trade as well as providing means for influencing domestic income shares.

There is no lack of awareness of the possibilities. In all parts of the developing world, the deprived are bringing pressure to bear, with varying success. Deterministic models of dependency give too little weight to the force of these demands—although they frequently have been important enough to provoke authoritarian regimes to try to repress them. Yet their presence continues to be felt even under these difficult circumstances. The legitimacy of such governments is being increasingly gauged by their responsiveness to income distribution issues and not the record of economic growth alone. The full consequences of such assertiveness are yet to be seen; they cannot be ignored. And they alter any easy supposition that increasing exports, even if produced by multinational enterprises, will not permit an improved standard of living of the poor.

Policy is equally at the heart of the political constraints. But this time it is international policy. One of the objectives of the New International Economic Order is a global environment that gives primacy to internal economic policy decisions. There will inevitably be external influences where there are external property rights and interests. The challenge is to channel them constructively and neither to define them as illegitimate nor to presuppose their constant benevolence. An appropriate goal is a guarantee of sympathetic neutrality. Neutrality does not mean acquiescence to expropriation without compensation nor guaranteed willingness to underwrite unlimited capital inflows regardless of economic performance. But it cannot also mean inequitable asset valuation or differentiated access to capital supply according to the politics of the regime.

We have come full circle. Those concerned lest a reform of present international economic relations merely benefit a handful of countries in the South and enrich only the oligarchs in those can take heart: the result turns on the kind of reform itself. International rules that are conducive to experimentation and do not rigidly define internal options can facilitate a more equitable internal distribution of the benefits of development. International rules that liberalize trade in labor-intensive products and assure continuing capital inflow can benefit the poorest countries. Neither is inconsistent with a reformist framework. Both ultimately place the major burden of development upon hard internal choices.

THE POSITIVE CASE FOR NEGOTIATION

I have thus far accentuated the negative. Each of the preceding issues is serious enough to call into question the wisdom of a strategy of accommodation. Any apparent immediate gains would very likely be illusory in an international economy whose bases had been significantly eroded. If the New International Economic Order were the gauntlet of a unified South seeking exit from the international system, taking with it essential resource inputs, there might be a case for principled resistance; if reform were only to aggravate poverty, there might be grounds for rejection of inadequate palliatives. Instead, a more rapidly developing South demands greater voice *within* the present structure, while within the South itself the potential wealth that might be created by a more equitable international order is increasingly at issue domestically.

The positive case for meaningful negotiation is more easily stated. The issue is not whether there should be a new order, but what kind. Bretton Woods has had its day. So, too, have primary reliance on bilateral resource transfers and appeal to GATT for resolution of trade differences. Those mechanisms provided a framework for postwar economic reconstruction that successfully restrained the forces of economic nationalism so rampant in the 1930s. For some two decades, welcome United States capital outflow and military expenditures provided the international liquidity that underwrote unprecedented expansion of global trade and production. American national self-interest was largely consistent with the needs of the West.[42]

That era of easy harmonization inevitably gave way to a more competitive one with the recovery of Europe and Japan and the

[42]For a discussion of Bretton Woods and the factors involved in its demise as well as further useful references see David H. Blake and Robert S. Walters, *The Politics of Global Economic Relations*, Prentice-Hall, Englewood Cliffs, N.J., 1976.

increasing conflict between domestic economic objectives and foreign responsibilities of the United States. It had been easy to be the world's banker when the export sector was unchallenged internationally and trade was a relatively insignificant economic interest. It was another matter when foreign assets dramatically increased in size, jobs seemed to be exported abroad to low-wage countries, and the burden of balance-of-payments adjustment was felt in slower domestic growth.

The present challenge is to amend the old economic order to make it more consistent with the realignment of international political and economic power that has occurred since 1945. It is difficult to argue that the present complex of market forces, increasing evidences of national self-interest, and decentralization of significant economic decisions represent an enduring response to the erosion of the old rules. It is at best a transition that has survived the rude shocks of the last few years surprisingly well. The doomsayers did not have it right when they foresaw trade and investment wars and perhaps even financial collapse. Private institutions, especially, have innovated in response to the reallocation of global reserves. But that does not make the status quo optimal and justify disinterest. Indeed, even as the earlier arrangements created to liberalize trade and assure collaborative balance-of-payments adjustments have been found wanting, a series of new global problems in search of multilateral solutions continue to fester: the Law of the Sea, population growth and adequacy of food supplies, control of the environment, among others.

Rules cannot be avoided. International economic relations constantly verge on neo-mercantilism. The national interest, narrowly defined, always seems to call for some measure or other that can yield temporary advantage. But the retaliation of others—sooner or later, overt or covert—converts advantage into loss, usually for all. Mercantilistic policies are self-fulfilling in their creation of the zero-sum game on which they are predicated. And unless kept in check, they have a tendency to spread rapidly.

This task of defining new rules must incorporate seriously for the first time the claims of the developing world. That is not because the focus in international economic relations has shifted from issues of production to those of distribution, as some have suggested. Bretton Woods, no less than the New International Economic Order, implied predictable distributional consequences, as accounts of United States–British divergence in the negotiations attest.[43] So, too, did the rounds of talks leading to reduction in industrial tariffs and recent realignments of currency values. But those accords primarily involved the industrialized nations. Until 1973, issues of economic interdependence and economic development were largely separate provinces. The latter could be dealt with by minimal coordination of development assistance and, in the extreme, concession of trade preferences of varying degrees of generosity. The former involved only those countries belonging to the Organization for Economic Cooperation and Development (OECD).

What the claims of the New International Economic Order ultimately question is the validity of that dichotomy. The developing countries now have increasing shares of world population and have begun to increase their share of trade and production. They are no longer marginal to the interests of the industrialized nations. For a long time, the South has been much influenced by decisions in the North; now interdependence has become two-way—and not merely in the recognized importance of commodities. Developing nations necessarily have an interest in new global monetary and financial arrangements when some of them have acquired large positive international reserves and others, impressive and burdensome international debts. They are vitally concerned with new rules for trade flows that can facilitate or burden the expanding role of the South in exports of manufactures and, for some, exports of foodstuffs.

These more inclusive global economic relations undoubtedly complicate matters. Wider participation in multilateral negotiations can lead to the coupling of the apparently irrelevant. Thus the developing countries insisted upon compensation for consent to the de jure scrapping of fixed exchange rates in the Jamaica

---

[43]See Richard N. Gardner, *Sterling Dollar Diplomacy*, rev. ed., McGraw-Hill, New York, 1969, on the great difference in where the burden of adjustment fell between creditor and debtor nations in the original British and American plans for an international stabilization fund.

IMF Accord—although it is by no means obvious that flexible rates worked to their disadvantage. A more generous IMF allowance for cyclical fluctuation in export proceeds than originally contemplated was the outcome. That linkage was not entirely logical. It partially reflected the absence of a broader context of negotiations, in which the relationship between the stability of import demand of the South and the prosperity of the North could be explored. Broadening the agenda can also narrow the focus of discussions of particulars within it. Varying degrees of interdependence involve nations differentially; obviously not all negotiations or agreements can or should be universal. Implementing such procedures will be possible only if the pieces are seen to fit within a more comprehensive whole and the interests of the South are seen to matter.

Not least among the benefits arising from a cooperative international economic framework are the avoidance of the non-economic costs inherent in a conflictual mercantilist order. The United States, and the industrialized nations as a group, no longer enjoys the hegemonic privilege of imposing cooperation. There must be wider consensus to avert consequences that potentially go well beyond smaller material global output. In a world in which modern weaponry and potential nuclear status abound, unresolved economic issues can spill over quite readily into military adventuresomeness. There is no pressing danger of a dramatic North-South confrontation. But as individual countries such as Brazil, Iran, Venezuela, Mexico, and Nigeria acquire greater power, smaller-scale hostilities are by no means out of the question. Already some observers are commenting on tensions between Brazil and Venezuela.[44] Historically the emergence of newer powers upon the international scene has been fraught with tension and, indeed, often accompanied by military conflict. The prospects are not improved within a hostile economic environment.

[44]See the nationally syndicated column by Elliot Janeway in the *San Francisco Chronicle and Examiner*, January 9, 1977. What is interesting is that the issue made the Sunday papers in the first place and that an economic issue—the oil price rise—is stressed as the reason for Brazilian aggressive designs.

There is therefore good reason for the North to make a sustained effort to reach an accommodation. United States resistance to reform can cripple reform efforts, but such resistance goes against its own economic interests. In recent years the United States has experienced an important contribution to growth from expanding trade. Between 1969 and 1975 exports increased from 5 to almost 9 percent of gross domestic product, partially in response to policies that ended the dollar's overvaluation and, with it the fixed-exchange-rate structure of Bretton Woods. International investments constitute an important application of resources for many of the largest corporations. Income from abroad has increased rapidly in recent years. Not since the nineteenth century has the United States been so integrated into the world economy. Those interests are better advanced and safeguarded by active espousal of a reformed international economy than by excessive faith in the continuing stability of the status quo.

TWO

Reforming the International Order

PRINCIPLES OF REFORM

However reformist, structural principles underlying the specific measures composing the New International Economic Order are fundamentally different from those of the old. In the first instance, there is a frank commitment to discrimination and non-reciprocity as legitimate means for distributing a larger share of the benefits of economic interrelations to developing countries. A second characteristic is an insistence upon larger, more automatic and guaranteed foreign-exchange availability—through not only privileged trade but also more accessible capital markets and more generous public resource transfers; exchange-rate policy is deemed insufficient to avert balance-of-payments constraints. Third, the spirit of the NIEO is interventionist and thus, at the least, suspicious of market processes.

In all these dimensions, the NIEO is a special kind of successor regime to the international order prevailing, with variation and evolution, for more than a century. These arrangements have emphasized the principles of nondiscrimination and reciprocity as central tenets of the trading system. Although in practice all the industrialized nations did not follow an unconditional most favored nation policy—the United States did not until the 1920s and deviated even thereafter[45]—the thrust of the system was

[45] Although the United States opted for the unconditional most favored nation clause in the 1920s, the United States–Cuba reciprocal trade treaty of 1934

directed toward universalized, liberal trade. First for Britain and gradually for the United States, as dominant nations, openness of markets and self-interest went hand in hand.

The old order also depended upon an automatic monetary adjustment to reestablish international equilibrium. The gold standard required only that the internal monetary supply respond to the balance of payments, thereby altering the domestic price level in the appropriate direction. Trade flows and the international structure of production would adapt straightforwardly to these changes in relative prices among countries. Although Bretton Woods was certainly less optimistic, it remained committed to fixed exchange rates and worked best under a dollar standard it facilitated but did not anticipate. There was in fact almost no synchronization of domestic policy or systematic efforts to assure an adjustment to the mounting United States balance-of-payments deficit. Despite the early establishment of GATT, a compromise substitute for the more far-reaching proposed International Trade Organization, the monetary regime rather than trade liberalization dominated at least until the 1960s. Foreign-exchange shortages of developing countries were conceived not as a structural but an exchange-rate problem.

Finally, despite abundant evidence of less than perfect competition, the free market remained the central paradigm. Cartels, foreign direct investment, even the appearance of quasi-state trading firms, were matters of national rather than international policy when they were the subject of policy at all. Developing countries were discouraged from nationalistic actions and on the contrary were encouraged to participate in the international market. For some of them, even the full concession of national sovereignty has been a relatively recent phenomenon.

The NIEO is thus a reaction by the South against a framework that has seemed inadequate to reflect the reality they faced and has seemed to serve best the interests of the principal and already

---

extended tariff reduction to no third nations on the grounds of contiguity. Yet the United States opposed Peru's application of the same principle in its trade with its Andean neighbors. See Dick Steward, *Trade and Hemisphere: The Good Neighbor Policy and Reciprocal Trade*, University of Missouri Press, Columbia, Mo., 1975, pp. 108–109, 232.

dominant actors. Principles had an elastic quality when they inhibited the North. Nondiscrimination could be put aside in the formation of the Common Market because of its political significance but was argued as a reason to exclude concession of preferences to developing countries. Arbitrary market barriers could be erected to satisfy "legitimate" domestic interests in the industrialized countries, even as nationalistic discrimination against foreign firms in the South was held to violate international law. And the market system itself, to the extent that it was operative, seemed only to widen disparities of income rather than afford equal opportunity.

Because there is a fundamental and mutual commitment to interdependence, as I have argued, there is a temptation for persons of good faith on both sides to eschew serious discussion of such apparently contradictory principles in favor of a search for a pragmatic bargain. The elements have already surfaced in the negotiations to date. There might be selective and more frequent discrimination in trade to apply once agreements vital to the interests of the developed countries had been reached; for instance, the coverage of preferences could be modestly extended while limits to their applicability were retained. A common fund to finance commodity agreements could be established, but limited in resources and carefully defined authority. A UN code on transnational enterprises could be accepted, but without concessions of substantive significance. In short, there could well be a limited reform modifying some of the objectionable features of the present system which could satisfy the minimum objectives of all.

Yet this is not the thrust of the reformism I would advocate. A modest effort is not fully adequate to the longer term and to a world that almost certainly will be fraught with other tensions. Continuing latent conflict could more likely manifest itself in another eruption like that in 1973–1974 in the absence of some consensus between North and South on the principles underlying specific rules. Part of the appeal of an ad hoc reform devoid of conceptual clarity is that it seems easier to attain—both internationally and domestically. That will be a matter of fuller discussion in Chapter Three. Suffice it to say here that durable reform may have to be integral in conception even if marginal in application.

I offer two simple principles to serve as the basis for a re-structuring of North-South economic relations. One is a joint commitment to extending and making markets more effective; the other is greater participation of developing nations in policing such markets and in making specific rules. The emphasis on international markets is not to be confused with advocacy of capitalism. Socialist countries that regulate their economies internally can conduct their external affairs on a market principle without prejudice to internal goals. A competitive model, with its inherent constraints on the exercise of economic and political power and its attractive allocative properties, is an attractive, normative ideal to guide the international economy. The reality of ever wider diffusion of political and economic power means that the premises of the competitive model are more nearly satisfied now than before. Explicit monitoring to assure that the market functions has a dual role: to prevent exercise of monopoly power and to guarantee that the international projections of state-controlled economies involve fair competition and not arbitrary practices. Inclusion of the developing countries in devising the specific rules that are necessary provides a guarantee that this is no collective, modern version of the imperialism of free trade. It is rather intended as a liberalism appropriate to a nonhegemonic global environment.

A virtue to the North of affirming and living by a commitment to fair markets is its ideological consistency; the industrialized countries need not retreat from their convictions so much as practice them. Implementation of that principle can also reward the South. Even much of the critical, *dependista* literature in the developing countries does not deny the virtues of a market system; it rather denies that the market can ever work because it will be and has to be manipulated to the disadvantage of the deprived. That is where this literature departs from well-intentioned liberals. Thus, Mahbub ul Haq, who seemingly takes the position of rejecting international market processes as inherently unable to function "either efficiently or equitably," turns around nonetheless to criticize the deviations: "The rich, in other words,

54

are drawing a protective wall around their lifestyles, telling the poor nations that they can compete neither with their labor nor with their goods but paying handsome tributes at the same time to the 'free' workings of the international market mechanism."[46]

It is late in the day to persuade the developing countries that the North does intend to accept the impersonal and occasionally harsh judgments of comparative advantage, but perhaps still not too late. A necessary measure of the sincerity of the commitment will be an active participation of the developing world both in assuring that the market prevails and in proposing substitute rules when it cannot and should not. Discrimination that compensates for real and temporary disadvantage and is applicable not merely between North and South but also among developing countries can be admitted where appropriate. Modern liberalism applied to international markets does not mean an unquestioning acceptance of the status quo. What it does impose is a healthy skepticism about intervention through regulation as an instrument of first resort and about arbitrary rules to redistribute the benefits of international interactions.

This conception of the international order rules out proposals for a centralized world development authority to direct the international flow of resources and guide their allocation among countries.[47] But it also rules out the present lack of coordination among the decentralized agencies—the World Bank, the IMF, a restructured GATT—that will retain responsibility for particular policies. What may be envisaged is a small technical secretariat attached to a coordinating committee of finance ministers which could serve as a locus for comprehensive economic negotiations. The frank intent is for a representative forum in which

[46]Mahbub ul Haq, *The Third World and the International Economic Order*, Development Paper No. 22, Overseas Development Council, Washington, D.C., 1976, pp. 5–6. Haq's analogy between the deficiencies of a domestic market mechanism in the presence of unequal distribution of income and an international market with poor countries is invalid. The international market enables low-income countries to be low-cost countries as well and thus to erode the inequality; low-income labor cannot itself combine internally with capital and technology to become a low-cost competitor.

[47]As proposed by ul Haq, p. 24.

rhetoric is not divorced from technical competence and shared language and skills can contribute to resolution of differences. It does not depoliticize the proceedings except in the most constructive sense; finance ministers are not without a sense of the political—at least if they intend to remain in office.

One measure of the validity of these principles is the policies they suggest. In the next section, therefore, a brief and by no means comprehensive overview of the principal elements of a potential reform program is provided.

Policies

Three priority areas in which significant measures can be taken to make market mechanisms operate more effectively are trade, international capital flow, and direct private investment. Each set of transactions occurs under circumstances that at present often fail to conform to the competitive model. The three together encompass the most significant economic interactions between the industrialized and developing countries.

1. Trade

The trade agenda must commence with the phased but rapid removal of the present barriers to developing-country exports. Escalation of tariffs biased against import of processed raw materials, quantitative restrictions on labor-intensive products produced more cheaply abroad, and arbitrary market exclusion seriously distort the operation of the market to the disadvantage of developing countries. Freer trade, not merely the checking of protectionist interests in the North, must receive the highest priority. In the absence of its attainment, many other policy suggestions themselves are debilitated. There can be no basis for repayment of accumulated debt, no assurance of efficient industrialization, no guarantee of greater production of foodstuffs and raw materials unless an expanding and competitive market in the industrialized nations is assured.

Dismantling the barriers will not be easy. Domestic interests are firmly entrenched. But a systematic means of moving toward that end, and sustaining freer trade, can perhaps be reinforced if the obligations toward freer trade are made more enforceable. Nations enter into an implicit contract in mutually guaranteeing access to their markets; failure to perform should not merely initiate recourse to injunctive procedures—as at present—but also be subject to financial recovery. When domestic interests petition for protection against enhanced international competition, the only international costs considered are those of potential retaliation. The damage to trading partners is ignored, while that to domestic producers is tangible and evident. This asymmetry contributes to a policy bias in favor of restriction. If the real costs to foreign suppliers were also rendered in financial form and compensation payments had to be made, the stability of a freer trade equilibrium could be enhanced. A first suggestion, therefore, is to negotiate a penalty mechanism to be administered by GATT.

A second suggestion is to accommodate differentiation by level of development through application of the market principle. Higher levels of protection for industry in developing countries need not immediately be reduced to the much lower level of the developed countries. It does take time to acquire productive efficiency. But developing countries can also be held to a more gradual schedule of reductions that is scaled to their degree of industrialization. Such liberalization can attack the hold of domestic monopolies operating behind antiquated and irrelevant protection that has been extended to goods that are largely supplied internally, at least in the more advanced developing countries.

Freeing of trade in a way that reflects the special interests of the developing countries has high priority. Labor-intensive manufactures, processed raw materials, agricultural products, and intermediate components are examples. Going along with such a thrust however, is the need to prevent unfair competition in the markets of the developed countries. Export subsidies that gain markets for one country at the expense of others are a particularly vexing issue. Few countries have failed to promote their sales abroad in one or another fashion. Those that have experienced the highest rates of growth of exports have frequently resorted to a battery of measures that have enhanced their domestic profitability. Not surprisingly, other nations have defended their producers against such unbounded competition.[48]

Action is required if the present situation is not to lead to irreparable deterioration in trade practices. One simple and implementable rule might help to standardize the variety of rules and practices. Uniform export subsidies could be permitted to the extent of the average level of import duties. Thus a country whose average tariff was 30 percent could set an export subsidy applicable to all subsidized goods equivalent to 30 percent of the value of export sales. (Rebates of indirect taxes on exports would continue to be permitted and would be specific to the product; they do not constitute subsidies.) Since import restrictions are smaller in developed countries, there would again be a differentiated allowance that had its basis in economic theory. A uniform export subsidy equal to the average tariff rate is approximately equivalent to a policy of free trade at an exchange rate devalued to the extent of the subsidy; instead of employing the subsidy and tariff, one could have depreciated the exchange rate, making imports more expensive and exports more competitive. The only differences are that capital account transactions would continue to be conducted at the overvalued rate, while tariff rates, but not the export subsidy, would typically vary among products. Because the subsidy would be high for those countries with very protective structures, significant internal fiscal transfers to exporters would be necessary. These could very well provide an additional incentive to accelerate the phasing out of unnecessarily protective tariffs, particularly as export proceeds increased in developing countries.

A third set of measures is required to deal with commodities: exports of raw materials and imports of food. The reason is the wide fluctuations of price inherent in such markets that inhibit their efficient working. Rising prices of food trigger export constraints and lack of availability of supply—a combination that for poor countries subject to the variability of nature can mean virtual disaster. Rising commodity prices have in recent years

[48]The Trade Act of 1974 set a time limit within which cases of alleged export subsidy must be heard, increasing sharply the number of complaints now investigated.

spurred speculation in commodities that has amplified the cycle, while the fluctuation and attendant uncertainty has made orderly investment plans for expansion in supplies difficult. Moreover, the management of national policy geared to long-run development objectives is complicated by the variability of import capacity.[49]

There are two alternative approaches to this problem of uncertainty. One emphasizes financial remedies; the other, more favored by developing countries, stresses physical intervention through buffer stocks. While these are not mutually exclusive—indeed, the integrated commodity program proposed by UNCTAD explicitly makes reference to the need for compensatory finance—they are quite different. Advocates of buffer stocks take a more optimistic view of the economies of scale of a centralized facility, and of planning more generally, and also place great weight on the assurance of physical supplies. Those who look with favor upon financial flows find greater virtue in decentralization and wider use of market arrangements to forestall uncertainty.

The issue of a common fund to finance a variety of commodity agreements is a related but separate matter. Its rationale turns on the advantages of diversification and of sheer size. If prices of commodities do not move together, savings can be attained because sales of one product generate the resources required for purchases of another. UNCTAD itself presents only limited evidence in favor of such a disparity in price changes and tends to stress the more economical access to loan finance that a consolidated facility would permit.

In many respects, the issue of buffer stocks has become excessively visible among North-South differences, serving almost as the gauge of progress in the wider agenda. Whether financed

---

[49]There is recent literature seeking to show that export variability makes a positive contribution to growth because it requires higher rates of savings. The observed simple correlation can better be explained by deliberate policy to industrialize and lower export dependence as well as inflows of foreign capital to compensate for export shortfalls. Cf. Oden Knudsen and Andrew Parnes, *Trade Instability and Economic Development*, Lexington Books, Lexington, Mass., 1975, and Pan A. Yotopoulos and Jeffrey B. Nugent, *Economics of Development*, Harper & Row, New York, 1976, Chap. 18.

individually or in common, buffer stocks do not guarantee higher export incomes. When price fluctuations emanate from demand, as the postwar experience seems to suggest, earnings will in fact be lower on average as a consequence of stabilization that only evens out price fluctuations.

This, of course, is what led to proposals for indexation that would guarantee the real prices of commodity exports and hence more directly attack the adequacy of long-run earnings. This suggestion has gradually been attenuated, even in the UNCTAD program, as the implications of such a rigid price have come to be more generally appreciated. Quotas would have to be assigned and enforced, with asymmetric benefits and costs for individual countries. The poorest countries would have smaller relative benefits from any scheme that raised real prices symmetrically. Thus for the 10 core commodities in the integrated program, the middle- and higher-income developing countries export 6 times more than they import, while for the poorest the margin is a smaller 4 to 1.[50] These proportions might well be applied to a declining volume of trade as substitution and technological change in response to higher prices had their effect.

As between centralized buffer stocks and enhanced financial flows to stabilize the real value of import proceeds, my disposition is to favor the latter as a more immediate, general, and efficacious solution. For particular commodities, larger stocks may be advisable and indeed necessary—as in the case of an international grain reserve. But they should be integrated with other measures that strengthen the capacity of the market to ameliorate the problem.

An expansion of IMF credit not merely to compensate for shortfalls in nominal export proceeds but also to offset adverse changes in the terms-of-trade meets such a test. It makes resources available to dampen fluctuations without altering real trends; the latter would require more fundamental reallocation decisions that went beyond commodity policy. Such credit would permit countries to invest in countercyclical stock accumulation at the source of production. With accurate information and, in-

[50]See UNCTAD, "A Common Fund for the Financing of Commodity Stocks," Addendum, Document TD/B/C.1/196/Add.1, p. 4, in which the imports and exports of the core commodities are shown by level of income.

deed, consultation among producers and consumers—who themselves also held stocks—market supply could be regularized and price fluctuation dampened. There would be no need for international agreement on uniform acquisition and sales prices—merely an agreement that consumers be allowed to purchase from stocks at the prevailing world price. This guarantee of access to supply, the decentralization of stocks, and the fact that the credits have to be repaid assure that the policy would not lead to monopoly control. Such credit could be further supplemented by experimentation with longer forward markets in which contracts written by developing countries might afford stabilizing speculation and a better climate for investment decisions.

The potential advantage of this policy alternative, relative to buffer stocks, is its administrative ease and probable financial savings. Once the questions of buffer stocks and indexation are separated, the ideological impediments to commodity agreements are less significant than the technical obstacles. A financial solution averts the need for closely coordinated decisions among producers and consumers. Yet because the flow of credit is tied to prices of imports as well as of exports, it provides an element of short-term, indirect indexation that is more efficacious than agreement on nominal commodity prices. In addition, the capital required for the common fund may well be much more substantial than the optimistic UNCTAD estimate of $3 billion. One independent simulation study implies a sum twice that to keep copper prices alone within reasonable bounds.[51] National stocks also will tie up capital, but with the difference that they can influence medium-term supply more directly.

A global food reserve poses rather similar problems, but with developing countries wanting to maintain lower rather than higher prices. They have emerged as significant importers, with projected grain deficits tripling by 1985 to some 85 million tons a year; the rise in price in 1973–1974 already has led to imports of $10 billion.[52] They can ill afford the added cost—and lives are

[51]Gordon Smith, "An Economic Evaluation of International Buffer Stocks for Copper," U.S. State Department, INR Contract 1722-620008, August 1975.

[52]Douglas N. Ross (ed.), *The Challenge of Overpopulation and Food Shortages*, Conference Proceedings No. 684, The Conference Board, New York, 1976, pp. 2, 17.

truly at stake. While some observers have emphasized that the recent crisis is symptomatic of long-term shortages, the more prevalent judgment is that the essence of the present global food problem is not a shortfall of productive capacity so much as its inefficient distribution among and within countries. The rise in real price occasioned by harvest shortfalls in the early 1970s in fact reversed a trend decline. It reflected the absence of large United States stocks that had compensated for such fluctuations in the past.

The need to recompose stocks is universally agreed. Yet little progress has been made. One reason has been lack of consensus on the sharing of costs between producers and consumers. Another and more fundamental cause has been disagreement about the purposes of the reserve and the role of the market in allocating global production. Despite their efficacy in keeping food prices low, one should not disregard the inefficiencies and costs to consumers of the large American food surpluses of the 1950s and 1960s—nor can one ignore the adverse impact on the agricultural policies of recipients of massive food aid from the United States. It does not make sense to return to such a past. Rather, a global reserve to ensure reasonably well against significant shortfalls in developing countries could be relatively small and inexpensive because aggregate grain supplies are not greatly variable.[53] Developing countries falling below trend production by specified amounts that vary with their level of development could have access to the reserve at average prices prevailing in a year of no shortfall. Thus both quantity and price guarantees are easily feasible.

Less feasible is a fund available to all buyers and sellers and holding quantities sufficient to avert price changes. For that purpose, freer trade is a far more efficient solution. It was not the abject failure of the free market alone that led to the food price rise in 1972–1974, but also its limited sway. The self-imposed insulation from the market of major exporters such as

[53]See D. Gale Johnson, *World Food Problems and Prospects*, Foreign Affairs Study 20, American Enterprise Institute, Washington, D.C., 1974, on this point and on the role of limitations to trade in the 1973–1974 crisis.

Canada and Australia and importers such as the Common Market, all of whom limited price increases and controlled trade, meant that the burden of international price adjustment, where it occurred, had to be even greater.

Unless the price mechanism is allowed to register scarcity more accurately, the necessary supply and demand adjustments to avert crisis are less likely to occur. It is striking that the recent food shortages have galvanized efforts in developing countries to deal with both the agricultural and the population problem. For the poorest countries, larger internal production of food supplies is the most efficient development strategy and should be encouraged. A global reserve to ensure developing-country requirements, along with freer trade, can provide much needed security. But the realities of economic interdependence require, in addition, serious efforts to engage all nations within a freer market; the developed countries can hardly preach about access to supply when it is denied in such vital merchandise of commerce as food.

This emphasis upon freer trade is not merely to suit an ideological fancy. The quantitative impact of such a policy on foreign-exchange earnings of developing countries is impressive. A serious and sustained effort to reduce trade barriers in the industrialized countries could mean more than $30 billion (in 1975 dollars) a year in increased export earnings for developing countries by 1985.[54] Even the Kennedy Round reductions—which excluded items of greatest immediate interest to developing countries—are estimated to have resulted in $1 billion in additional developing-country exports. By contrast, the gains from present preference provisions seem to have been substantially smaller, placed by some estimates at no more than $100 million.[55]

[54]Robert McNamara, *Address to Board of Governors*, October 1976, p. 21.

[55]Mordechai E. Kreinin and J. Michael Finger, in "A New International Economic Order," U.S. Department of Treasury, Office of the Assistant Secretary for International Affairs Discussion Paper, 1975, cite various detailed studies and this conclusion (pp. 7–9).

Later but still uncertain estimates suggest a greater increase in exports from preferences—as much as $300 million to $500 million. But as long as there are value limits and quantitative restrictions the benefits are limited, while with

Commodity agreements, if concluded, will yield lesser variation in price but probably no significant increase in foreign exchange. It is doubtful that the developed countries will agree to any scheme that raises real commodity prices in a systematic way. Yet even supposing indexation were accepted and the real price of the 10 UNCTAD core commodities doubled, then a generous estimate of the annual net gain by 1985 would be of the order of $18 billion (1975 dollars). Apart from their improbability, those benefits would have to offset the costs of rigid prices in reduced exports, which are here ignored. By way of comparison, the expanded IMF compensatory facility had already in 1976 increased foreign-exchange credits to more than 25 developing countries by between $1.5 billion and $2 billion even without modification to compensate for import prices.[56]

Systematic expansion of trade opportunities, coupled with efforts to provide orderly competition and to reduce uncertainty through market incentives, thus can make a difference. The more advanced Third World countries of the South can be expected to gain particularly from such a policy because their share of the trade of the developing countries is large. But the poorest countries, too, by policies directing more of their production to the external market, may actually improve their relative economic position. A grain reserve directed especially to the needs of the poorest, and more generous capital flows, can also assure that Fourth World needs are not excluded.

2. Financial Flows

A second important set of transactions for which the market at present provides only imperfect guidance are international

---

universally freer trade they would not be similarly constrained. For these larger estimates and useful discussion, see R. E. Baldwin and T. Murray, "MFN Tariff Reductions and LDC Benefits under the GSP," *Economic Journal*, vol. 87, no. 345, March 1977, pp. 30–46, and Zubair Iqbal, "The Generalized System of Tariffs Examined," *Finance and Development*, vol. 12, no. 3, September 1975, pp. 34–40.

[56]The estimate of the effect of doubling the *real* price of core commodities is based on a $17 billion value (in 1975 dollars) of exports in 1970–1973, assumed to grow at 2 percent a year. See *International Financial Statistics*, International Monetary Fund, Washington, D.C., vol. 29, no. 12, December 1976.

financial flows. These have changed markedly in recent years in favor of a larger private, as opposed to public, component. Between 1967 and 1974, the composition of developing-country external public debt increased from 27 to 35 percent privately supplied; the total amount outstanding more than tripled. This meant that private credits accounted for almost two-fifths of the dramatic increase in debt in recent years. In the higher-income developing countries the reliance on the private sector was more marked still; thus in Latin America, of the $30 billion increase in debt private sources of credit, especially banks, made up almost two-thirds.[57]

This expansion of private-sector activity is consistent with the greater scope for market influence that has been advocated. It has contributed to an improved growth record in the developing countries and, after the oil crisis, a source of funds that partially insulated them from the downward trend in the world economy. Access to the private market bypassed the political and economic costs of official bilateral flows and gave scope for the application of a more objective profitability standard. Bank lending provided foreign exchange that could be used immediately. Yet larger private flows have also brought new problems. The allocation of private resources has favored the higher-income developing countries rather than the poorest. Private banks quite rightly searched out the most promising application of their resources. The increased assignment of funds to the poorest countries from official sources did not rectify the balance, simply because the growth of official lending was not as rapid. Differential capital availability contributed to differentiated growth that even more sharply divided the Third World from the Fourth in the late 1960s and early 1970s.

On the other side, the past acquisition of that large debt now poses a potentially serious burden of adjustment in many of those higher-income countries. The supply of private credit to even highly regarded developing countries is not entirely within their control. It has been to a considerable degree a reflex of economic conditions within the industrialized world. Abundant credits

[57]These debt data are taken from World Bank, *Annual Report*, 1976, Table 4. The Mediterranean countries are excluded from the developing-country total.

were first made available during the recession of 1971–1972 when Eurodollar interest rates plummeted. Banks manifested a herd instinct, as favored countries were besieged by eager lenders. Terms were generous, and few candidate countries resisted the attraction. It seemed a very positive opportunity. Foreign financial markets could replace the inadequacy of internal intermediation, while external resources supplemented domestic savings.

In accumulating debt, these countries took on a certain obligation for repayment in return for uncertain potential benefits. Such a trade-off is sensible when foreign resources are necessary to sustain capital formation, either as a supplement to savings or as a source of foreign exchange. Then future growth provides the basis for repayment. But the accumulation of debt in the early 1970s went beyond such bounds of necessity. Moreover, the terms of repayment, while seemingly attractive, did not possess the grant element inherent in public resources. Only at receipt is a dollar of private credit equivalent to a dollar of public credit; thereafter it sets up a stream of larger and more immediate outflows.

The recession that began in 1974 in the industrialized countries and the influx of deposits from the newly rich oil states facilitated an increased flow of bank credits and a rollover of the old. But now augmented debt was a matter of necessity rather than choice if developing-country growth was to be maintained. Interest rates have become dramatically higher and credit maturities shorter. Banks have not disguised their desire for the developing countries to curtail their expansion plans and reduce their import requirements: in some instances these private institutions, rather than the international ones, have begun to impose and monitor policy targets.

The next few years will witness a need for a large flow of external resources to developing countries merely to amortize and service the past debt. This need coincides with a greater need for net capital inflows to compensate for the recession-induced decrease in growth of exports. Banks quite naturally show reluctance to lend as risk increases, thereby, of course, making default more likely. International loans, even more than the domestic bank portfolio, are quality- rather than price-rationed. Clearly, developing countries must adjust to the new higher oil prices and to the decline in real income they represent. But external pressures for conservative policies can be exaggerated. If the surpluses of the oil exporters had not been channeled to developing countries, world income would have fallen significantly. Their deficits increased demand for industrialized-country exports measurably in the last few years.[58]

Thus the market mechanism has not proven fully adequate—for either the higher-income or the lowest-income developing countries. The call for a debt moratorium and the insistence upon larger public resource flows are responses to these felt deficiencies. They do not take account of the further potential danger that more rapid recovery in the industrialized countries will reduce the real supply of private credit to developing countries.

The problem has three dimensions. One is the need to assure continuing intermediation in financial markets to prevent an unnecessary decline in global income. A second is restoration of a better balance between private and public sources of funds, reducing the exposure of the former while enhancing the influence of the latter. Third is the longer-run requirement that developing-country exports expand rapidly enough to pay back the debt. Credit can forestall the immediate consequences of the oil price rise, but it cannot avert the eventual need to accommodate. Thus an essential requirement for the effective functioning of financial markets is freer merchandise markets. The two go hand in hand.

As far as financial flows themselves are concerned, three measures are called for. The first responds to the need to reduce uncertainty in private bank flows and to continue the recycling of petrodollars. An exchange of part of the present commercial bank portfolio of developing-country loans for World Bank bonds could be quite constructive. No immediate increase in official

[58]John A. Holsen and Jean L. Waelbroeck, in "The Less Developed Countries and the International Monetary Mechanism," *American Economic Review*, vol. 66, no. 2, May 1976, estimate that explicit balance-of-payments borrowing by developing countries of $20 billion in 1974–75 sustained developed-country aggregate demand by 1 percent, or perhaps $30 billion (p. 175).

lending capacity would be created, but the reduced exposure of commercial banks would permit them to continue to play a role in expanding credit on their own account. In turn, the World Bank could renegotiate the interest rates and terms on outstanding debt it had so acquired to lessen the burden on the most vulnerable developing countries. Even so, because of short maturity and high yield on the assets, the Bank's receipts could quite possibly be enhanced. In return for temporarily greater risk, it could earn larger profits that could subsidize loans to the poorest countries. And risk for the financial system as a whole could be reduced by such further intermediation.

Only a proportion of commercial bank loans could be absorbed by the multilateral banks, since private bank lending now has considerably surpassed that of the official banks. But even an exchange of $5 billion to $10 billion over the near term would reduce present pressures dramatically and appreciably alter developing-country perspectives. To ensure that a representative mix of loans and not merely the most marginal, would be offered, one might have the commercial banks select some part of the portfolio for exchange, and the official banks would select the rest.

This short-term swap averts a present crisis. It does so in a way that is consistent with the objective of defining a more prominent role for multilateral public capital flows. For even if commercial banks could resume a more aggressive lending posture, it still might not suffice to adequately intermediate the oil-exporter surpluses. There is no reason why the private institutions that receive deposits should be entirely responsible for their placement. Private purchases of World Bank liabilities, permitting the Bank to increase its lending, and closer cooperation between private and public institutions through joint participation, can make the financial system work much more effectively. Lending by commercial banks should not be a dominant source of development finance; their proper domain is much more short-term and oriented to projects yielding more immediate repayment. Longer-term commitments and the policy dialogue with the developing countries require a guiding hand from the official institutions.

If the international banks are to play that role, they must be able to increase their size. That then imposes the second policy requirement—an increased governmental subscription to their capital. This authority does not require a counterpart public contribution of actual resources. What is needed is the opportunity to tap the private market and to perform more adequately the intermediary role between the surpluses in the developed world and the oil-exporting countries and the deficits in the developing countries. The cost in public funds is therefore a small fraction of the increase in lending capacity.

Larger official flows, coupled with a reduced surplus for the oil exporters as their real imports increase—thereby giving a positive impulse to world trade—can in the context of freer trade prove adequate to the needs of the Third World. The continuing requirements of resource transfer to the poorest countries, however, will likely exceed what increase of international bank capital can permit. Nor can one depend on national generosity; the experience of declining real official bilateral aid in the last decade is sobering proof. Even were this not the case, reassertion of larger aid targets is unlikely to be effective. An adequate response to the problem of the Fourth World requires a more automatic, continuing, and truly international supply of resources.

Thus a necessary third measure is earmarking of receipts from one or more international taxes for redistribution to the lowest-income countries. The revenues could be obtained as a share of the profits emanating from exploitation of common ocean resources, levies on pollution of the atmosphere and seas, or a tax on exports of nonrenewable resources. In all three instances, there are persuasive arguments that producers within the present nation-states fail to take into account the full and appropriate social (global) costs inherent in their production processes. Such taxes would therefore be justifiable intervention not merely for the sake of equity but also for efficiency. The levies would be progressive in effect. It is the richer states that exploit the international fisheries, that will exploit the ocean bed's metallic nodules, and whose consumption of minerals and manufactures would bear the lion's share of any export tax.[59] These receipts, not requiring an annual debate and vote in each of the industrial

[59] I am assuming that the export tax would largely be passed on to importers (because demand is relatively inelastic) and ultimately to final consumers.

democracies, could begin to dent the gross inequality in the distribution of world wealth. (Note, however, that even with a revenue tax, exploitation of seabed resources might harm developing-country exporters as their land-based production faced increased competition. Adequate compensation to developing-country producers could require transfers unrelated to taxes if their incomes were adversely affected by such new common property resources.)

Even by the end of the next decade, studies suggest that taxes on profits derived from exploitation of seabed minerals could yield close to a billion dollars annually, rising sharply thereafter. Full capture of the rents from fisheries might produce twice as much. A 2 percent tax on the value of mineral exports could easily generate revenues of more than $4 billion. These sources taken together imply a flow of funds that would supplement a projection of current grant levels by more than 50 percent by the middle of the next decade. Equally significantly, it would establish a precedent for mobilizing the resources of the global community to deal with problems of global magnitude.[60]

These new resources should be allocated to the Fourth World on the basis of need. Universal satisfaction of the minimal requirements of nutrition, health, education, and housing is the proper goal. Yet there must also be scope to reward nations for their own efforts both to meet such immediate requirements and to go beyond them. National policies cannot be an exclusive basis for distribution of official resources, but neither can they be ignored.

In particular, it would be folly not to incorporate the question of population growth integrally within the global economic dialogue. National population policies inadequately take into ac-

---

[60]For estimates of potential revenues from fisheries and manganese module exploitation, see Richard N. Cooper, "The Oceans as a Source of Revenue," to appear in J. Bhagwati (ed.), *Proposals for a New International Economic Order*, MIT Press, Cambridge, Mass., forthcoming. George Bulkley presents somewhat larger estimates of revenue potential of undersea mining in his thesis, "An Econometric Evaluation Using Computer Simulation Techniques of the Impact of Different Legal Regimes upon the Size and Distribution of Benefits from Mining Minerals on the Deep Ocean Floor," University of California, Berkeley, 1977 (unpublished Ph.D. dissertation), which I have used here.

count the full consequences for the global community of excessive population growth—just as decisions at the family level ignore the implications for national societies. Rapid population growth makes more difficult the already serious problem of equitable development. It need not be left to chance. International resources can provide financial incentives to reinforce, not to impose, what is rapidly emerging as a global consensus. Countries that are desirous of reducing population growth rates should be granted the financial means to do so; those that are most successful in implementing national policies that are not merely directed at family planning but also go directly to the economic and social status of the poor should be rewarded more than others. It is appropriate to link the issue of population growth to the eradication of absolute poverty in this way, for the two are clearly related. Such a thrust can sustain the resolve of the industrialized countries to stay with the task of mobilizing adequate resources for the Fourth World.

3. Investment and Technology Flow

A third set of economic interrelations that a reformed international order must address involves private investment and technology transfer. The private sector of the developed countries has been the most prominent means of transferring technical knowledge and managerial capacity and diffusing modern industry. That know-how has been disseminated throughout the world in unprecedented fashion through the workings of the market. Yet direct private investment continues to be viewed with suspicion and resentment and as an inadequate instrument for making available to the South the technological capacity of the North. That dissatisfaction explains the passage of a Charter of Economic Rights and Duties of States designed to enhance the sovereignty of host states while checking the power of the transnationals. And efforts within the UN and other international forums for a code of conduct to limit the actions of foreign private firms have been regularly pursued.

There is a persuasive case for supplementing the automatic constraint of the market with some kind of regulatory action. Monopoly power is the rule rather than the exception for foreign enterprises.[61] It is the rare firm that invests abroad without some control in that market, in the form of either import restrictions or exclusive franchises and enforced by unique access to technical production or marketing processes. Entry by competitors cannot be relied upon to drive down the rate of return to normal levels, nor can imports from other foreign sources.

Few firms possess absolute market power, however. There are other transnationals with similar products and skills, competitors that are increasingly of different nationalities. American, Japanese, and German firms now bid among themselves with greater frequency, matching now on the supply side the competition that formerly was much more vigorous among potential host countries. This environment favors more active countervailing intervention by host countries in determining the conditions of entry and operation of transnational enterprises. Necessarily, as the commitments of the firm grow, its own relative power diminishes; the ardor displayed by the host country in its initial courtship converts to a cooler, more considered evaluation of actual performance. Market guarantees, export subsidies, tax privileges—all become subject to renegotiation.

An important source of bargaining strength for the foreign firm in this context is its command over technology. The price of the technology, whether implicit in profits or explicit in the guise of royalties, bears little relationship to its actual cost. Its additional application abroad involves little further expense, but rather amortizes a total research and development effort. Indeed, that opportunity is one of the principal incentives for foreign operation. Firms can bargain knowing full well that the opportunity cost of replicating the technology is much greater than the asking price, while the latter still can yield handsome profits.

The transnationals and host countries thus operate in an imperfectly competitive market in which each of the actors possesses power and encounters constraints. The firm can play one government off against the other to maximize its advantage; on

___

[61] For a useful, far-ranging discussion of the characteristics of the multinational enterprise and its implications for conventional economic analysis, see John H. Dunning (ed.), *Economic Analysis and the Multinational Enterprise*, Praeger, New York, 1975.

the other hand, once established, its environment is very much determined by host country policy. The state can try to appropriate excess profits, but its treatment of investors will influence not only those firms already in the country but also those who potentially might come. It is a market far different from the classical competitive ideal.

Steps can be taken to improve it, however, and to assure that the manifest need for investment resources and technology in the South does not redound to its disadvantage. Such measures go beyond the capacity of individual developing countries, lest the search for temporary advantage lead each to deviate from the rules and provoke a less satisfactory outcome for all. The industrialized countries have an obligation to participate because their national interest in an equitable and efficient international economic order transcends the short-run interests of their private sectors.

A first requirement is much fuller disclosure. Transnational enterprises should be expected, as a counterpart to their privilege of wide-ranging international operation, to report much more completely on their activities to a central, international repository. Any report must include information on pricing policies and profits in all the various countries where the firm transacts business. Transnationals engage in intrafirm transactions that defy the "arms length" simulation of the market; at best, one can have an ex post reckoning. Disclosure opens the option for the host states to take corrective action as they see fit. Essential, too, is information on royalty payments and adequate descriptions of the technology for which they are made. The lack of a functioning technology market is explained not merely by the heterogeneity of the transactions but also the ignorance surrounding them. Finally, there should also be regular interchange of information between the tax and regulatory agencies of the industrialized countries and those in the developing countries. One standard of business ethics should prevail internationally, and there is no better warrant of the commitment of the developed nations that it be an honorable one than such cooperation.

These measures do not usurp national authority for particular policies that accord with the development objectives and philosophy of individual countries. They tread a fine line between centralization of information and decentralization of decisions. As such, they do not prevent the transnational from exercising its unique genius of organizing its economic operations globally, a circumstance that involves taking advantage of different objective conditions such as market size, location, adequacy of skills, and the like. Each country should have an opportunity to influence the kind and amount of technology that is transferred, by varying the incentives it is prepared to offer. Any attempt to enforce uniform behavior will infringe upon the choice of development models without assuring a more equitable distribution of international income. It is a static approach that ignores differences among countries as well as the dynamic nature of the bargain between firms and host countries. One can only enforce freer dissemination of information and rely upon the shrewdness of host nations to negotiate more satisfactory results.

A new approach to the resolution of nationalization disputes is also indicated. While relatively few in number, expropriations have frequently led to bitter conflict. Diplomatic interventions by industrialized countries occasion a virulent reaction in the South because they seem the ultimate manifestation of the power of the North to defend its private interests—right or wrong. Conversely, the foreign business community regards unjustified nationalizations, and the inability to enforce compensation, as evidence of the higher risk that justifies the greater rates of return so objectionable to host countries.

No simple rule will avoid all disputes, partly because they reflect an amalgam of economic and political considerations; indeed, one purpose may be a calculated desire to stimulate conflict. But the dimensions of that conflict can be narrowed and some disputes averted by devising a solution that recognizes the limitations of the legal framework. The industrialized countries have long favored international arbitration to resolve disputes; facilities have been established in conjunction with the World Bank, but they are infrequently used. Few developing countries are willing to make any concession of sovereignty to an outside, neutral agency because doing so would deprive them of the very countervailing power they are trying to exert against the enterprise. They wish, on the contrary, to force the home state to value good relations more than the private loss and thereby to discourage it from pressing the case.

That reluctance to accept arbitration is reinforced by lack of consensus on a standard of asset valuation. Many developed countries, including prominently the United States, interpret international law as requiring compensation equivalent to the ongoing value of the firm. However, a book value measure is favored by the majority of countries in the South, not merely for foreign but also for domestic nationalization. There is little prospect of a mutually satisfactory proceeding when the very basis of valuation is in doubt.

There are good reasons to seek to end the impasse by international agreement on a standard of book value (adjusted for inflation). The net value of the enterprise measured in this accounting fashion will in fact approximate the capitalized value of a stream of normal profits; otherwise the firm would not have made the investment. The book value will exceed the ongoing value when the investment is a disappointment relative to initial expectations; it will be smaller when there is realization of windfall, unanticipated profits. But to the extent that the latter are not the result of decisions internal to the firm, their social expropriation is reasonable. That is precisely the justification for nationalization which insistence upon compensation at market value defeats.[62]

Acceptance of this standard finesses the larger legal principle inherent in denial of the right of diplomatic representation—the Calvo Doctrine espoused by many developing countries (according to which foreign investors must submit to the legislative authority of the host country). National sovereignty and international law would coincide in practice. A cooperative, joint

[62]The book value of the initial investment should equal the anticipated returns capitalized by the risk-inclusive normal profit rate under competitive circumstances. If higher returns are in fact earned, then they presumably contain a monopoly rent that should be subject to expropriation. One of the problems with the ongoing-value criterion is that firms do not wish to discount the anticipated returns by the high, ex ante rate of discount they use in their own internal calculations.

governmental effort or an outside agency could then more readily deal with disputes in a constructive fashion. Industrialized countries have an interest in the payment of fair compensation and not the maximum compensation desired by the firm. That difference must be emphasized and puts a different light on defense of property rights.

There can be a further deterrent effect of the policy change, reducing the likelihood of expropriation. Book value tends to be known with a fair amount of precision, making the potential costs of compensation a more certain magnitude. Governments will have to decide whether taking over the enterprise is worth it. Of course there will still be differences concerning past taxes that should have been paid, claims for return of unjustified profits, etc. A consensual standard of valuation is not a panacea. But its achievement can contribute to a more rational climate for evaluating foreign property rights, and it can moderate the role of sheer economic power. As such, it would permit developing countries to opt for interdependence without fear of sacrificing their internal, national goals; yet at the same time the policy makes clear the intent of protecting the legitimate right of foreign investors to "prompt, adequate and effective competition."

I emphasize these two thrusts as examples of the possibilities for international regulation of corporate behavior within a market framework. Others have stressed diffusion of information and accelerated technology transfer under governmental auspices, the creation of appropriate technology through international centers, etc. These activities are important, especially in the agricultural sector. But the greater priority is to harness more effectively the constructive potential of private foreign capital and technology. For some time to come it is likely to remain the dominant instrument of rapid industrialization in developing countries. Replication of the research and development effort in manufactures already being undertaken in the North is not an efficient alternative. Pooling of effort within the South can make adaptations to that technology more accessible and should be encouraged. But still more important is creating an environment in which the private sector of industrialized countries and developing-country governments interact more beneficially.

THREE

Prospects for Reform

The principles and policies enunciated above will not inspire immediate and unanimous acclaim in either North or South. This package does not involve large resource transfers. For the greatest part, the potential increase in foreign exchange earnings relies on expanded trade and credit and thus on a significant developing-country contribution as well. Nor will powerful interest groups within the industrialized countries welcome more liberal trade or enforceable international rules governing transnational enterprises. This reformism, because it is broad-ranging, may arouse greater opposition than apparently more radical, but in fact partial and inadequate, measures such as a common fund to finance commodity agreements.

The proper sequence to eventual international agreement must begin not with global conferences but with domestic consensus. Developing countries have seen many other such liberal proposals; the South remains to be convinced of the sincerity of the commitment of the North. That requires an internal public debate to galvanize support for a policy of nonhegemonic interdependence. The inadequacies of the status quo must be understood. It is not an even-handed policy to deny market access to imports from developing countries but insist on nondiscrimination against foreign capital. It is not justifiable to derive significant national advantage from investment abroad but then refuse to permit the products of such subsidiaries to compete freely in world markets. It is not consistent to contemplate means of controlling the export of technology but expect free access to needed raw materials.

In short, a truly interdependent new order must rely on symmetrically freer market forces, not on immediate national advantage, for the distribution of benefits.

The principal costs to the industrialized economies of such an interdependence are the reallocation of domestic resources from present inefficient applications. Freer trade would accelerate an already discernible longer-term trend in economic activity. Because of affluence and the unprecedented expansion of world trade the industrialized economies already have seen rapid growth of service activities at the expense of the more traditional labor-intensive industrial sectors. Income is derived from abroad not merely from the sale of goods but also through the return on investment and on service and management contracts. There has been a dramatic change in the internal composition of the labor force. Women have increased their participation in the new white-collar jobs thus created. Educational attainment and requirements have increased. Organized labor increasingly represents those segments of the labor force threatened with international competition rather than directly benefiting from it.

These domestic adjustment costs must be faced. Whatever the favorable aggregate economic effects of a more liberal policy, some individuals lose. Yet the losses are small and manageable. Recent estimates of the consequences in the United States of a 50 percent reduction in all tariffs (but without a change in textile imports or agricultural exports) indicate an overall loss of 151,000 jobs and the creation of 136,000, with a somewhat more unfavorable balance within manufactures alone. Predictably, professional and technical workers as well as agricultural laborers gain at the expense of semi- and unskilled operatives. Phased over a 10-year period, even in the import-sensitive industries, normal growth should eliminate any problem of unemployment. Nor does the regional distribution of the impacts modify the "main conclusion . . . that the United States can participate in a substantial tariff-cutting negotiation without causing adverse trade and employment effects."[63] The same would likely hold true for other industrialized countries.

[63]Robert E. Baldwin, "Trade and Employment Effects in the United States of Multilateral Tariff Reductions," *American Economic Review*, vol. 66, no. 2, May 1976, p. 148.

Admittedly, a greater reduction on items of special interest to the developing countries would exaggerate the employment effect, but not so much as to make the policy unfeasible. A time when domestic policy in the industrialized democracies is increasingly facing up to the problem of noninflationary job creation is, paradoxically, perhaps the best moment to move ahead boldly on the trade front. One can exploit the opportunity to create permanent opportunities for employment in new sectors rather than falling victim to the appeal for protectionist expedients. Job creation explicitly compatible with much freer trade may be a better application of public resources—for both North and South—than generalized increases in foreign assistance. Such adjustment aid could perhaps even be visualized as a form of official development assistance, making the trade-off between freer trade and greater aid more transparent.

The threat of inflation, another serious domestic concern in the North, also is diminished by a more liberal international policy. Consumers have learned to make their interests in lower prices more vocal; no longer are producers alone decisive in their espousal of less foreign competition. As freer markets come to mean more adequate supplies and brakes on price increases, potential support for a liberal order could swamp the reluctant nay-sayers.

For the United States, the novelty of interdependence has created a special reluctance. The prospect of a more service-oriented and internationally open economy means a potential vulnerability that is disturbing to some.[64] The example of the rise and decline of Great Britain as an industrial power seems to warn against such a model. As an analogue, however, it is not compelling. First, the degree of openness of the American economy would be altered only modestly by much more liberal trade; the ratio of imports to gross domestic product stands today at less than 10 percent, far smaller than for any other industrialized country or for historical Britain. Second, the lack of tech-

[64]Robert Gilpin emphasizes the risks associated with foreign investment rather than with free trade. Some risks apply to the latter as well, and not merely because the two are interrelated. See Robert Gilpin, *U.S. Power and the Multinational Corporation*, Basic Books, New York, 1975, chaps. VIII and IX.

nological dynamism in Britain was itself fed by the closure of markets in industrialized Europe and the United States and was not the result of free trade. Industrial exports embodying research and development would be favored, not handicapped, by a more liberal international regime. Nor, finally, would an import surplus repaying past investments make the United States a *rentier* economy, without incentive for investment in continuing domestic industrial growth. The internal market is simply too important.

Rather, history suggests another and more valid lesson. It was not possible at the end of the nineteenth century to establish an international order that lent itself to peaceful diffusion of power and emergence of relatively powerful new nation-states. That opportunity and challenge has now been repeated a century later in the guise of the North-South engagement over a new international economic order. Until those larger stakes inform domestic policy in the industrialized countries, the prospects for meaningful international economic reform must remain in doubt.

Ultimately there must be an appeal to a sense of equity as well as a sense of necessity. The United States is perhaps uniquely poised to respond. The rhetoric emerging from the globe's South is no more shrill than that which came out of the American South and West at the end of the nineteenth century:

Wall Street owns the country. . . . The great common people of this country are slaves, and monopoly is the master. The West and South are bound and prostrate before the manufacturing East. . . . The politicians say we suffered from overproduction. Overproduction when 10,000 little children, so statistics tell us, starve to death every year in the United States. We want money, land and transportation. . . . We want the accursed foreclosure system wiped out.[65]

Populism did not achieve its specific demands, although it initiated a continuing search for means by which government might mediate the impact of a market economy increasingly subject to

[65] Mary Elizabeth Lease of Kansas, one of the leaders of the Populist campaign, is the author of this particular broadside. Quoted in Carl C. Taylor, *The Farmer's Movement, 1620–1920*, Greenwood, Westport, Conn., (reprint of 1953 ed.), p. 283.

the influence of powerful and organized forces. Many of its policy proposals would have been counterproductive by denying the need for a continuing reallocation of resources in response to market signals. It was the long-run adaptation to an evolving industrial economy, not the freezing of the economic structure, that ultimately reduced hardships.

Nothing more or less than a similar adaptation is proposed internationally. Measures that grossly sacrifice efficiency for the sake of immediate equity will meet a fate no kinder than did the claims of the Populists; and their status within a functioning polity gave them more effective voice than the South possesses in the global community. The impossibility of such measures being taken on a global scale is no great loss. Internal mobility of capital and labor compensated historically for rigidities introduced by regulation. That option is not open internationally. The long-run transformation of national economies is the principal means by which developing countries can hope to improve their situation. Efficiency and equity can go hand in hand in the international market if it is allowed to work.

Leadership within the North can mobilize popular support for a liberal and comprehensive program. Events since 1973 have afforded vivid evidence of how individual livelihoods can be negatively affected by international economic policies. The task now is to convert the current apprehension into thorough understanding and endorsement of interdependence. There are ample opportunities to signal a new public will in the North. Bilateral foreign assistance allocations will represent an early test. Even if an international fund were agreed upon, its financial contribution initially would be limited. Public resources are urgently needed to sustain the real value of bilateral programs as well as to meet past and future multilateral commitments. Decisions favoring adjustment assistance against more protection, not reluctantly but positively, will also be an important gauge of national sentiment. More than rhetoric, concrete decisions will pave the way to more far-reaching global agreement.

Once the domestic groundwork has been laid, global accord will be within reach. The euphoria of 1974 has given way to greater pragmatism within the South. Developing countries are prepared to bargain and to respond to a comprehensive program offered by the North. The contrast between the Sixth and Seventh Special Sessions of the UN is informative. But instead of a large list of initiatives, what will be more productive is agreement on principles and implementation of priorities. Those proposed here would find support within developing countries if they believed these priorities were more than a diversionary reiteration of the imperfect status quo. As one of their spokesmen has said, "the poor nations are seeking greater equality of opportunity, not charity from the uncertain generosity of the rich."[66] No new structures are necessary. CIEC is already in place to provide an immediate framework for negotiations.

There is now greater appreciation in the South that the new order will take time to construct and that its accomplishments will be cumulative. No agreement, moreover, can be a guarantor of more rapid and equalizing development. That responsibility, and the resources contributing most to it, reside with the developing countries themselves. Unless domestic policies mobilize savings, channel investment efficiently, and provide for fair distribution of the rewards of economic growth, and unless the poor can be made more productive, the shape of international economic relations will be of little significance.

The new order advocated here does not represent a radical change. Its reforms create an environment linking interdependence and development and facilitating both. Third World countries would continue their accelerated development; a larger commitment of resources to the problem of absolute poverty and the wretched standard of living in the Fourth World could establish the basis for more consistent performance there. The specific policies proposed differentiate among developing countries, seeking to aid the poorest but without penalizing the middle- and higher-income nations. Inevitably, Brazil, Mexico, Venezuela, Iran, and some few other high-income representatives of the South would have their power enhanced by the participatory framework and the possibilities for continuing mediation be-

[66]ul Haq, *The Third World and the International Economic Order*, p. 8.

tween industrialized and developing countries. That constructive role should substitute for more adventuresome undertakings.

It is, in short, a reform worthy of commitment: principled but also pragmatic, familiar yet innovative, efficient yet promising more equal opportunity. The Great Depression of the 1930s spawned the Keynesian Revolution and renewed recognition of the relevance of mercantilistic statecraft. The oil crisis of the 1970s will have had as profound an impact if it leads to the recuperation of liberal international economic principles as the basis for relations among states.

Delinking North and South: Unshackled or Unhinged?

Carlos F. Díaz-Alejandro

ONE

Introduction

Delinking (or decoupling) the North and the South has become one of those popular slogans that so often either structures or substitutes for thinking in the area of development and international relations. This is an essay at understanding the mood and the substance behind this influential concept. A critical but not unsympathetic stance will be taken.

Precise definitions of *delinking* vary among different authors. To some it means a complete cutoff of commercial and financial relations between a given developing country, or a group of them, and the centers of capitalism. Proponents of this version of delinking regard such a cutoff as a necessary condition for true development, by which they mean balanced, equitable, and self-reliant growth. The traditional case for freedom in trade and capital movements is thus stood on its head. But even among revolutionary governments there have been few followers of this pure delinking thesis. A modified version of the thesis, which

NOTE: Earlier drafts of this essay benefited from detailed comments and criticisms from Andrés Bianchi, Jaime Campos, Benjamin I. Cohen, Richard N. Cooper, Max Corden, Marcelo Diamand, Gerald K. Helleiner, Nurul Islam, Charles P. Kindleberger, Nicolas Lardy, Jorge Braga de Macedo, Vahid Nowshirvani, Maurice Scott, Frances Stewart, Paul Streeten, Dan Usher, and Laurence Whitehead. They should not be held responsible for the opinions found in this paper; indeed, some disagreed with a good part of its substance and style. I am also grateful to Gail Ross for expert typing and editing.

may be labeled *selective delinking*, will also be explored in this essay. Selective delinking lacks the dramatic clarity of its purer cousin, but it may be closer to what many in the Third World, particularly those actually in positions of decision-making responsibility, regard as a desirable strategy. While pure delinking is nowadays associated with advocacy of socialist revolution in the Third World, selective delinking can be pursued by a broad variety of political regimes. As will become clear, selective delinking makes more economic sense to this author than does pure delinking.

However, whether pure or selective, delinking cannot be evaluated solely on the basis of economic criteria. The case for delinking is primarily political and sociological rather than economic, at least as such terms are understood by most mainstream Northern economists. This should not make the orthodox scoff. Even the purest neoclassical economist would be hard pressed to deny that international economic relations are highly politicized and that decisions on foreign trade and finance will influence internal political balances. Furthermore, the purely economic justifications for laissez faire in international economic relations have been subjected to numerous qualifications by postwar theoretical developments. The new orthodox case for free trade now includes heavy doses of more or less practical and political judgments. Once this tricky arena has been entered, one surely cannot ignore the judgments of others with different economic viewpoints.

The essay is organized as follows: The next section will sketch old and new critiques of laissez faire in international economic relations. Advocates of delinking are heirs to this tradition; indeed, it could be argued that once misguided models and the more spectacular rhetoric are peeled away, what remains in the delinking case is mostly a new packaging of the many valid points made throughout history against the extreme case for laissez faire. The pure delinker and the extreme advocate of laissez faire can be viewed as two straw men locked in fierce battle. The essay will continue with a search for the precise policy prescriptions made by proponents of pure delinking. Some delinkers see little need to go beyond calls for socialist revolution and a cutting

off of ties with capitalist markets. Delinking for them is fundamentally a political banner and a debating slogan: the less its
proposals are developed and examined, the greater is its use-
fulness as a rallying cry for revolution or at least for exciting
students and exasperating the orthodox. But other interpretations
of delinking, as already noted, are also possible, and a modified
selective-delinking strategy for less developed countries (LDCs)
will be presented. An evaluation of that strategy brings out some
difficulties but also interesting themes and ideas on how to expand Southern options in the world economy.

Up to this point, the essay will consider international economic
relations from the viewpoint of a single given LDC that is trying
to restructure its society, taking the world economic system as
given. But while a single country has limited room to maneuver
when facing international markets, the Third World as a whole
could help rewrite the rules of the game so as to expand the
narrow alternatives each nation faces individually. The time is
ripe for such rewriting, as present rules and practices trouble
both South and North. Buyers and sellers of raw materials, borrowers and lenders in world markets all fret under present arrangements of doing business. The fourth section, therefore,
begins what can be regarded as a second paper, examining the
world economy as a whole, and investigates how a partially
delinked world would look as well as whether such a vision is
viable. That desirable international framework will be viewed
as permissive of different types of LDC socioeconomic regimes;
its objective is to accommodate change and reform, not to bring
them about. Pure delinkers might, of course, regard this as an
exercise in "renegotiating the terms of dependence," while reformist Northerners eager to launch a worldwide war on poverty
and injustice will find that framework too restrictive.

The fifth section will touch briefly on other aspects of world
economic reform and on some Northern apprehensions about
the reform process. A few remarks will also be made on the
problems and opportunities created for the Third World by the
more active participation of socialist countries in the world economy. The essay will close by emphasizing the limits of what can
be expected to be achieved by manipulating LDC and world

trade and financial policies and making a few other general observations on North-South relations.

One last introductory remark: The essay, particularly in its first half, touches on matters that throughout history have led to bloody contests between groups, each containing individuals of principle. Those in the front lines of such battles would discuss issues raised here with a passion and commitment I cannot duplicate. What follows is a perception of the substance, as well as of the sound and fury, of that struggle as viewed from a comfortable academic tower.

TWO

The Critique of Laissez Faire

The critique of laissez faire in international economic relations predates and is more developed than precise policy proposals on how and how fast to delink South from North and on how far that process should be carried out. The criticisms are many, but not all are consistent with each other. Not all come from the left; fascists, traditionalists, and others on the right have historically been suspicious of openness in trade and finance. Some of the arguments summarized below are weak; others command careful thought. All have helped to create an antiorthodox intellectual climate out of which the delinking views have arisen. The review will be brief; bibliographic materials listed at the end of the essay elaborate the points made here.

While economic arguments against laissez faire will be discussed first, it should be stressed that the basic argument for delinking is political. It can be summarized as follows: Extensive and unregulated international trade and financial links for a given LDC are perceived by its policy makers as limiting their freedom of action, both in the present and in the future. The links are said to reduce national autonomy. What is disliked on political grounds is then damned with economic arguments which, regardless of their motivation, may or may not be sound or quantitatively important.

Economic history provides a powerful reason for skepticism regarding the benefits of international trade and finance for what is now the Third World. It may not be irrelevant to quote at length from the alleged father of laissez faire on this point:

The discovery of America, and that of a passage to the East Indies by the Cape of Good Hope, are the two greatest and most important events recorded in the history of mankind. Their consequences have already been very great: but, in the short period of between two and three centuries which has elapsed since these discoveries were made, it is impossible that the whole extent of their consequences can have been seen. What benefits, or what misfortunes to mankind may hereafter result from those great events no human wisdom can foresee. By uniting, in some measure, the most distant parts of the world, by enabling them to relieve one another's wants, to increase one another's enjoyments, and to encourage one another's industry, their general tendency would seem to be beneficial. To the natives, however, both of the East and West Indies, all the commercial benefits which can have resulted from those events have been sunk and lost in the dreadful misfortunes which they have occasioned.[1]

When this was written, the horrors of the Opium War, the Congo, and other nineteenth-century imperialist abuses were yet to come. Other authors note that some Southern regions that were closely linked with capitalist centers during the nineteenth century, as in the case of the East and West Indies, are now far behind countries that at that time (say, early in that century) were delinked from those centers, for example Japan.

[1] Adam Smith, *An Inquiry into the Nature and Causes of the Wealth of Nations*, Clarendon Press, Oxford, 1976 (Glasgow Edition), book IV, chap. VII, part III, vol. II, p. 626. Smith did not expect a change in these circumstances to arise from the workings of the Invisible Hand. A change would come, as indicated in the following quote, via something more like the confrontations brought about by OPEC and the discussions regarding a New International Economic Order: "At the particular time when these discoveries were made, the superiority of force happened to be so great on the side of the Europeans, that they were enabled to commit with impunity every sort of injustice in those remote countries. Hereafter, perhaps, the natives of those countries may grow stronger, or those of Europe may grow weaker, and the inhabitants of all the different quarters of the world may arrive at that equality of courage and force which, by inspiring mutual fear, can alone overawe the injustice of independent nations into some sort of respect for the rights of one another."

Nineteenth-century European latecomers as well as Japan and the United States also had mixed feelings about across-the-board laissez faire in international economic relations. They were happy to import English skilled workers and machines but doubted whether such liberality should apply to competition for local infant industries. Alexander Hamilton and Friedrich List first sketched the infant-industry argument for protection which, suitably qualified and refined, has survived to our day.

The early British technological monopoly and later examples of market power in international trade and finance naturally led to another qualification to the optimality of laissez faire from the national viewpoint. Under those circumstances, a nation could gain most from international intercourse by restricting its foreign links somewhat, in a manner similar to that of OPEC. Britain restricted her technology-intensive exports of goods and services, with varying degrees of effectiveness, until the diffusion process made such measures totally inoperative. It is said that the United States under the Nixon administration considered adopting similar measures; other contemporary industrialized countries are also concerned about the leakage of their technological expertise to the South.[2]

As already noted, nineteenth-century European imperialism opened new frontiers to international trade and finance, relying not just on the persuasive power of Ricardian theorems on comparative advantage. In lands of recent settlement and later in colonies and ex-colonies, it was not long before additional pitfalls to excessive openness were perceived, even when such openness arose from a genuine belief in laissez faire policy rather than being externally imposed through destruction of local food crops and forced labor. Monocultivation made an economy vulnerable to external shocks and could reduce what later was called its "capacity to transform." Favorable economic and social linkages from the production of some export crops were deemed

[2]The British export prohibition for machinery is discussed by A. E. Musson, "The 'Manchester School' and Exportation of Machinery," *Business History*, vol. 14, January 1972, p. 49. See also Charles P. Kindleberger, "The Rise of Free Trade," *Journal of Economic History*, vol. 35, no. 1, March 1975, pp. 29–30.

small, and their potential for diffusing new technology and encouraging entrepreneurship within the local economy came to be doubted. In addition, the benefits from international trade and finance were seen by many as being unjustly distributed not only between the countries of the center and those of the periphery but also within the periphery and within the center countries themselves.

Before 1914 these arguments were submerged by benefits arising from a prosperous Pax Britannica and the sheer political power on the side of openness. The disasters that befell the world economy during the 1914–1950 period and the breakup of old empires shattered the prestige of the British-led laissez faire position. John Maynard Keynes, who as a student at Cambridge in 1903 spoke for motions "in favour of the support given by the present Government to the Principles of Imperialism" and said "that Home Rule for Ireland is beyond the sphere of practical politics," toward the end of his life argued that the future lay with state trading, international cartels, and quantitative import restrictions.[3]

Pessimism about the prospects for the exports of the less developed countries was rampant by the late 1940s. Demand for LDC exports was expected to grow slowly if at all, because of the assumed low responsiveness in the demand for primary products to higher incomes in the North, the widespread introduction of synthetic substitutes, plus the expectation of sluggish growth in the industrialized economies. LDCs, it was thought, could do little to offset the impact of these conditions; if they tried to give their exporters better incentives, little would be achieved either because of the difficulty of actually increasing supplies of the exportable goods or because foreign demand would not increase sufficiently in response to lower prices. Indeed, attempting to expand exports when faced by stagnant and inelastic foreign demand could lead to immiserizing declines in the LDC terms of trade. These arguments were vigorously advanced from a

[3]R. F. Harrod, *The Life of John Maynard Keynes*, Penguin Books, Harmondsworth, 1972 (originally published 1951), pp. 110–111 and p. 672.

Southern viewpoint primarily by Raúl Prebisch and his disciples at the UN Economic Commission for Latin America (ECLA).

The mood in the industrialized countries was no more favorable to openness in international trade and finance. Many worried about the conflict between openness and the need to stabilize domestic economies, a preoccupation also widespread in LDCs. Possible gains from trade seemed no match for the gains to be reaped from domestic stabilization; reduced openness appeared a small sacrifice to pay for domestic policies assuring full employment. Given the record of the international economy since 1914 and the uncertainties and anxieties surrounding the years immediately following the end of the Second World War (soon to be reinforced by the outbreak of hostilities in Korea), these were not unreasonable positions to hold circa 1950. Already in the early 1930s, giving up hope for an international order that would allow Britain to achieve both free trade and full employment, John Maynard Keynes scandalized his contemporaries by advocating import tariffs as a second-best policy to promote employment. Keynes also noted that the quest for international markets and investment opportunities could threaten peace. Thus, his much quoted 1933 delinking remark:

I sympathize, therefore, with those who would minimize, rather than those who would maximize, economic entanglement between nations. Ideas, knowledge, art, hospitality, travel—these are things which should of their nature be international. But let goods be home-spun whenever it is reasonably and conveniently possible; and, above all, let finance be primarily national.[4]

Classical orthodoxy on the benefits of laissez faire was further challenged by postwar theoretical developments. It was rigorously shown that freer trade policies could make some members

[4]Ibid., p. 526. This cannot be dismissed as simply depression economics. In his essay on national self-sufficiency, Keynes pointed out that a close dependence of one nation's economy on the policies of another was not likely to assure international peace. John Maynard Keynes, "National Self-sufficiency," *The Yale Review*, June 1933, p. 757.

of the community absolutely worse off; in other words, not only were the gains from trade unequally distributed within a country, for some groups there could also be losses under laissez faire. In addition, the new welfare economics emphasized that unless those benefiting from a certain policy actually compensated those made worse off by it, one could not say that the policy was desirable.

Still, within respectable academic circles at the center, second-best theorizing opened a Pandora's box of models that by assuming this market imperfection or that instrument limitation, could lead to a disconcerting variety of results regarding the effects of freer trade on welfare and desirable policies. Under certain assumptions, it could be shown that free trade would lead to a worsening of a country's welfare; autarky would be preferable to free trade. Even growth could be shown to be immiserizing for a country under some circumstances. True, the major message of these models was that while government action was required to correct distortions (so complete laissez faire was out), it was unlikely that first-best policies would involve trade restrictions (so free or freer trade was still desirable). But if first-best policies are not feasible: "Once one departs from first-best and is willing to go well down the hierarchy of policies a great deal can be justified. In any particular case one has to justify the need to go down the hierarchy—and this depends on the particular constraints and noneconomic considerations one is prepared to accept"[5]—quite a change from the days when free trade was proclaimed by Richard Cobden to be "the international law of God."[6]

If such cautious agnosticism prevails within established academic circles, the growing number of radical and Third World economists have added with greater abandon to the Hamilton-List-Manoilescu protectionist tradition, from doubts about trends in the terms-of-trade through infant-consumer or infant-engineer arguments to new theories about unequal exchange. The latter

[5]W. M. Corden, *Trade Policy and Economic Welfare*, Clarendon Press, Oxford, 1974, p. 412.

[6]Jacob Viner, "The Intellectual History of *Laissez-faire*," *The Journal of Law and Economics*, vol. 3, October 1960, p. 61.

take as an axiom for the world the principle of equal pay for equal work and apply it to analyze trade between center and periphery in the world economy. That trade is found not only to be unequal but also frequently to lead to immiserization of the developing countries; the surplus of the Third World is seen as being systematically drained by trade and financial links with the capitalist center. The theoretical economic models expounding these views, while often murky, have gained popularity, even among many who have no idea what is in them. Those advocating the unequal-exchange thesis are close to delinkers and dependency theorists; all of them are critical not only of orthodoxy but also of ECLA-type import-substitution policies, which foster LDC industrialization by relying on protected domestic capitalists and foreign investors.

The purely technical arguments pro and con openness in trade and finance have a way of becoming less compelling when quantification is applied to them. Free trade enthusiasts are embarrassed by calculations showing that the gains from removing all remaining trade barriers for most countries (North or South) typically come out to be fractions of 1 percent of gross national product (GNP) when static neoclassical tools are used in such estimations. They are put in the awkward dilemma of admitting that all the shouting is about peanuts or that their favorite tools do not capture the real benefit of free trade. The antiopenness group, it should be stressed, tends to be even less quantitatively oriented in its arguments. Indeed, its strong suit has to do with broader socioeconomic arguments, to which we now turn.

History, argue many of those opposing openness, shows that when a Southern country linked up, usually under duress, with the capitalist center, the opening-up process involved the transmission of not only goods, technology, and finance but also cultural and social germs to which Western countries had perhaps become immune but which ravaged the body politic of the peripheral societies. Under the new order, the sundry trade and financial links are intermediated on the Southern side by a small comprador/landlord class that undoubtedly benefits from the process and uses that position to reinforce its political power. More often than not such power is a reflection of that of the hegemonic country setting the rules of the game for international links, so the interests of this class are tied more to those of the foreigners than are those of the mass of their fellow citizens. Put another way, most gains from trade are captured by this small class and invested in reproducing their economic and political power with a minimum of diffusion of economic and political benefits.

The potentially positive learning effects of openness are blocked by the imperfect nature of local markets, by specialization in technologically stagnant commodities with unstable world prices, and by control of the local government by a dependent comprador/landlord class so that public goods and social overhead capital, which even competitive markets could not provide, are not produced in the necessary quantities, thereby retarding progress. Education, for example, is not something for which this class would show enthusiasm, nor is it likely to encourage better peasant techniques for food self-sufficiency. Local industry will be acceptable only if it does not clash too directly with the established interests, and local entrepreneurship will be smothered. At every turn the state apparatus will tilt decisions toward further dependence, which will in turn further debilitate local capabilities and initiatives.

Because the international links have rendered the Southern country wide open and porous, the argument continues, the foreign hegemonic power has many ways of disciplining any wayward tendencies on the part of reformist offsprings of the reactionary class that may arise. If, by sloth or incompetence, that class failed to maintain its grip over the rest of its fellow citizens, the leading foreign power would come in to assure that local law and order is consistent with profitable international links.

From these hierarchical structures, several consequences will follow. The comprador/landlord class will ape the culture, technology, and consumption habits of the center, in turn setting the example for the rest of the local population, particularly the ambitious and the upwardly mobile. That which is foreign will be automatically deemed superior. Imports of goods, technology, and capital will create habits and compulsions similar to those of drug addicts. Local traditions and even language will be viewed as inferior, and national self-respect will be low. Some theorists have argued that the new consumption habits will typically be highly capital- and import-intensive; if so, they will reinforce pressures toward inequality in domestic income distribution and dependence on foreign links. As Osvaldo Sunkel has put the argument, international integration will lead to national disintegration. This may even be reflected in the cancerous growth of one or two cities within the dependent country, which will exploit their local hinterland even as they are exploited and manipulated by foreigners. Indeed, authors like André Gunder Frank have stressed the chainlike nature of metropolitan-satellite relationships, with the center exploiting the periphery while within the periphery larger cities exploit smaller ones, and so on down to the most isolated rural regions located at the bottom of the pyramid.[7] Contrary to the beliefs of some nineteenth-century writers such as Domingo Sarmiento, who saw cities as the civilizing agents of the barbarous countryside, urban centers are regarded as instruments of domination and exploitation of the hinterland.

Some delinkers stress one possible consequence of this vision. As a Southern country becomes more deeply entangled in this type of international link, its per capita income may grow, but such growth renders it *less* able to reach a position of national autonomy and true development or the convulsions needed to achieve such goals become increasingly catastrophic and traumatic. This is because such growth ("development of underdevelopment") reinforces political and social structures that oppose autonomous and equitable development. Thus, to those having this view, the outlook for development in Cuba, Tanzania, or Cambodia is far better than that for the Ivory Coast and Puerto Rico. The latter case is often given as a nightmarish extreme of local impotence, a country defenseless against the whims of foreign investors and tourists and incapable of providing dignified employment within its boundaries for its sons and daughters.[8]

---

[7] André Gunder Frank, *Capitalism and Underdevelopment in Latin America: Historical Studies of Chile and Brazil*, rev. ed., Monthly Review Press, New York and London, 1969.

[8] "We have been regretfully forced to conclude that Puerto Rico has very little scope for financial policies which would insulate the Island from overseas economic and financial developments" (p. iii). "Even with the best of policy

This view of links with the capitalist centers leading to a sociopolitical structure that is both reactionary and subservient to foreign interests is one applied not just to the past but also, suitably modified, to the present. The modifications involved are basically two. On the external front, transnational corporations (TNCs) appear as the key institutional mechanism controlling international links in both trade and finance. Those corporations are the natural offspring of nineteenth-century capital after several decades of further concentration and internationalization. On the internal front, the local comprador/landlord class has been subject to some facelifting to accommodate new groups—especially technocrats, the "new" military, and the state bourgeoisie—and some postwar aspirations for better social services and at least the appearances of national autonomy. The dominant class could thus become less homogeneous than before, increasing the possibility of friction among its components, some of which could ally themselves with nondominant or popular groups. Such fragmentation coupled with increasing needs for legitimacy (e.g., to satisfy nationalist aspirations) would increase the fluidity of the political game. But the essential nature of the beast, many observers argue, has not changed even if there is some debate as to whether national and state bourgeoisies do or do not have as much room to maneuver today as they did in nineteenth-century dependent countries.

Indeed, some delinkers argue that the revolution in world transport and communications makes openness the enemy of balanced and equitable growth ("true development") today even more than in the past. During the nineteenth century the interests of world capitalism were served by a high degree of international mobility of all kinds of labor as well as capital. Today world capitalism is interested mostly in a high degree of mobility for skilled labor plus, naturally, the highest possible mobility for that

and the best of luck, the Island faces a severe unemployment problem for several years" (p. vii). *Report to the Governor; The Committee to Study Puerto Rico's Finances*, December 11, 1975. This committee, incidentally, did not include a single Puerto Rican. The report argues that any small capitalistic open economy, whether independent or not, will face essentially similar difficulties in trying to devise effective policy tools.

capital controlled by large firms forming the core of world capitalism. So rules regulating international factor mobility have reflected such secular changes in the interests of hegemonic capital. Whatever international mobility for unskilled labor remains, as in Western Europe, is regulated and controlled in a manner that would raise howls of protest if applied symmetrically to capital movements.

It is often argued that TNCs that can arrange for mobility of skilled labor and that rapidly diffuse the latest consumer goods and fads generated in the capitalist centers make LDC upper and middle classes associated with them more loyal to the TNC-run world economic system than to their less opulent fellow citizens. When conflicts arise between transnationals and reformist LDC governments and the transnationals depart, many in those upper and middle classes will echo the biblical pledge of Ruth. Under more normal circumstances LDC upper and middle classes will feel grievously deprived if they do not have access to the goods and services provided by the transnationals and others in the capitalist centers. Their youth in particular will be seduced by that center's glitter. In those LDCs where demonstration effects are also transmitted via tourism, the children of the rich will dream about parties at the local Hilton, while the children of the poor will dream about the chance to wash dishes there if they are unable to get the opportunity to do so in New York or Paris.

Under those circumstances, the argument continues, trying to motivate the best and the brightest youth by material incentives will doom the developing country to persistent, or even growing, inequality and a continuous aping of the frequently visited center. If attitudes are to be changed and appeals to moral and patriotic motivations are to be effective or, indeed, if modest reliance on material incentives is to have any bite, a shutting off of the garish Northern influences will be necessary. The young people are unlikely to go back to the people's farm once they have seen Disneyland. When viewed in this light, even moderate reformist proposals to freeze (not to cut) the real income of the upper classes can be seen as naïve; those classes will be satisifed only if they can keep up with the latest advances in the consumerism of the center. Put another way, the argument is that profit rates and wages for skilled labor will be given from the outside to the dependent country that is unable to control highly mobile financial and human capital. Wages for unskilled labor in these countries will simply be the residual left after the mobile factors take up whatever is necessary to keep them up with international standards.

Ruling groups in contemporary dependent Southern countries will constantly stress to their fellow citizens the key importance of maintaining good relations with foreign investors, providers of concessional aid, and foreign customers. Workers will be told that unless they keep their wages low and their mouths shut, either cheaper foreign goods will destroy their source of livelihood or foreign investors will find more docile labor elsewhere. A subservient link is also likely to exist between military and intelligence agencies of the dependent country and those of the hegemonic power. The creation of a good investment climate will worry dependent ruling groups more than domestic nutrition levels. Opinions about government decrees heard at the International Monetary Fund (IMF) will carry more weight than those heard a few meters from their offices. As much of the political power of these ruling groups arises from their knowledge of how to persuade powerful foreigners to smile upon their country, they will scoff at proposals for greater self-reliance. Government officials of dependent LDCs will return from their frequent visits abroad announcing new credits and other foreign concessions that are proclaimed as being ways to save the local economy. Official development aid will be sought as a complement, not a substitute, for the investments of TNCs. The latter will act as a discreet but powerful lobby favoring concessional Northern loans to well-behaved Southern countries.

It is further argued that local industrialists, who often started their careers as importers, limit their activities mainly to areas (e.g., automobile parts) that are deemed uninteresting by TNCs or are auxiliary to TNC enterprises. State enterprises are larger and may control more strategic activities. But in most dependent LDCs neither private local industrialists nor state enterprises are deemed capable of carrying out innovations beyond those of an adaptive nature. Either a dependent mentality or a web of national and international regulations, it is alleged, limits their capacity to generate significant autonomous technological change. Furthermore, the timid sergeants of local industry can be manipulated by TNCs to oppose reforms in those (or other) regulations while the TNCs pretend to respect local political processes. A capital flight stampede can always be triggered as a first line of defense against the pretensions of reformist leadership. Often no further disciplinary action will be required.

In this environment, the foreign connection will be critical for civil servants, local entrepreneurs, and even academics. Myths about the insufficiency of local saving and initiative and even about the national character will flourish in that debilitating atmosphere and may even cease to be myths after years of dependence. Joint ventures between local and foreign capitalists and licensing agreements to obtain foreign technology become new forms of dependence rather than first steps in the road to autonomy.

In short, the argument is not just that the international links are the conduits through which the dependent country is drained of its surplus for the benefit of the dominant countries. The international links also penetrate and deform the internal sociopolitical structures of the peripheral country, leading to the waste and misallocation of whatever is left behind by the foreigners. A decreasing number of delinkers argue that under these circumstances the dependent country is unlikely to industrialize and certainly will not be able to develop its heavy and capital goods industries. Most delinkers will now admit that dependent industrialization and growth are possible, but they argue that such processes will feature not only the polarization and unevenness of classical capitalist expansion but an exaggerated and even more monstrous version of it.

These are vigorous arguments, much more so than the often turgid technicalities of unequal exchange.[9] It remains to be seen

[9] Paul A. Samuelson concludes a recent article reviewing the technical parts of Arghiri Emmanuel's challenge to the fundamentals of the theory of comparative advantage by asserting that it has thrown no new light on why countries are rich or poor and has neither discovered a flaw in nor improved upon the

what policy proposals or recipes for political actions flow from them. Only one seems clear: the need to eliminate the political power of the reactionary class or group controlling the state apparatus. Is it necessary to delink to achieve this? Will delinking ensure desirable political change? And once the political change is achieved and secure, is there any further need to remain delinked?

---

theory of comparative advantage. See Samuelson, "Illogic of Neo-Marxian Doctrine of Unequal Exchange," in David A. Belsley, et al. (eds.), *Inflation, Trade and Taxes*, Ohio State University Press, Columbus, 1976, p. 107; also Arghiri Emmanuel, *Unequal Exchange: A Study of the Imperialism of Trade*, Monthly Review Press, New York and London, 1972.

It may be noted that Emmanuel's theories have also been sharply criticized by Marxist authors. The valid economic insights provided by the literature on unequal exchange may be said to represent elaborations of arguments developed by Arthur Lewis and Hla Myint, in which low productivity in LDC subsistence agriculture generates an ample supply of cheap labor for the sectors producing exportable staples. Under those conditions, it is unlikely that LDC export prices can keep up with those of exports from industrialized countries. Under colonial rule, public expenditure on research was focused on the export sector; surplus labor, if not available nearby, was brought in from other colonies, regardless of the long-run social consequences of such decisions.

An alternative view of the unequal-exchange thesis hypothetically compares the terms-of-trade between center and periphery that would exist if there were unrestricted worldwide labor migration with those obtained without labor mobility. The former conditions would be more favorable to the periphery than the latter. Note that observations of actual trends in terms of trade cannot disprove the validity of this counterfactual experiment.

THREE

The Search for a Delinking Strategy

While criticisms of openness abound, arguments by delinkers often terminate abruptly with "therefore, true development is possible only if the South cuts off links with international capitalism." Pleas for a little elaboration on what needs to be done bring some hints but no blueprints. Those hints often make reference to countries that seem to have delinked successfully. This section will begin with a rapid look at some of those experiences, particularly that of China. Next a synthetic summary of what needs to be done will be presented based on my interpretation of the literature. The reader should be warned that this could very well be rejected, partly or totally, by many delinkers, particularly those who regard as utopian going beyond the bare statement that a break with the world market is the primary condition for development. History, they would argue, will show the way beyond such a break. This section will close with a critique of the synthetic argument.

PRAXIS

Historical cases of delinking are not plentiful. Indeed, during the 1950s and 1960s, even as criticisms of openness multiplied at the academic level, expanding world markets operating under the rules of the game established by the Pax Americana of 1945–1973 lured many Southern countries into growing links with international capitalism, to the exasperation of pure delinkers, as indicated by Giovanni Arrighi and John Saul:

Even socialists, however, have tended to operate in terms of the conventional model of development based upon the expansion of cash crops for the export market, increased industrial capital formation in consumer goods industries, and the import of foreign—generally private—capital, the requisite amount of infrastructural investment being the responsibility of the state. This is, of course, in essence the ideal type of "perverse growth" in Africa which we discussed [earlier].

Even in the heyday of Guinean socialism, for example, there was little attempt to question ties with international capitalism in the industrial and extractive industries. . . . Not that the redefinition of such a neocolonial relationship is easy: investment codes of varying degrees of stringency have in fact been tried. . . . But if the international economic environment has been a harsh one for such efforts, it is also true that the will to divert international ties in a socialist direction has not been a sustained one.[10]

Some delinkers have made references to historical examples of self-reliance following socialist revolutions. But closer examination of the historical record of the immediate aftermath of important socialist revolutions, such as those in the Soviet Union, China, and Cuba, while showing that indeed some species of delinking occurred during and immediately after those events, also indicate that delinking was not so much a choice of the revolutionary authorities but was imposed through blockades by the hegemonic capitalist countries. The United States' partial or total embargoes against the Soviet Union, China, and Cuba lasted many years after the revolutions in those countries; indeed, that against Cuba still goes on. It is not without a certain irony that pure delinkers now advocate what in the past was triggered by capitalist hostility to socialist revolution.

The case of China, which for many years was not very well known because of the hostility of first the capitalist countries

---

[10]Giovanni Arrighi and John S. Saul, "Socialism and Economic Development in Tropical Africa," in Arrighi and Saul (eds.), *Essays on the Political Economy of Africa*, Monthly Review Press, New York and London, 1973, pp. 23, 33.

and then the Soviet Union, was vaguely perceived by some as the great example of delinking. The vast size of that country and its ancient, autonomous culture gave it advantages in the road to self-reliance which few, if any, developing countries have (with the exception of India). Yet available evidence indicates that there has not been an absolute decline in the level of Chinese foreign trade.[11] During the 1950s the growth rate of foreign trade exceeded GNP growth; at that time China also received substantial foreign aid from the Soviet Union. For recent years, Chinese foreign trade expressed as a percentage of GNP does not appear to be much below that of India, another large and low-income country. Is it perhaps that China is exporting mostly new and sophisticated industrial goods? Hardly; its export bill is one-third foodstuffs and includes such "colonial" items as inedible raw materials, pig bristles, walnuts, prawns, gum resin, animal hairs, rice, textiles, ores, footware, glass, chinaware, furniture, carpets, and sports and travel goods. In the future, China could join the ranks of important oil exporters, making further imports of machinery and technology difficult to resist. Self-reliance need not mean a closed-door policy, according to Chinese experience.

China, of course, does not follow a policy of laissez faire regarding international economic relations. Trade is rigidly controlled by the central government, and imports are based on pay-as-you-go policies. Soviet credits have been repaid; the Chinese foreign debt is negligible. Indeed, China runs her own foreign aid program. The points raised earlier regarding Chinese trade simply indicate that self-reliance and similar concepts, if they are to be meaningful, must be more subtle than cutting off all trade with the capitalist North. They also suggest that the doctrine of self-reliance, as practiced by China, is much more rigorous regarding finance than regarding trade. Capital formation must be financed by domestic savings, but some capital goods

[11]See, for example, John G. Gurley, "Rural Development in China 1949–72 and the Lessons to be Learned from It"; and Percy Timberlake, "China as a Trading Nation," both in *World Development*, vol. 3, nos, 7 and 8, July–August 1975, pp. 455–471 and 575–586. See also Donald B. Keesing, "Economic Lessons from China," *Journal of Development Economics*, vol. 2, 1975, pp. 1–32.

may be imported. The pro-trade stance during recent years of the Soviet Union, Vietnam, Cuba, and many countries of Eastern Europe (and not just among themselves) strengthens this modest conclusion. Indeed, one must wonder whether the inward-looking trade policies of the Soviet Union and Eastern Europe during the 1930s, 1940s, and 1950s had more to do with depressed or dislocated world market conditions and the cold war than with the allegedly inevitable incompatability, or at least conflict, between planning and foreign trade. As with China, the expectation is that socialist countries grouped around the Soviet Union will expand their links with capitalist nations at a rate as fast or faster than their growth in domestic production. Vietnam, whose vocation for national autonomy few would dispute, appears to find no conflict between self-reliance and active participation in foreign trade with capitalist nations; its exports include rubber, coffee, tea, other farm products, handicrafts, and anthracite coal. Trade offices are maintained in Hong Kong and Singapore. Vietnam has also joined the IMF and the Asian Development Bank; it has welcomed a mission from the World Bank, whose president is Robert McNamara. There are reports that Vietnam is contemplating an investment code allowing business ventures with foreign capitalist firms for the development of natural resources, notably oil, coal, and bauxite. Some delinkers see North Korea and Albania as the remaining champions of pure self-reliance, perhaps with the addition of the peculiar case of Cambodia.

There is no reason why the search for delinking experiences should be limited to countries that have experienced socialist revolutions. Several Latin American countries reinforced the trade-limiting effects of the Great Depression and the Second World War during roughly 1930 to 1955. Burma and Tibet, the latter before being absorbed into China, discouraged links with the outside world; the spiritual tranquility of the local population may have gained from such policies, but no great developmental breakthroughs have been reported as a consequence. The Japanese experience is richer; after it was forced to couple by Commodore Perry, it sought to keep the links limited and under control. The Revolutionary Government in Peru has followed a policy of selectivity regarding its foreign links; as in the Cuban case, however, its development plans rely heavily on growing exports of primary products.

The delinking experience need neither lead to nor be initiated by socialist development; it may involve an independent capitalist state or new social forms not easily labeled. One of the clearest cases of delinking occurred in Paraguay from 1814 until about the middle of the nineteenth century, under the leadership of Rodríguez de Francia. This extremely repressive regime is difficult to catalog. During 1975 and 1976, the new Cambodian authorities have followed a Francia-type delinking policy, calling it "socialism." It is too early to say whether this policy is a temporary phase to accompany harsh domestic restructuring or is expected to continue over the long run.

In the view of some delinkers, the domestic repressiveness of regimes such as that of Cambodia is historically justified (or at least of secondary importance) either because it is deemed necessary for the creation of a sovereign and just society or because it reinforces the divorce with foreign capitalist centers, denying those centers the materials and surplus on which they grew fat before the revolution in the peripheral country. Thus, even when the repressive Southern regime displays quasi-fascist traits, so long as it denies the capitalist North of access to its actual or potential surplus it may be regarded as historically progressive by some delinkers. There is also in this view the expectation that Northern imperialism will weaken without a steady diet of Southern raw materials and surplus.

It is doubtful whether further historical research or the contemplation of the writings of the various species of delinkers would yield a single and generally accepted summary of what delinkers want or predict, much less a single vision of how the ideal they envision is to be achieved. Many delinkers and dependency theorists are more interested in articulating a viable ideology for radical change than in setting forth testable hypotheses or specific policy proposals.

As noted earlier, this field is crowded with key words or phrases that imperfectly transmit the mood of dissatisfaction with openness. Self-reliance, autocentrism, economic independence, autonomy, and delinking are seen as good, while laissez faire, world markets, disarticulation, and dependency are bad. To my mind, the best case for delinking can be structured around the key word or concept of selectivity. It is selective delinking (or selective relinking) that is of interest as a possible Southern strategy. What follows is an attempt to present the best synthetic summary of such a strategy, borrowing some of the language and faith of delinkers. It is not meant to reflect the complete views of any one delinker living or dead nor necessarily the views of UNCTAD (UN Conference on Trade and Development) enthusiasts. My own evaluation of what I regard as the best case for delinking will await the full presentation of this case.

DELINKING POLICIES: A SYNTHETIC SUMMARY

There are many dimensions to selectivity regarding the international links of a developing country. But the fundamental precondition for a policy of selectivity is, of course, the power to be selective. A colony or a puppet regime cannot be selective about its international links; an incompetent, corrupt, or porous regime is unlikely to be selective in a manner conducive to the welfare of the majority within the country.

Even granted a measure of political autonomy, the hope that openness, laissez faire, and export-led growth by themselves will help a country reach its development targets is bound to be disappointed sooner or later, leading to Puerto Rican–type situations in which the people of a country lose control over their economic fate. When hit by unfavorable external circumstances, such countries can do little but wait for the magical reappearance of tourists and export-led growth. The privilege of autonomously starting recovery is reserved for the hegemonic industrialized countries. The dependent nations can only plead with the leaders to please lead; otherwise they must sit and wait. So, the argument continues, steady and long-term development can be achieved only if the development plan makes sure that the engine of growth is within the country. This means that in order to avoid undesirable ties of dependence, exports should be promoted only insofar as the plan calls for imports of goods or technology.

Naturally a self-reliant country, particularly a small one, can suffer from unfavorable external circumstances, but unlike the dependent capitalist country, it will not let those circumstances paralyze its development efforts. New lines will be tried, resources will be mobilized toward goals made more promising by the new circumstances—this is another way of saying that the engine of growth is within the nation. In short, international links may be useful to help the country achieve some development targets under some conditions and specific historical circumstances, but it is fatal to regard openness as a good thing per se and to let external links and foreign demand determine the direction and pace of the country's economic growth.

Laissez faire openness and the international links it generates are seen as undesirable for reasons already discussed. Those delinkers who also advocate revolution argue that during the revolution the key thing is to maintain control of the state. International links may distract the country; indeed, those links may be used by international reaction and domestic enemies to destroy the revolution, so a complete cutoff during this historical stage may be desirable (e.g., Cambodia in 1975–1976 versus the campaign against Salvador Allende in Chile during 1972–1973). After the revolution a selective relinking to support the development plan where necessary is fine, but always via institutional mechanisms such as national state trading monopolies subject to central control. Some greater degree of decentralization, however, may eventually be desirable and possible, particularly in small countries (e.g., Hungary in the 1970s), and indirect incentives could partially guide foreign trade (e.g., Yugoslavia). It is a debatable point whether domestic enterprises should be allowed to specialize completely in foreign trade or whether no single enterprise should be permitted to have more than, say, a quarter of its sales directed to foreign markets. Strict exchange control, however, is likely to remain a permanent fixture of a selectively delinked country. Concessional finance from abroad, except under very special and temporary circumstances, is incompatible with self-reliance.

It is an error to suppose that partial delinking or even total delinking is either a necessary or a sufficient condition for the seizure of state power by forces regarded as progressive by de-linkers. Partial delinking via import controls, prohibitive tariffs, exchange controls, and regulation of foreign investment may simply strengthen a reactionary regime and give domestic priv-ileged classes fresh sources of power and booty. Foreign trade and financial policies are subsidiary; the central issue is who controls political power and thereby the gains from whatever international trade there is. Indeed, under certain historical cir-cumstances, a movement toward greater openness of the econ-omy could strengthen progressive political forces and weaken local feudal and absolutist controls.

A very important dimension of selective relinking is the ability to choose the international capitalist markets in which the South-ern country will participate. In the same way as the first re-quirement for a strategy of selective relinking is the power to be selective, effective selective participation in world markets re-quires local expertise on how to go about shopping in those markets. This necessitates a core of experts whose loyalty to the national interest of the Southern country is unquestioned and unclouded by links to extranational business centers. It is only superficially paradoxical that an economy like China's, with a relatively low ratio of foreign trade to GNP, has a better rep-utation in international trade circles as a judicious buyer and a skillful seller than do wide-open Third World countries such as Kenya. Cuba and Tanzania, also selective delinkers, share the Chinese reputation.

Once local expertise in the mysteries of foreign trade and finance is in place, à la China or Japan, selectivity may be guided by two criteria: characteristics of traded goods and services and characteristics of the markets where such goods and services can be bought and sold. As noted earlier, if self-reliance is to mean anything, it must mean that basic needs of the country are not at the mercy of the caprice of external markets or vulnerable to external blockades. A self-reliant country such as China will prefer to face even natural calamities on its own. This need *not* mean that foreign trade in basic needs, such as foodstuffs and energy, will be totally avoided. It does mean that a substantial margin of preference will be given for local production of these goods and that international purchases of such goods will be diversified geographically while ample locally controlled stocks should prove a wise investment.

A Southern country seriously embarked on policies of self-reliance plus reduction of domestic inequality is unlikely to show much interest in the international market for Pepsi-Cola and Alfa-Romeos. Exports of luxury goods and services (e.g., tourism) would be easier to justify, although the spillovers of production of exportable luxury goods and services onto domestic consumption could be significant. It is said that Polish exports of luxury consumer durables to Western markets have influenced goods sold domestically. The demonstration effects arising from tourism are obvious and powerful, as are the effects resulting from the export of unskilled labor, for instance in Algeria and Yugoslavia.

International markets differ markedly in their degree of competitiveness or standoffishness. A Southern country selectively relinking will prefer, *ceteris paribus*, to deal in international markets that are as competitive as possible unless its power is such that it can effectively manipulate those who in turn control those international markets (e.g., OPEC with the "seven sisters"; the Soviet Union with some transnational corporations). On the export side, this consideration should dominate the distinction between primary and manufactured goods; a Southern country will profit more at less expense to its autonomy by exporting a staple traded in fairly competitive world markets (e.g., cotton) than by exporting some bits of electronic goods whose only market is organized and run by a transnational corporation. Standardized goods will be more likely to have competitive markets than will those not so characterized. But a Southern country historically associated with a differentiated, specialized commodity (e.g., Cuban cigars or Chinese handicrafts) will struggle to maintain such a monopoly position.

It may also be useful here to mention the distinction between auction markets and customer markets. The former are models of standoffishness: each transaction is made with no tomorrow in mind. In the latter "a kind of intertemporal comparison shopping develops by which yesterday's offer influences today's demand, as a result of an implied commitment of the seller to maintain his offer."[12] Auction markets are quite feasible for standardized goods and services whose characteristics are easy to define and recognize. Such markets show resiliency even under insecure international conditions. For many goods and services, however, particularly durable ones with imprecise or difficult-to-define characteristics, customer markets are common. In such markets buyer and seller may be hard put to define exactly what they are buying or selling. These are particularly troublesome markets in the international setting because they must rely on such intangibles as confidence, predictability, and continuity. Historically, such intangibles were usually provided by organizations closely associated with hegemonic powers providing and enforcing the international rules of the game. Entry into these markets has been particularly difficult; a change in the relationships and hierarchies implicit in them is likely to be abrupt and traumatic. Delinking from customer markets will inevitably be bruising; when the time to relink comes, the relationship will be qualitatively different from what it was before. It will not be a matter of selling a bit more or less sugar or cotton internationally.

Today and tomorrow are difficult to separate in most markets for technology, machinery, and financial services. Buying a machine today is likely to imply requirements for parts and repairs tomorrow; confidence must exist between lender and borrower; blueprints alone can be auctioned off only as abstract art. What should be the stance of a Third World country wishing to be a selective delinker toward these markets? Policies to expand local expertise, to build up the knowledge to buy knowledge are even more necessary to deal in these markets than to deal in auction markets. The Third World country will build its own customer relationships with selected foreign companies, selected partly on the basis of their willingness to do business independently of the political pressures that may be applied by their home governments. The Third World country will search for the breaking up of the package of finance, technology, management, and market

---

[12]Arthur M. Okun, "Inflation: Its Mechanisms and Welfare Costs," *Brookings Paper on Economic Activity*, vol. 2, Washington, D.C., 1975, p. 361.

access offered by TNCs. When possible, the selective country will borrow funds in the Eurodollar market, seek attractive offers for desired machinery, and sign contracts with independent management consultants. It will try to build long-term links with each of those business associates while trying to keep them independent of each other; the packaging of those inputs and the knowledge and control of how they all fit together will be retained at home by the national planners.

Another important dimension of selectivity is the choice of trading partners. The following overlapping criteria illustrate the nature of that choice: socialist versus nonsocialist countries, LDCs versus non-LDCs (or even greater selectivity within the LDC group), small versus large countries, ex-colonial master versus all other countries, neighboring versus distant countries, private firms versus public enterprises, large versus small private firms. The desirable choices in this area will be guided by both political and economic considerations. By combining selectivity of commodities and of partners, one can obtain a vast number of possibilities.

The promotion of commercial and financial links among LDCs, if necessary (or, some would say, preferably) at the expense of such links with the North, has emerged as a popular policy recommendation labeled "collective self-reliance." Since differences in productivity and real wages among LDCs are relatively small, intra-LDC trade will *not* involve unequal exchange, it is maintained. Proponents of this view argue that collective self-reliance should be quite different from traditional proposals for creating LDC common markets or free trade areas and that it should not be in conflict with national self-reliance. Third World countries should not only give preference to their mutual trade but also make sure that the new links are direct and do not go through the intermediation of the capitalist center. Trade should not be left to market forces but should be planned. Producer cartels should be formed by the Third World, and its technological knowledge shared free of charge. Southern countries, finally, should form their own multinational enterprises to exclude the presence of Northern TNCs. The package is viewed as one capable of receiving the support from admittedly heterogeneous (both politically and economically) Third World countries and is regarded as correcting past colonial and neocolonial distortions of trade patterns.

The manipulation of other international links in various specific historical circumstances could clearly advance diversification and insulate Southern countries from undesirable dependence on excessively powerful partners. The political point is obvious, and perhaps little more need be said on it. Selective links with the smaller nonhegemonic capitalist countries and with their firms could provide Southern countries with important technological inputs at negligible cost to their freedom of political action.

The search for ways of limiting undesirable spillover effects of international links on the domestic economy and polity has also led some countries to be selective as to the domestic location where such links are allowed. The Chinese, for example, have crowded many of their international links into the Canton fairs since 1957.[13] The Tanzanians are said to encourage tourism into their country only in regions isolated from the bulk of their population. Many Third World nations are quite happy that their natural resources, exploited in combination with foreigners, are located in remote parts of their countries. The controlled use of enclaves to reap gains from trade while minimizing spillovers from contacts with foreigners goes back for many hundreds of years to both Eastern and Western antiquity.

In the balancing of economic and political considerations, a selective Southern country will try to enter world markets when the capitalist cycle is generating bargains. Those bargains are more likely to apply to LDC exports rather than imports; attention has already been called to widespread delinking during the 1930s in contrast with the 1960s' relinking. One may note in

[13]About half of China's $14 billion foreign trade transactions in 1975 are said to have been arranged at the fair. These two-month-long events are held on the edge of Canton. After arriving from Hong Kong by train, traders need never venture farther than across the street where their hotel is. Some find these arrangements reminiscent of the practice, under the Ching Dynasty, of restricting foreign traders to a special area on the outskirts of Canton where they were allowed to deal with only a small group of semi-official Chinese merchants. See *New York Times*, May 15, 1976, p. 31.

passing the conjecture by Albert Hirschman that an LDC's long-term development may best be served by alternating phases of partial delinking and relinking with the capitalist centers, presumably timed to minimize the economic opportunity cost of delinking.

AN EVALUATION

Sympathy for delinking proposals will depend more on political positions than on technical expertise. Even the strategy of selective delinking sketched above requires doses of revolutionary change and centralization of political power that will concern the social democrat, distress the liberal, and alienate the conservative. The falangist/militarist may not mind these aspects but may not be happy about the purposes for which the power is used. Technical points are ways of elaborating on these fundamental political attitudes toward the great bet that is revolution. What follows is both a critique and an elaboration of some of the points involved in the delinking strategy outlined above.

The Keynesian delinking remark quoted earlier contained an implicit criticism of some political aspects of the selective delinking practiced in, say, China by stressing the international nature of ideas, art, and travel that presumably should be allowed to flow freely among nations. He also went on to argue: "Yet, at the same time, those who seek to disembarrass a country of its entanglements should be very slow and wary. It should not be a matter of tearing up roots but of slowly training a plant to grow in a different direction."[14] It is unlikely that he would have shown enthusiasm for the 1975–1976 Cambodian delinking policies or for Chinese restrictions on outward migration. The dialectics of justifying domestic excesses for the sake of external confrontations with the capitalist center, one hardly has to add, contain enormous potential for human suffering.

The question of who will decide which links to keep and which to cut arouses legitimate concerns. The strategy of selective linkages also places great demands on the organizational and

[14]Keynes, "National Self-sufficiency," p. 758.

117

planning skills of Third World countries, demands that could be excessive at some stages of development. A delinking strategy can be a high-risk option, economically as well as politically, for those choosing it.

In blaming openness for maldevelopment, national disintegration, lack of national entrepreneurship, and an inequitable distribution of income and wealth, the argument of the delinkers induces the expectation that delinking by itself will unshackle native energies, generate innovations, integrate the nation, and lead to fast and equitable growth. But most countries seeking balanced development and the widespread diffusion of technical expertise, with or without delinking, have found the task difficult and requiring efforts beyond the area of foreign trade policy. Neglect of a minimum of old-fashioned microeconomic efficiency has thwarted the plans of more than one reformist or revolutionary LDC regime. Such neglect makes the country vulnerable to new forms of dependence despite the rhetoric and intentions of its leadership. For example, errors in Cuban economic management during the 1960s reduced that country's room for maneuver during the 1970s. Similar observations could be made about the Peruvian experience during the last few years.

Suppose an average developing country, previously linked to the capitalist North under neocolonial conditions, goes through revolutionary spasms and a drastic delinking phase and then embarks on a policy of controlled and selective relinking. Can we say anything regarding the likely levels and characteristics of its imports and exports under the new internal order? A few years ago it was popular to argue that redistributive policies, by curtailing the direct and indirect luxury consumption of the rich, would lead to a substantial drop in import requirements. Both empirical studies (not perfect but suggestive) and reformist and socialist experiments in countries such as Chile, Cuba, and China indicate that such an argument is weak and that redistributive policies will have a minor effect on the import total. This effect, at any rate, will be swamped by the import requirements of a vigorous development plan, even one characterized by spartan and equalitarian consumption habits. Particularly in countries lacking capital goods industries and with inelastic food sectors, pressures on imports will be great; those arguing that, by suitably modifying technology, a self-reliant country can increase investment without adding to import requirements still have to come up with examples in which such a trick has been performed.

Note that, contrary to much trade and development literature, a substantial reorientation of a country's growth program in the direction of equitable development will be reflected faster in the structure of its imports than in the composition of exports. This is in line with classical thinking on the subject which emphasized, in attacking mercantilism, that imports are the payoff to foreign trade or the tangible expression of the gains from trade. Both Cuba and the Dominican Republic export sugar, and the Cuban export bill does not look very different than it looked in 1958 (indeed, the Colombian and Brazilian export bills have changed more drastically since then). The impact of revolution must be sought in the import bill. Over the long run, however, export diversification both geographically and by products should become a pillar of national autonomy.

Little can be said with certainty regarding what selective delinking will do to the ratio of imports of goods and services, or of exports, to GNP. Perhaps a presumption exists that it will be somewhat lower than what would have been registered under laissez faire, assuming high capital formation also under that alternative regime. But surely the success or failure of selective delinking, viewed as a handmaiden of development, cannot be measured or evaluated by observing how these ratios evolve.

Recent research suggests that a country's participation in foreign trade (although not in foreign finance) as measured by, say, the ratio of imports to GNP has more to do with its per capita income, population size, and natural resource endowment than with its social system or domestic income distribution. One is tempted to talk about iron coefficients. Even if some flexibility in such relationships is accepted, it remains true that the costs to different Southern countries of a false leap into delinking will vary and will largely depend on these factors. Generally speaking, the opportunity cost of such a leap will be higher the greater the endowment of natural resources facing favorable world demand (greater for Libya than for Paraguay) and the smaller the population (greater for Chile than for Brazil). What about per capita income? Here the situation may be more complex: A very poor country with a very large subsistence sector may have little to lose but its links. A middle-income Southern country, if it also has a large population and thus a substantial internal market, may experiment with delinking at relatively little cost. But the interaction of these three objective influences—per capita income, population, and resources—on openness as well as their connection with political factors are difficult to establish neatly beyond the obvious statements already made. One may note, however, that many of the horror stories of dependency occur in small countries; it is debatable by how much a small country can modify its dependence on the outside world either by changing its social system (e.g., Cuba) or by reaching high levels of per capita income (e.g., Denmark).

The notion of greater intra-LDC interchange and cooperation is an idea whose time has come. But there is little political or economic sense in suggesting that, say, Paraguay should give across-the-board preference to trade and financial links with Brazil and Argentina at the expense of its links with Sweden and Denmark. Even if only LDCs of similar sociopolitical views or with a common cultural background were to participate in a collective self-reliance scheme, it is doubtful that such a plan should imply a serious and permanent reduction in links with the rest of the world. China, after all, can be viewed as a large agglomeration of many developing regions giving preference to each other but not shutting off the rest of the world. The disappointing record of LDC customs unions should also warn against turning collective self-reliance into another of those fads in the international arena which regularly serve to distract LDC policy makers from crucial domestic problems. Yet some suggestions present in the discussions about collective self-reliance could prove to be valuable to the Third World. The creation of Third World multinational enterprises is one of these ideas that is already being carried into practice. The OPEC could play a critical supportive role in this area. Intra-LDC interchange should certainly be dramatically expanded in case of sluggish growth in Northern demand for LDC exports, arising from either

Northern protectionism or stagnation. Institutional mechanisms for activating this line of defense against a deteriorating world economy should be kept in good working order even under prosperous world circumstances.

Doubts about the benefits an LDC can derive from foreign aid or foreign direct investment under present world circumstances represent the strongest weapon in the arsenal of delinkers. These doubts, of course, are not limited to delinkers, but they have stressed them most emphatically. At least since the late 1950s, the Chinese version of selective delinking has demonstrated that poverty can be conquered and significant growth achieved, even in a country with one of the lowest per capita incomes in the world, without recourse to foreign concessional finance or, indeed, to any type of foreign finance. At the same time, in many LDCs substantial inflows of concessional aid and direct foreign investment have weakened local initiative, discouraged tax reform, and reduced savings coefficients. Autarky makes more sense in finance than in trade; exchange controls can be justified more easily than reluctance to trade.

It should be clear to the reader that nothing said by pure delinkers has shaken my belief in the proposition that foreign trade and contacts *may* make a given LDC and all its people better off. Yet nothing said by laissez faire enthusiasts convinces me that this will always happen spontaneously. The central point which I would emphasize is that focusing attention on trade and financial policies is wrong if one is seeking enlightenment on whether a given regime is leading its people toward equitable development. Indeed, I would conjecture that most Third World countries will increasingly move in the direction of greater vigilance over their foreign trade and financial links even as they seek to expand those links regardless of their social systems. After all, Brazil and Cuba find it easy to cooperate in international sugar policy, and the differences in the oil policies of Saudi Arabia, Venezuela, and Libya are much smaller than those in their domestic arrangements. Both Iran and Hungary are frequent borrowers in the Eurodollar market, and so on.

If a Southern country is run by a reactionary oligarchy, it is far-fetched to suppose that somehow inducing changes in its trade and finance policies will affect power and wealth distribution in that country in the near future. That oligarchy may or may not follow laissez faire and policies of openness; if it suits the consolidation of its power, the oligarchy may renounce foreign aid and become an ardent selective delinker or a vociferous Third Worlder. It is more likely than not to be interventionist regarding domestic control over foreign trade; there are few more foolish misconceptions than to suppose that import controls are a badge of progressiveness.

A country with a popular and self-confident government interested in the welfare of the majority of its population and following a "basic needs" strategy is very likely to actively participate in international trade and, more selectively, in international markets for finance and technology. It will be vigilant as to the institutional mechanisms through which those interchanges occur. It will manage the international links carefully: direct and indirect controls will be substantial and particularly strict in the areas of international finance and direct foreign investment. The optimal degree of delinking will be regarded as different for different types of transactions. Vigilance over trade flows, however, could very well rely on general incentives and disincentives. Such a government will seek to curb luxury consumption and will appeal to both material and moral incentives to generate the efforts necessary for development. It may even try to offset the external pressures of consumerism by countervailing publicity. Some may wonder why this common-sense package of policies need be given a special label; indeed, it may be argued that the above describes current practice in several small industrialized countries. But in most LDC circumstances, making sure that potential gains of foreign trade and contacts are realized and distributed equitably among the people represents a sharp break from the past and is a far from trivial achievement. Accomplishing that while not tampering with the free flow of "things which should of their nature be international" would be a spectacular one.

FOUR

Toward a World
Safe for Selectivity

Various forms of selective delinking have been discussed thus far under partial-equilibrium assumptions, i.e., for a single given LDC and taking as given the international rules of the game as they existed circa 1976. This section will examine the extent to which existing international arrangements are compatible with the aspirations of those LDCs choosing some kind of selective delinking. I have argued elsewhere that reconciliation of national autonomy with international specialization should be sought in arrangements encouraging commercial transactions carried out at arm's length whenever possible, with component parts of those transactions clearly decomposable and reversible through time.[15] This viewpoint will be followed in this section and will be regarded as compatible with selective delinking. Possibilities as well as problems with this approach will be illustrated by reference to some important international markets. The blueprints not found in the writings discussed previously will not be found here either. The purpose is to provide some suggestions that should guide the process of searching for desirable international rules.

At the risk of boring the reader, I must stress that even more than in earlier sections I now move away from most of the delinking proponents. Perhaps a lengthy quotation from one of

[15]See my "North-South Relations: The Economic Component," in *International Organization*, vol. 29, no. 1, Winter 1975, pp. 213–241.

the most authoritative delinkers, Samir Amin, will highlight differences as well as similarities in approaches to the general-equilibrium issue discussed in this section:

Saying that development of the periphery requires the setting up of autocentric national structures which break with the world market means expressing an undeniable contradiction. Capitalism has unified the world, in its own way, by imposing upon it the hierarchy of center and periphery. Socialism, which cannot exist unless it is superior to capitalism in every way, cannot be a juxtaposition of national socialisms. It must organize the world into a unified whole without inequality, and cannot be completed until it has attained this objective. However, the road that leads to this end passes by way of the self-assertion of those nations that are victims of the present set-up, and which cannot assemble the conditions for their prosperity and full participation in the modern world unless they first of all assert themselves as complete nations.

What the fully socialist world will be like, how the national entities (if they survive) will be linked together in world unity, it is too soon for us to say or even guess at, and to try to answer these questions is to fall into utopianism. All that can be said is that certain principles can be laid down. Socialism cannot be based on the market, either on the internal scale or on the world scale.[16]

NATIONAL AND INTERNATIONAL MARKETS

Many orthodox Northern observers gloss over differences between national and international markets; the relatively fine performances of the former under some circumstances are assumed to make a case for the latter without further ado.

Adam Smith as well as other classical writers emphasized the political and legal structures necessary for the emergence of efficient, decentralized markets. Primarily they had in mind national markets, involving transactions between parties of the same nationality. They took for granted that a fruitful domestic division of labor would not prosper without a framework of law

[16]Samir Amin, *Accumulation on a World Scale: A Critique of the Theory of Underdevelopment*, vol. 1, Monthly Review Press, New York and London, 1974, p. 33.

and order and respect for and enforcement of contracts. The written and unwritten rules and regulations fostering and guiding national markets have evolved in most countries over many years, gradually achieving legitimacy and social acceptability.[17]

If it is misguided to expect that without the necessary political and legal framework efficient markets will arise spontaneously within nations, at the international level such expectation requires quasi-religious faith. Historically, international markets have been limited to sporadic, auction-type transactions or have been carried out under the protection of a leading power. Under those circumstances, one can expect the rules to be determined and the contracts to be enforced by that power and its major allies. In particular, customer relationships and implicit futures markets will be quite sensitive to shifting political balances in the world. Contracts between parties with different backgrounds and perceptions will always be difficult to negotiate; without an obvious international enforcer of contracts, there will be few and their number will decrease the longer the expected transactions stretch into the future.

It has been the historic role of the hegemonic power to provide public goods or the infrastructure for international markets, especially for those markets going beyond once-and-for-all transactions. Rome took pride in clearing the Mediterranean of pirates, in its road system, and its laws and coinage. At least since then the ruling elites of the hegemonic powers every so often express weariness of their leadership role. Yet such a role, with all its alleged burdens and costs, is seldom given up without a fair dose of kicking and screaming. Indeed, transitions from eras characterized as Pax Romana, Pax Britannica, and such to those

---

[17]A leading author on the history of economic thought, D. P. O'Brien, emphasizes that while the classical economists recognized and appreciated the value of the market, they were clear that it could operate only within a framework of restrictions that were partly legal and partly religious, moral, and conventional. See D. P. O'Brien, *The Classical Economists*, Clarendon Press, Oxford, 1975, p. 272. This view of markets contrasts with that of the Chicago school, which argues that economic interests determine outcomes regardless of institutions and political frameworks and that markets will arise whenever and wherever they are paying propositions.

following them have often been traumatic and violent for the world. During the last century, the transition from British to United States leadership and the accommodation to the rise of Germany and Japan were accompanied by two great wars and a Great Depression. The process of democratizing institutions within Western and other countries advanced secularly also in fits and starts, but that progress was far superior to anything achieved in the international setting.

The international market for labor perhaps shows in the clearest fashion the importance of political power in making the rules of the game within which the "free play of market forces" is allowed to operate. The richest countries, even at the height of their belief in laissez faire, were less enthusiastic about labor than about capital mobility. During more recent years, international labor mobility has been tightly controlled, and its ebbs and flows are dictated by the convenience of industrialized countries. When such mobility bursts out of bureaucratic control, as in the case of Caribbean and Mexican migration into the United States, the cries of alarm within the host country surpass in shrillness those of the most ardent Third World protectionist faced by smuggling. One need not be an expert in general-equilibrium economic analysis to see that barriers to labor mobility will have a powerful effect on the whole configuration of world prices for goods and factors of production, i.e., on both world efficiency and income distribution. The welfare of most of the population of the Third World is not increased by such barriers.

The international market for capital is hardly free of institutional features closely linked to political manipulation. Financial flows may go through open security markets or through corporations, via long-term bonds or via bank credit; they may be a result of purely private deals or supervised by some international agency, all depending on political decisions taken by industrialized countries. The power to initiate significant changes in those markets rests exclusively in their hands; the burden of adjusting to those changes often falls elsewhere. According to circumstances and Northern convenience, one may hear Northern officials call for laissez faire and the law of supply and demand for, say, international private lending to the LDCs or instead call for a "rule of law" that could well lead to a credit cartel under the supervision of the IMF. Northern private commercial banks will swallow their enthusiasm for private enterprise and run for help to their home governments and the IMF when they see their bargaining power decline vis-à-vis that of LDCs.

In short, an intelligent person expressing faith in the efficiency of international markets really is making more a political than an economic judgment. That person is expressing trust in the wisdom of the hegemonic power and its allies to enforce more or less sensible arrangements and to be sufficiently flexible to adjust to new pressures and events. It is only a slight exaggeration to say that if national markets have historically grown subtly out of the barrel of a gun, international markets have grown crudely out of gunboats.

HISTORICAL TOLERANCE FOR SELECTIVITY

From the viewpoint of this essay, it is of special interest to inquire regarding the historical tolerance of dominant powers toward the exercise of selectivity by peripheral countries in their international linkages. The answer is not encouraging. Examples have already been given, such as the Opium War or the United States embargo of Cuba, in which hegemonic powers strenuously opposed one form or another of selectivity. On these matters, the periphery has more often than not faced a package deal on a take-it-or-leave-it basis, and offers from hegemonic powers to participate in the international division of labor were not to be refused lightly. A sound mainstream economist, R. G. Hawtrey, writing in the twilight of the British Empire, reflected well the center's intolerance of peripheral selectivity:

Those who protest against imperialism and militarism are often led to take a stand on the defense of right against force, and to contend for the sanctity of sovereign rights. It is part of their case to uphold the weak against the strong, and it is easy to be sarcastic at the expense of the civilising mission of a country which uses its power to dispossess the natives of a promising district and to hand over their land to profit-seeking exploiters.

But it is futile to shut one's eyes to the problems that arise in such cases. It is no solution to insist on indigenous sovereign rights; that would be to preserve barbarism as in some parts of the world we

127

preserve big game. . . . Let them retain unspoiled as far as possible their folklore and their picturesque customs and surroundings, but we cannot ask them to abjure change, and to cut themselves off from contact with the intellectual, artistic and social movements of the rest of the world. . . . And if we stipulate that what is valuable, attractive or even harmless in their culture ought to be preserved and to be made a component in their progress, that does not mean either that they are to be kept as they are, at the cost of interposing an insuperable barrier in the way of the development of the resources that lie around them and under their feet, or that a medicine man with a council of village elders should decide on the terms of a mining concession, the route of a new railway, or legislative proposals on the subject of companies, patents, bankruptcy or land tenure. . . . Mankind has become dependent on the systematic use of the material resources of the world, and cannot afford to allow those resources to be withheld from use through the shortcomings of communities which rule over them. . . . What is needed, far from being a more rigorous respect for sovereign rights, is some means other than force or overriding sovereign rights. There must be a new principle of growth. . . . When we seek to eliminate force from the system, we find that force is fulfilling an indispensable function, the supersession of decayed or atrophied sovereign authorities by healthy and vital ones.[18]

Hawtrey also expressed concern about "the continuance of cruel and horrible practices" among the natives who sat on natural resources. His language is today reserved for the privacy of select clubs in center countries, but his spirit is clearly present *inter alia* in discussions regarding the Law of the Sea conference and statements to the effect that LDCs cannot expect to have access to the markets of the developed countries unless they show friendliness to Northern transnationals. Cloaked in deep philosophical concerns, his spirit is also present among those who wonder about the right of LDCs to determine the rate at which they allow their natural resources to be exploited, in the access to supplies discussion, and even among those who would use food aid leverage for noble purposes.

[18]R. G. Hawtrey, *Economic Aspects of Sovereignty*, Longmans, Green and Co., London, New York and Toronto, 1930, pp. 138–140 and 152–153. In the latter pages, Hawtrey argued that by 1930, "the impurities expelled from the Imperialist powers" had reappeared among the subject peoples, who, according to him, had become more narrowly nationalistic than their masters.

Is it then naïve to plead for a world safe for selectivity? It will be argued that present and expected world political realities, particularly the consolidation of polycentrism and the nuclear stalemate, make the search for international rules allowing for various degrees of selective delinking a realistic and desirable program for a broad coalition of elements in the South *and* in the North. Reasonably standoffish world markets may grow out of five or six nuclear guns aiming at each other.

THE OLD INTERNATIONAL ECONOMIC ORDER: BRETTON WOODS VERSUS HAVANA

Serious multilateral efforts at comprehensive rule making for global economic relations have been rare in history. Before recent discussions on a New International Economic Order, the major effort centered around proposals for an International Trade Organization (ITO). In the midst of the struggle against nazism and fascism, which had offered the conquered peoples of Europe a new order, the more far-sighted thinkers from Britain and the United States realized that something more than a return to the dismal interwar economic circumstances had to be proposed. Plans for a better postwar world, first employed in the battle for the hearts and minds of Europeans by the British and United States governments, gradually expanded and led to proposals for an International Trade Organization. It will be recalled that what is now known as the Bretton Woods system was only part of the grand architectural design of postwar planners. Institutions such as the IMF, the International Bank for Reconstruction and Development (IBRD), and the General Agreement on Trade and Tariffs (GATT) were only fragments, even if substantial fragments, of that design. Without the ITO they would have been regarded by the more enlightened planners in, say, 1946 as providing an unbalanced and incomplete world economic order. Those planners were right.

The Senate of the United States, without floor debate, failed to ratify the Havana Charter creating the ITO. It was alleged by critics in the U.S. Congress, which throughout its history has generated tax and trade legislation of great complexity and with many loopholes, that the Havana Charter was too riddled with exceptions and special provisions. The United States, it was feared, would stick by its principles while foreigners would use escape clauses. Other United States critics saw in the ITO a kind of supergovernment with power to plan world trade and interfere with domestic economic policy. The ITO Charter was criticized for not doing enough to spread the United States system of "free enterprise," for not providing firm protection for private foreign investment, and for failing to adequately protect the interests of the United States in its voting arrangements. Influential business organizations, such as the National Association of Manufacturers, stressed that acceptance of the ITO Charter would weaken efforts being made publicly and privately to create a "proper climate" for private investment; this would postpone the day when LDC governments would realize that in their own interests they would have to provide more freedom and security for potential investors.[19]

Viewed in historical perspective, it is not surprising that the ITO was stillborn; vested interests within the two superpowers that emerged from the war had little to gain from having their political and economic might checked by rules drawn up in cooperation with Lilliputian powers. Each superpower could pretty much unilaterally set the rules of the game in its own sphere of influence; the hard-nosed realists in each camp could think of many reasons to sink the ITO. Only institutions designed so that the influence of the United States and of its close allies was clearly dominant, such as the IMF, the IBRD, and the GATT, emerged (but slowly) from the frustration of idealistic war and postwar planning.

Could the ITO have evolved into what is nowadays called a "New International Economic Order" (NIEO)? That counterfactual hypothesis is most intriguing. The ITO Charter, it will be recalled, allowed for commodity agreements in which both

[19]See Percy W. Bidwell and William Diebold, Jr., *The United States and the International Trade Organization*, International Conciliation, Carnegie Endowment for International Peace, March 1949, no. 449; and William Diebold, Jr., "The End of the I.T.O.," *Princeton Essays in International Finance*, no. 16, October 1952.

consumer and producer countries would be represented equally. The prewar abuses of the tin and rubber cartels (which were *not* led by LDCs) were to be avoided. Access to supplies, a concern during the interwar period causing fierce rivalry among major powers, was to be regulated and assured. It is not difficult to imagine the ITO Charter preoccupations with restrictive business practices and private cartels and its direct foreign investment provisions, in retrospect so mild and yet so resented then by the United States business community, evolving into a code on international investment, technological transfer, and TNCs. One may note that the ITO investment code had nothing to do with the Charter as originally conceived; it was a late addition originating, ironically, in United States business pressure to obtain the very climate that business leaders later said would not be promoted by the code. The Charter also opened the way for international coordination of domestic stabilization policies. Its provisions for freer trade, suspected by India and by the Latin American countries at the Havana meeting, may have allowed for sensible infant-industry protection in LDCs while discouraging the worst excesses of import-substitution policies. The multilateral and globalist spirit of the Charter, which made ample room for socialist countries, state trading, and public enterprises, would have encouraged freedom of action for the Third World, a freedom severely limited by the cold war.

Political and economic circumstances during the 1960s and early 1970s led to an erosion of Pax Americana rules for international economic relations. New rules have not yet been established; no single power is able to impose them, and negotiations, as in the international monetary sphere, have proven laborious. The tendency has been to let international markets emerge and become stronger; those markets have increasingly become the mechanisms through which interdependence becomes tangible, and they substitute for more explicitly political mechanisms. Thus, the Soviet Union and Eastern European countries have borrowed in the Eurocurrency market without needing explicit political decisions to encourage this arena of East-West cooperation. Currency markets have substituted for political negotiations on par values. Management consultants and new firms have introduced greater fluidity in areas previously dominated by a few TNCs.

On the whole, the Third World has benefited from the loosening of political hegemones and the emergence of relatively open international markets. For example, during the 1950s a Southern country in need of external credit had few choices except to submit to IMF dictates: private bankers in those days would not move without the IMF green light. During those years, the IBRD would not lend to Southern public enterprises wishing to develop their countries' natural resources: international private capital, it was argued, was available and willing to do that job for them. Both the IMF and the IBRD have changed their tune, not because of a general advance of enlightenment but fundamentally because both short- and long-term financing alternatives available to Southern countries have increased. The Eurodollar market, which was neither foreseen, proposed, nor encouraged by either UNCTAD or most private enterprise enthusiasts, has done more for at least certain types of Third World countries than clever pleading and arguing with the IMF and the IBRD could have accomplished. The expansion in potential markets and sources of technology (Japan, Germany, the Soviet Union, and other LDCs) has also provided a more favorable international environment for the South than that which existed during the 1950s. Both the selective-exit option and the voice of the Third World inside and outside international organizations have become more robust.

Yet the current state of affairs appears fragile and precarious. There is a widespread feeling that the present international economic order is serving neither the purposes of the South nor those of a North plagued by inflation, recession, and economic insecurity. In some cases, as with bank lending, the North has become deeply concerned with the consequences of competition. Explicit political decisions setting up comprehensive rules to guide international economic relations seem to be called for—and this, I would argue, should be the fundamental rationale for the agitation in favor of an NIEO. Those rules could, in some cases, consolidate and expand advances registered in some international markets, such as the Eurocurrency market, which have been shown to reconcile international economic interdependence with domestic autonomy. In other cases, international markets require substantial reforms and improvements if they are to achieve that reconciliation. In yet other areas, such as the oceans, Antarctica, space, and other commons of humanity, more explicit political mechanisms will have to be created. Enlightened groups in both South and North have an interest in seeking arrangements allowing for the option of selective delinking wherever possible (though this may not be so in all areas). A review of some arenas of economic interaction between North and South will follow, with an examination of their potential for efficient yet standoffish interdependence as well as for selective delinking by countries choosing to opt out.

INTERNATIONAL COMMODITY MARKETS

Perceptions regarding the efficiency and equity of international commodity markets differ sharply between South and North. Less known perhaps is the divergence in perceptions about these markets between experts in international politics and history and certain types of mainstream economists, both from the North. The latter emphasize the long-term but ahistorical workings of demand and supply in hypothetical markets characterized by the long-run predominance of competition so that prices will eventually tend toward equality with social marginal costs. Their faith in the universality of this vision is matched by the often stated proposition that "commodity agreements don't work," so that they will never work; cartels of any sort sooner or later break down. Some of these economists may concede that commodity markets are a bit erratic at times; even this statement came under doubt in the 1960s. And even if such instability existed, "it was not clear" that it was economically undesirable or harmful to South or North. Departures from laissez faire in those markets, therefore, are presumed to be inefficient.

The Northern expert on international politics, typically with more knowledge of history than the orthodox economist, emphasizes how until at least the Second World War the struggle

133

over access to cheap raw materials was a constant and important source of friction among industrialized powers. The British and French empires certainly did not pretend to give to all nations equal access to the raw materials of their colonies, nor was their cynicism so great as to claim that it was all the equivalent of an international competitive market. It was not only the latecomers to the imperialist scramble, such as Germany, Italy, and Japan, who fretted over this state of affairs. As late as the time of the Atlantic Charter, frictions arose between the United Kingdom and the United States over what was to be meant by equal access to raw materials qualified by "respect to existing obligations." Even today one hears within the United States and Europe blunt comments (privately expressed) reflecting concern about Japanese competition in the demand for Third World fuels and raw materials.

The orthodox economists become impatient with all this looking back. But it might be helpful if such economists could clarify when, exactly, international commodity trading ceased to be dominated by big-power politics and began to be characterized by desirable competitive characteristics. Was it perhaps always that way and were the Japanese, Italians, and Germans simply stupidly preoccupied with access? Or did the competitive world market spring full-blown from the ashes of Hitler, Tojo, and Mussolini? Orthodox faith needs to be strong not just to neglect history but also to see the invisible hand at work in invisible markets. Thus, it is now alleged by some that the bauxite market is being cartelized. The last time I asked, no one could tell me where I could find the bauxite market. The banana market is somewhat less ghostly, but the forces at work there are hardly anonymous.

Postwar reluctance by the governments of industrialized countries to deliver on ITO-type commitments on the commodity question must be explained not by abstract faith in laissez faire but by their confidence in the strength of their several lines of defense and control in this area. The best economic brain of his generation and a man who knew commodity markets at close range, John Maynard Keynes, favored commodity agreements for the postwar world. In 1938 he argued that the risk of holding surplus stocks until they should be wanted was beyond the scope of private enterprise, while the fluctuations in the prices of commodities were too violent to serve any good economic purpose. After the war, however, governments of industrialized countries felt that existing conditions would make it in their interests to avoid extensive commodity agreements. First, they expected to see plenty of excess capacity in raw material production; a new world slump was deemed likely by many. Second, for many commodities, a good share of production and marketing was organized by TNCs from industrialized countries eager to pick up not only signals from the market but also those emanating from their home governments. To a large extent, those TNCs managed the markets, holding stocks and planning the necessary investments. At least for some goods and favored customers, they ran effective commodity stabilization schemes. The intimate links between oil companies and their home governments throughout history are well known (and only now loudly and publicly deplored by more than a handful of Northern economists); it is doubtful that such links were absent for TNCs involved in other commodities. Third, in case of sudden unexpected shortages as in the Korean War, "voluntary" arrangements could be organized to keep prices relatively low and supplies flowing from friendly LDCs. This technique was also used during and immediately after the Second World War; life was made extremely hard for Third World countries, such as Argentina, who chose to stay out of such arrangements. When the threat of excess demand disappeared, the return to the free play of the market would be announced and the rhetoric of cooperation for "common safety, common growth" would be dropped.

Even before October 1973 world commodity markets presented a wildly heterogeneous picture. The truly international market for sugar, for example, was separated from the major industrialized markets by protectionist and discriminatory policies. International trade in meat was (and is) subject to unexpected shocks originating in changes in the commercial policies of industrialized countries, particularly the European Economic Community. Even where production conditions guarantee a large number of potential suppliers, control over marketing, primarily

135

by TNCs, limits the resemblance of those markets to textbooks ideals, as in the case of bananas. The International Resource Bank proposed by Henry Kissinger in May 1976 starts from the assumption that international markets for trade and investment in minerals are seriously flawed.

As LDCs have attempted to exert greater control over the production, processing, transport, and marketing of their raw materials, the heterogeneity of commodity markets has increased; in spite of the outcry of those in the North who fear not the destruction of efficient world markets but their reduced capacity to manipulate those markets,[20] the greater LDC assertiveness in this area may eventually lead to looser, more competitive arrangements for some commodity trading. But this need not happen. In some cases, the new LDC organizations may seek alliances with the TNCs managing world markets. In others, the LDCs could attempt establishing their own network of special relationships with good customers, which could lead to new oligopolistic structures. Transition from the old to the new order in commodity markets, particularly those in minerals, could be plagued by severe price instability.

Can this sea of imperfection be improved by the adoption of Keynes-ITO-type commodity agreements that will no doubt introduce some imperfections of their own? Would those agreements be compatible with the option of selective delinking? Can a country keep at arm's length from customers and fellow producers belonging to the same agreement? If standoffishness were the only guide to the organization of international markets, spot auction markets in standardized and clearly defined commodities requiring a minimum of mutual trust or expectations of continuing links would be the most desirable mechanism for organizing interdependence. Buyers and sellers, each having their own stocks,

---

[20]A minor but revealing example of attempted manipulation of world commodity markets by Northern powers is given by United States opposition to World Bank loans to finance palm oil production in the South. Palm oil has become a major competitor to soybeans, whose market has been dominated by the United States. Sri Lanka, by comparison, would find it more difficult to oppose the expansion of tea production elsewhere. See *The Economist*, May 8, 1976, p. 44.

would come and go as they pleased as if each transaction were a once-and-for-all encounter. With true weights and measures, the spot price of the standardized commodity would give all the relevant information for the transaction. Each country could organize its auction or several could cooperate in arranging for a regular meeting place with a trusted auctioneer.

Such a picture has considerable appeal, but it also has short-comings. Some more continuity may be desired between buyers and sellers of at least strategic commodities such as food and fuel; even with reasonable stocks of food at home, it may not be wise to be willing to buy from a different baker, butcher, or brewer every week with little notion about what prices and quality will be. Explicit contracts covering future transactions or implicit ones involving customer markets may be more efficient and increase security. They may also encourage a more efficient pattern of investment. Creating the framework within which a little more voice can be heard could have advantages over just relying on the exit and search options. Note that the gradual move away from the pure spot-auction-market (or "silent trade") situation requires increasing trust between buyers and sellers, not just trust that future obligations will be carried out faithfully but also trust that if circumstances unforeseen at the time a contract was signed occur, both sides will be sensible regarding suitable modifications to the deal.

The greater assertiveness of the Third World in international commodity markets has shaken up established patterns of trust and customer markets organized and led by TNCs and indus-trialized countries; hence the turmoil and anxiety. New networks of trust will not be easily formed. In this task, Keynes-ITO-type commodity agreements could be helpful and not incompatible with the reconstruction of international commodity markets that are more fluid and competitive than past and present ones. In-deed, insofar as such agreements increase trust between buyers and sellers and expand the flow of information, the apparently paradoxical result that commodity agreements will strengthen markets *may* result, e.g., by providing a framework for long-term sales agreements and for future contracts of longer maturity than those now available.

It is now clear that the role of international commodity markets as guides to the allocation of fresh investments for the future production of commodities, a role at which these markets were never particularly good by themselves, is in a serious crisis, particularly in minerals. It was noted earlier that for many commodities, TNCs from advanced countries historically provided not only marketing but also production and investment decisions; the visible markets were often minor appendixes to the invisible ones internalized by those corporations. Third World assertiveness in production, marketing, and investment in oil, copper, bananas, etc., has upset these cozy arrangements. Before a new framework is established, instability in commodity markets could become more severe than it was during the last 20 years.

The search for international arrangements in commodity trading which are truly efficient, are perceived as fair, and allow for a minimum degree of arm's length relationships will not be easy. It is not helped by those who assume that all is well at present (excepting, of course, the only imperfection recognized by them: OPEC) and that international commodity markets are of such a nature that any tinkering will necessarily reduce their efficiency. This is bunk. More helpful are those who at least call for a closer study of how these markets operate; it seems that faith in markets is best maintained by minimizing detailed knowledge of how they operate. It is not clear why future contracts do not stretch further into the future and whether anything could be done to encourage that possibility. Some observers within the industrialized world who advocate more expansive economic policies to combat domestic unemployment, but who fear the inflationary consequences of rising prices for raw materials in erratic world markets during the cyclical upswing, have also joined the search for improved markets in this area. Excess capacity and high unemployment in the North are surely bizarre weapons with which to fight higher prices for Southern raw materials. It would also be peculiar if Northern defenders of international interdependence were to advocate purely national buffer stocks to deal with this problem.

In a world in which managed floating of exchange rates under international surveillance has become acceptable after many years of rigid rates, the eventual acceptance of managed floating of, say, copper prices after many years of unregulated fluctuations may not be impossible or undesirable. The managing may be done by a central authority or by key countries subject to international surveillance. Third World countries could also put an increasing part of their wealth into stocks of raw materials they export and import so as to have a greater say in their marketing. Some inevitably will see this as cartelization; in most cases there will be no substance in the charge.

INTERNATIONAL MARKETS FOR TECHNOLOGY AND CAPITAL

Historically, the Third World may be said to have been basically an exporter of commodities and an importer of technology of different types, embodied and disembodied. Technology, or most consumer and producer goods embodying it, is difficult to pin down and describe in the same way a metric ton of refined sugar can be described. Buying a radio implies something about future purchases of parts and servicing; this will be true, *a fortiori*, when buying electric generators and blueprints for building petrochemical plants. One moves sharply in the direction of customer markets for manufactures, even more dominated historically by Northern countries than commodity markets, some of which have a greater potential for becoming auction markets. Beneath normal steady-state operation, customer markets are fraught with potential conflicts: "An established customer-supplier relationship introduces a bilateral monopoly surplus that can be split between the competing buyers and sellers. In the short run, most customers would pay a slightly higher price to their suppliers without shopping and most suppliers would, if they had to, sell for a shade less to their customers. This interdependence puts a premium on maintaining the relationship."[21] But clearly the larger the bilateral surplus to be shared, the more vulnerable the relationship will be to changes in the environment inducing one of the partners to rethink the deal.

[21]Okun, "Inflation," p. 362.

139

The technology market is characterized by large gaps between the marginal cost involved in selling one more bit of that particular commodity and the marginal value to the buyer of acquiring it. It is also characterized by a tendency toward a lopsided distribution of information between buyers and sellers. All this refers to existing technology; naturally, the pricing of already existing knowledge may be said to have some influence on the creation of new knowledge, at least under some institutional circumstances. Few economists ever argue that in spite of difficulties in defining technology and the products embodying it, pure laissez faire policies should be applied to such an unusual market. It would be very strange to argue that way for international markets. Rules and codes of conduct in this area which go beyond archaic nineteenth-century patent agreements seem necessary to reconstruct international markets along efficient, equitable, and reasonably standoffish lines. At present, restrictive business practices banned in the domestic markets of some industrialized countries are frequently found in international markets for technology.

The topic of technological markets is closely interwoven with that of transnational corporations and direct foreign investment. The frequently lamented hypersensitivity in this area of Southern countries as well as that of countries such as Australia, Canada, and France has at least placed the transnationals and direct investment firmly on the agenda of economists, political scientists, and government leaders. This is no mean achievement, as before the "emotional" and "irrational" Third World and Australian-Canadian-French outbursts, general complacency reigned among establishment scholars and observers regarding those phenomena. Harry G. Johnson has put the matter candidly: "As regards welfare effects, it has been generally and rather uncritically assumed that the impact of a package of capital, technology, and managerial skill must be beneficial to the host country. Closer investigation of this issue, however, shows that the gains are not so obviously inevitable or significant."[22] The erosion of such uncritical assumptions, one may conjecture, would have been much slower without Third World agitation.

[22]Harry G. Johnson, *Technology and Economic Interdependence*, Macmillan, London, 1975 (published for the Trade Policy Research Center), p. 50.

Industrialized countries have long recognized the dangers that corporations with substantial market power can represent for efficient national markets as well as for political stability. The assumption that bigness in national markets inevitably turns into smallness when thrown into international markets will not do. Jacob Viner wrote in 1960, "In any case, monopoly is so prevalent in the markets of the western world today that discussion of the merits of the free competitive market, as if that were what we were living with or were at all likely to have the good fortune to live with in the future, seem to me academic in only the pejorative sense of that adjective." He went on to argue: "But given the prevalence of the dangers of substantial intrusion of monopoly into the market, the logic of the laissez faire defense of the market against state intervention collapses and there is called for instead, by its very logic, state suppression or state regulation of monopoly practices."[23]

The ITO Charter, it was already noted, contained modest proposals for international antitrust action. But little survived, and in these matters a crude nineteenth-century laissez faire prevails in international markets on the whole. Perhaps only the populist agitation of the South can succeed in changing this state of affairs, which does little for the welfare not only of the South but also of the vast majority of Northern populations. Concerned Northern agencies, such as the European Economic Community Commission, have been timid in pressing minor reforms such as making groups of companies publish separate accounts for each of their operations as well as consolidated accounts for the group.[24] Transnationals, for all their protestations of good citizenship, appear reluctant to show their returns separately for

[23]Jacob Viner, "Intellectual History of *Laissez-faire*," pp. 66–67. Viner also noted: "It is not reasonable to treat an existing income distribution, for the purpose of analyzing the market, as if it just 'happened,' as if it were independent of influence by the market and as incapable of influence on the market, through the effect of aggregate human exercises of will and economic power, as the Rocky Mountains or storms and earthquakes are free from human control" (p. 67).

[24]"Total Exposure?" *The Economist*, May 1, 1976, pp. 71–72. The same journal has criticized the OECD code of conduct for transnationals as unnecessarily weak while declaring itself a good friend of transnationals. See the article entitled "Multinational Mummery," June 26, 1976, pp. 61–62.

every subsidiary in each country. Tax authorities of industrialized countries have shown themselves eager to protect the privacy of transnationals; interchange of tax information among countries has advanced little. Northern diplomatic pressure routinely has been brought to bear on LDCs that try to reduce exorbitant monopoly privileges attached to Northern patent holders within LDC markets, even though most experts agree that neither LDC welfare nor world efficiency gains from the maintenance of such privileges. Perhaps as early as the 1980s, the most enlightened citizens of the United States and the Netherlands will recognize that their freedoms and economic welfare were better served during the early 1970s by the international battles of Salvador Allende to regulate transnationals than by the complacency of Richard Nixon or Prince Bernhard.

So a world safe for selectivity needs international rules to curb abuses of economic power and restraints of trade by corporations. At present, even countries that have vigorous antitrust enforcement for their national markets have legislation practically encouraging collusion among their corporations when they deal in international markets. It is a favorite gambit of transnationals when faced by statements calling for their international regulation to lament the incomprehension of the world and to proclaim that they are withdrawing into their home country for the foreseeable future. The year 1976 heard many such declarations, particularly from United States–based transnationals, and this time there may be more substance to these announcements than in earlier times. Such withdrawal, in fact, may be a development not to be regretted. Some of the expansion of United States transnationals during the 1960s could be interpreted as medium-term speculation against an overvalued dollar; such motivation has now disappeared. More alternatives to transnationals in the financial and technological markets as well as a revision by many LDCs of misguided import-substitution policies can also be expected to dampen the flow of direct foreign investment to Southern countries. The fertility of the research and development laboratories of the transnational corporations may also be on the decline, as in pharmaceuticals, eroding their basic source of monopoly power, and the 1980s may witness a faster rate of diffusion of existing knowledge instead of fresh substantive (rather than gimmicky) breakthroughs.

The unpackaged interaction via trade, finance, and technology markets can be encouraged in a number of other ways. A broadening of LDC access to the national capital markets in the North would encourage the unpackaging process. Preferences given in some Northern countries to outflows of direct foreign investment as compared with outflows of long-term portfolio investments could be eliminated. The internal political dynamics of many Northern countries are such that the governments are pressured by their transnationals to tie commercial relations with LDCs to how willingly those Southern countries allow inflows of unregulated direct foreign investment; the margin of LDC selectivity is thus significantly reduced. Acceptance by the North of the Calvo Doctrine, pending the establishment of truly international rules on foreign investment, would be desirable.[25]

It should be stressed that the goal is to have a world in which access to unpackaged capital and technology is one of the options. Even under those circumstances many LDCs may prefer to stop short of complete unbundling. It is said, for example, that some Latin American and Eastern European countries have chosen joint ventures with foreign investors even when those investors had given them the option of just purchasing technology. The host countries thought that *some* equity participation by the supplier of technology was a way of guaranteeing that the technology supplied would be the best possible for the venture and that it would remain so. Other LDCs may feel that they have not yet reached the stage at which they can efficiently bring together on their own the different parts of the investment pack-

---

[25]The Calvo Doctrine states that investors from abroad must accept the exclusive competence of host country tribunals to settle any litigation and must renounce recourse to home governments or to international arbitration. Anything else would discriminate against local investors. An investment by foreigners in a country is interpreted as ipso facto acceptance of this doctrine. As noted by Walter Lippmann as early as 1927, in the last analysis, the security of United States investments abroad must rest on the faith of the host nations that such investment is mutually profitable. See his "Vested Rights and Nationalism in Latin America," *Foreign Affairs*, vol. 5, no. 3, April 1927, p. 363.

age. When, as in the area of minerals and fuels, the activities of TNCs can quickly generate substantial tax and foreign-exchange revenues, those LDCs will not hesitate to allow an inflow of foreign investment even under rather old-fashioned conditions.

FIVE

Other Reforms and Northern Apprehensions

While I have warned the reader that this essay is no exercise in constitution writing for a world safe for selectivity (and that it would not produce a timetable for reform), it may be useful to mention other areas where world markets could be made more efficient and equitable while broadening the range of LDC selectivity. Some of the points raised are only loosely connected with either delinking or selectivity, but any serious attempt to improve the present world economic order would have to take them into account, even if no fundamental restructuring is contemplated. They are sketched here to meet the challenge of those who explicitly or implicitly argue that the present order is as good as one can possibly hope for and who ask for further specific criticisms in addition to those raised earlier. This section also discusses the disconcerting hostility shown by some Northern observers toward the call for a new look at world economic arrangements. As one can expect a growing participation of socialist countries in world markets during the next two decades, a very brief look is also taken at the problems and opportunities this could raise for the South.

OTHER ITEMS ON THE AGENDA

(1) In a world safe for selectivity, actions such as the persistent United States commercial blockade of Cuba would, of course, be illegal. The claim by some United States government officials

that after many years of such an embargo, after several United States–inspired attempts on the lives of Cuban leaders, and after a United States–inspired invasion of that island, the Cuban government is an international outlaw and still owes the United States a large sum of money would be laughed out of court. More generally, ways should be sought to separate the areas of commercial transactions from those of political relationships.

(2) Deficient and unstable foreign-exchange earnings weaken the LDCs' capacity for autonomous decision making and increase their vulnerability to external pressures. There is much that LDCs can do on their own even under present difficult international circumstances to remedy that deficiency and instability. But the international setting can also be vastly improved. Both secular and sporadic Northern protectionism, particularly in labor-intensive, standardized manufactures, in agriculture, and in the area of processed minerals and raw materials, still represent a significant barrier to Southern efforts to "earn their own way." In those areas, apparently low (nominal) tariffs hide large effective rates of protection. For example, tariffs on chocolates and cigars appear low, but they exceed those on cocoa beans and tobacco leaf, thus discouraging processing industries in LDCs. Northern tariff and nontariff barriers to trade, which include some domestic subsidies to their depressed industries and regions, have also encouraged the destruction of competition in world markets. The so-called voluntary export-restriction programs, for example, generate pressures for firms to coordinate their actions in the affected area.

It should also be stressed that sporadic Northern protectionism, such as the European decision to abruptly shut off its market to meat imports, threatens international capital markets. If Argentina, for example, based its foreign-borrowing plan on expected earnings from meat exports, sudden (and, under GATT rules, illegal) closing of foreign markets for its meat could lead to a revision of its debt-servicing schedule. Indeed, under those circumstances the world community should accept the servicing of Argentine debt in the form either of beef or of bonds redeemable in beef at some average of recent world prices. More generally, it is difficult to see how in a world in which industrialized countries deny entry to unskilled LDC labor, shut out LDC exports—often in an unpredictable manner—and go through cycles of boom and bust with little regard for their side effects on the Third World, one could expect a smooth and tranquil servicing of LDC foreign debt.

GATT, it will be recalled, was originally designed to be a part of ITO. Many Southern countries originally decided to wait until the ITO Charter was ratified before joining GATT. Some are still waiting. Rather than participating actively in the successive rounds of tariff cutting sponsored by GATT, Southern countries have sought preferences for their manufactured exports via UNCTAD. Ex post, both the emphasis on preferences and the neglect of the GATT tariff-cutting rounds appear to have been tactical mistakes. UNCTAD proposals, after all, had eventually to lead to action in the GATT. It may be noted that many LDCs have been reducing their own tariff levels in recent years without asking for reciprocity from Northern countries.

Greater Southern participation in GATT could be especially useful in the framing of new rules on export subsidies. At present, some LDCs use those subsidies to compensate for overvaluation of their currencies, on "infant-exporter" grounds, and to offset Northern protectionism. Northern countries have, on some occasions, imposed ad hoc countervailing duties on Southern exports benefiting from those programs, claiming that the procedure involves dumping or disrupts markets. The same Northern countries use subsidies of various kinds for ostensibly domestic reasons, such as regional or industrial policies, which have the effect of reducing potential markets for Southern exports.

(3) One can foresee a growing participation of state enterprises and governments from North, South, East, and West in international transactions. In steel, for example, state mills account for a majority of output not only in socialist countries and many LDCs, but also in Britain, Holland, and Italy. The framers of the Havana Charter wrestled with the issue of how to reconcile such participation with the goal of letting each international transaction be guided by purely commercial considerations under fair play rules. This is not an easy matter to settle, but it does not loom as an impossible barrier to standoffish commercial trans-

actions. Bringing the provisions for state trading in the Havana Charter up to date and incorporating them into an expanded and reformed GATT should be encouraged. While those provisions are untried and often debatable, they represent useful building blocks.

(4) Not all arenas of international economic interaction can be expected to avoid a fairly high and persistent degree of politicization. Such is the case with humanity's commons, including the oceans and Antarctica. Concessional aid for the least developed countries will also involve some politicization. Inevitably in these matters the North will seek weak international organizations (unless their voting is arranged as in the IMF and IBRD) and flexible rules that put a minimum of restrictions on their economic, political, and technological power. The South, particularly its weakest components, can be expected to seek rules more along the lines of automatic negative world income and wealth taxes. The rents generated by humanity's commons are natural candidates for the latter type of automatic redistributive mechanisms.

(5) The supply of international money in recent years has hardly been an example of economic rationality. International money is not ruled by a well-defined body of laws and regulations with a balanced allocation of rights and responsibilities among nations. Complaints in this area regarding hegemonism have not been limited to LDCs. Influential international organizations are sometimes run, and their voting power is allocated, as if they were profit-making institutions.

More items could be added to the agenda. But the points already covered perhaps show that expansion and consolidation of the area of efficient international arm's-length transactions are possible but require greater attention to global rule making. Those rules should embody multilateral principles; selectivity would certainly be curtailed in a world characterized by rigid regional hegemones led by either Northern or Southern powers. For explicit politics to be taken out of daily market transactions, the politics implicit in present international markets needs to be tackled head on via rule making. It could be argued that the central virtue of the agitation for a New International Economic

Order, particularly in its ideological dimension, has been to focus the attention of the world on the need to reexamine the implicit politics of existing (and missing) rules.

NORTHERN DELINKING AND NORTHERN PERCEPTIONS

A few years ago, Arthur Lewis proposed the following mental experiment: What would happen to the development of the South if all the industrialized North were to sink into the ocean? Extreme delinkers, of course, would argue that the effect would be strongly positive; enthusiasts of export-led growth and openness, the opposite. The experiment can also be carried out in reverse—by asking about Northern welfare should the South disappear. Here many more observers would give the selective delinkers' answer to the first experiment: There will be some negative effects and some positive ones; some countries will have more of one type than of the other; but on balance and in the long run, the net effect will be small. It would appear that the case for Northern delinking may be more powerful than that for Southern delinking.

On closer inspection this is not so obvious. A complete cutoff, even if conceivable for the United States, is out of the question for Europe and Japan. Even within the United States, some groups and institutions depend heavily on the Third World for their profits and welfare. A selective delinking of the type discussed earlier, accompanied by the adoption of new global rules of the game, however, should be very attractive to liberal and progressive groups in the North. Naturally, TNCs and others benefiting from their present freedom of action in world markets will take a dim view of such changes and will typically argue in favor of the status quo. But even here some changes in attitudes may develop; for example, corporations worried about future supplies of raw materials may come to support commodity agreements, while financial groups whose lending may replace direct foreign investment in the exploitation of Third World natural resources could support, *a fortiori*, those arrangements.

Recent years have witnessed the way the lack of international

149

controls over the power of TNCs can have negative repercussions for the economic welfare of their home countries as well as for the stability and integrity of their system of government. A situation in which certain deeds are illegal at home but legal abroad or when committed against foreigners creates Frankenstein monsters who soon forget the dividing line with a cosmopolitan spirit worthy of a better cause. Unfortunately, some Northern thinkers still fall for the line that attacks on the transnationals are attacks on their countries. Liberal observers and scholars in developed countries often show annoyance at Southern emphasis on the history and past sins of Northern public and private organizations. Reluctantly it is conceded that, yes, *perhaps* the *allegations* of historical abuses of power by Northern institutions *may* have a kernel of truth, but naturally they are *likely* to have been grossly exaggerated. (Fame and glory surely await the graduate student who shows that the Opium War led to a Chinese takeoff that was aborted by later attempts to restrict trade.) But all of this is in the past; things are now different. Guatemala? Vietnam? The Dominican invasion? The Cuban blockade? The attack on Suez? The Chilean destabilization? Well, these were secondary slips, explained by quirks and aberrations of gruff but basically well-meaning Northern personalities or stupid (but never evil) blunders of silly bureaucrats, intelligence officials, executives, or generals.

To many of these Northern observers, the history that can be neglected begins yesterday and perhaps even today. When something like the Vietnam War or the Dominican invasion is occurring, the situation is deemed too complex for "simpleminded" positions. The sensible mainstream observers and scholars are fierce in demanding that critics prove their allegations that something is wrong. Few of them will be found publicly condemning official policy, even if in private it becomes increasingly fashionable to express concern. By the time the thing is over and its lunacy obvious to all, it is time to look again at the future and neglect to dwell on the past, which, one is told, would never happen again because the lesson has been learned. What happens to all those who supported or went along with the discredited policies? Their lessons learned, they are in high positions, fresh for new adventures. What happens to those who were right at the time? Such impudence is intolerable; they go the way of Eugene McCarthy or George McGovern. One does not typically get to be President, cabinet member, or adviser to the mighty by being too far ahead or behind the sensible mainstream. Other than a few (preferably dead) personalities, no one is left to shoulder responsibility for the past. Making models to analyze the future is much preferred to dwelling on such "meaningless" history.

The contrasts and similarities of this process with the rewriting of history practiced in Eastern Europe, the Soviet Union, and China are intriguing. In the East, history is simply rewritten from above. Western democracies, with their faster turnover of leaders, have another mechanism for avoiding historical and systematic analysis and for explaining events deemed undesirable ex post as a consequence of peculiar personalities and blundering bureaucrats, leaving the future fresh for new "blunders" that later will be similarly explained. The critics can never catch up: while the events are happening, no conclusive proof of their wickedness is possible; when proof becomes available, the events are "irrelevant history." One may note that TNCs carry this process one step further by changing not only their top management but even their names: when Chiquita Banana gets caught with her pants down, some in the top management are disgraced (unfairly if necessary), and while United Fruit disappears, United Brands goes marching on.[26]

The mood of many liberal Northern observers in the mid-1970s

---

[26]Corporate manipulation of Northern ideological symbols also changes with great speed, and little remains stored in the national memory. Corporations such as Alcoa, Anaconda, Ford Motors, Gulf Oil, International Telephone and Telegraph, United Fruit, and United States Steel, which during 1974–1976 had some difficulty proving their respect for the law, in 1964 formed (with other corporations) what they called the "The Rule of Law Committee," which drafted what later came to be known as the Hickenlooper Amendment, empowering the U.S. President to cut off aid to any country nationalizing, expropriating, or seizing property owned by United States citizens without speedy and full compensation. See Eugene F. Mooney, *Foreign Seizures: Sabbatino and the Act of State Doctrine*, University Press of Kentucky, Lexington, 1967, pp. 106–113.

is particularly disconcerting. Great eagerness and moral righteousness have been spent denouncing Third World elites. It appears that only the Third World has elites; the First World has "leaders" and leaders whose leadership is often glorified and rationalized. Third World and UNCTAD representatives are said to be arrogant, emotional, irrational, lazy ("they don't do their homework"), stupid ("they don't know their own interests"), corrupt, tyrannical, mean to each other, selfish, moralizing, lawless (sometimes "international outlaws"), loudmouthed, revanchist, power-hungry, and often less interested in the welfare of their own people than the Northern observer is. Proposals put forth by the Third World are closely examined for flaws that once found provide justification for leaving things as they are. The flaws, of course, are frequently there, and the charges against Third World leaders are also frequently true. But one would like to see the same moral zeal applied to evaluating the actions and motivations of First World elites and ruling groups and the analytical talent invested in producing constructive counterproposals. In short, the building of a moderate world order in the 1980s could use more of the likes of John Maynard Keynes, James Meade, and George Marshall. One may also reflect that the charges of irrational, incompetent emotionalism so often leveled at the Third World leadership may partly explain the great popularity of OPEC among poor countries. Surely OPEC and its leaders could not be so stupid if they have become so rich.

Warnings by Northern liberals about "the threat from the Third World" have also encouraged latent Northern populist xenophobia and protectionism, reflected both in the fury with which affluent consumers react to high coffee prices and in the anger of Minnesota beet growers at low sugar prices. Shoe and textile producers in the North have suddenly become ardent critics of Southern despotism.

The North-South debate has certainly shown that there is no shortage within either region of talented theatrical debaters and imaginative name callers. Perhaps such catharsis was necessary. Looking ahead, it can be argued that semantics will remain important. In particular, the Third World could benefit by using certain Northern ideological traditions to legitimize Southern theses. For example, rather than attack abstract, nonexistent free markets, Southern champions could emphasize how reality in international markets often violates at least the spirit of antitrust regulations within Northern countries.

SOME ISSUES RAISED BY EASTERN RELINKING

Socialist participation in world markets, outside COMECON (the Council for Mutual Economic Assistance), has been far from negligible but subject to ad hoc arrangements. The intellectual efforts of the drafters of the ITO Charter to devise rules for trade between centrally planned and market economies were to be reflected mainly in early postwar textbooks on international trade. During the late 1960s and early 1970s socialist presence in world markets has risen, and their interest in a framework for international economic relations should follow.

The socialist stance toward Third World demands for a New International Economic Order (NIEO) has been cool on the grounds that socialist countries have had neither colonies nor neocolonies and therefore owe no reparations to the South (a line fortunately not adopted by Sweden). Confident of their bargaining power and in their mechanisms for controlling trade, some elements in the socialist countries may continue to avoid commitment to whatever concessions are made to the South by the industrialized, capitalist North and also to global rules regulating international economic relations. The smaller socialist countries could be more interested in any such rules than the Soviet Union has been, however. China, which has shown considerable interest in the NIEO, could also contribute to the reconstruction of international markets, although her size is likely to tempt her to try to have her own superpower status in these and other matters.

It should be noted that there are some potentially harmful elements in the trend toward East-West economic cooperation for the South. First, Eastern Europe is already an important competitor in Western Europe and other markets for labor-intensive manufactures. Second, the same is already true of some primary products and could become even more so if the mineral riches of Siberia are tapped with the help of Western and Japanese corporations. Third, the efficacious use by Eastern Europe of the Eurodollar market could crowd out many Southern countries. Finally, the multiplication of contacts between the socialist countries and Western government agencies and TNCs poses some questions: Will recent efforts by some United States agencies to bring the Soviet Union into rate-setting shipping conferences be extended to other areas, to the detriment of competitive forces in the world economy? Will the TNCs attempt to use their leverage to, say, limit socialist competition in the transfer of technology to the Third World? These undesirable possibilities should not be exaggerated, but neither can they be dismissed with ideological clichés.

On balance, however, a more active socialist participation in world markets is likely to benefit the South, expanding options particularly in the areas of export markets and of suppliers of capital goods and technology. But as emphasized by Carlos Andrés Pérez, the President of Venezuela, in his visit to the Soviet Union during November 1976, socialist coyness about participation in the North-South dialogue looks increasingly unjustified and raises doubts about socialist willingness to actively support Southern aspirations. Practical difficulties standing in the way of closer links between the East and the South should not be underestimated, either. These include nonconvertibility of socialist currencies, lack of historical contacts, meager trade and transportation links, and fears of socialist planners that joint venture arrangements with LDCs would introduce additional uncertainties into foreign trade planning.

SIX

Concluding Remarks

It is well to emphasize what should *not* be expected from my version of a world safe for selectivity. There will be nothing in the rules of such a world to assure either democratic politics or economic justice inside each nation participating in international markets. Southern countries are and will remain very heterogeneous not only in their economic situations but also in their political systems and in the attention they give to the welfare of their poorest citizens. Some of the countries will choose to remain very open, partly to buttress their domestic political regimes with external support. Others may go through various degrees of delinking. The rules should make room for all of these options, but all countries would be expected to participate in rule making. To repeat: the point is not to devise an international order that will *assure* progressive changes in the South. The point is to create an order that will accommodate a variety of experiences, particularly progressive changes in the South, and that will not be hostile to and sabotage Southern efforts to achieve greater economic autonomy as the old international economic order has often done. Some unpleasant Southern regimes may benefit from such a standoffish world, but better ones may gain much more from it in the future.

Why not argue for a worldwide war on poverty and oppression? To those familiar with the rise and fall of the Alliance for Progress, the answer is obvious: no Northern government has both the credibility and the resources to launch and lead such a program seriously and globally, not now and not in the 1980s. Proposed global bargains between Northern and Southern elites of the type involving more aid in exchange for more redistribution and democracy are at best utopian and at worst a new version of an old confidence game. The sincerity with which some Northern individuals deplore poverty and oppression in the South is to be respected; but it strains the imagination to believe that major Northern governments, particularly those of large countries, could place such concerns at the center of their policies toward the South in any sustainable fashion in the near future. Indeed, much remains to be done by such governments on their home fronts to eliminate poverty and injustice.

So even if all rules allowing for selectivity in international markets were accepted or, indeed, even if all Southern demands now embodied in calls for an NIEO were to be immediately accepted by the North, it is doubtful that the mass of the poorest citizens in the South would feel much improvement in their welfare, at least in the immediate future. Booming Southern exports would no doubt lead to increases in Southern growth rates, but I doubt they would, by themselves, significantly influence Southern income distribution during the 1980s, particularly in the largest LDCs. This is just another way of saying that the central development problems for most LDCs are internal. Indeed, it could be argued that Third World leaders and intellectuals have spent too much time on international economic issues and too little time on domestic ones. Battles for domestic reforms seem less glamorous and more dangerous than those for an NIEO; Third World leaders carried away by the temptations of global statesmanship may find themselves engulfed by old-fashioned national economic disorder. The argument that nothing can be done domestically unless the external framework is changed is unconvincing for most LDCs under contemporary circumstances.

But this, of course, is no reason to dismiss calls for establishing an NIEO or searching for new international rules. There is a touch of hypocrisy in the upsurge of Northern elite concern about the indifference of LDC elites to poverty and democracy in the South, an indifference that to some observers seems a sufficient rebuttal to calls for an NIEO. The spectacle of Ferdinand Marcos lecturing on the evils of concentration of income and wealth is indeed revolting, but so was the spectacle of Richard Nixon lecturing Salvador Allende on the need to respect international law. It is important to maintain such ethical sensibility, but it is also important not to use it as an excuse to block needed reforms. Most people would read the historical record as indicating that very seldom do hegemonic Northern governments let concern for the poor and oppressed in the South determine their major long-run policies toward LDCs; to pretend that they do is far-fetched. Relations between major Northern countries and those Southern countries that have seriously battled poverty or have maintained democratic frameworks have not been significantly better than those with other LDCs. Neither Tanzania nor pre-1975 India was more popular in Washington than were South Korea and Brazil.

Northern solidarity with the poor and oppressed of the South could be reflected in some government programs as well as in the activities of private individuals and organizations. In some cases, such actions could be channelled via international organizations. Northern scientists, for example, not satisfied with researching improvements in ballistic missiles or plastic surgery, may seek to devote their talents to seeking breakthroughs in tropical agriculture or tropical diseases. It is not inconceivable that subsets of Northern governments, particularly those of small countries, and Southern governments with similar sociopolitical outlooks of a progressive cast could form informal alliances for progress. In much the same way as the UN calls for Scandinavian troops whenever trusted units are needed to keep the peace, Scandinavian-type countries could be trusted to lead and organize the Northern side of global programs against poverty, even if finance comes mainly from the ocean revenues or from the larger countries. Thus, even a selectively delinked world could have some room for modest and pinpointed doses of concessional finance, as much for the sake of Northern consciences as for the sake of the Southern poor. Mobilization of world public opinion to check abuses of human rights wherever they occur is also highly desirable, although it is a matter requiring a degree of delicate handling and purity of motive that may be beyond persons likely to be found in any national government.

A global international economic order allowing for selective delinking should reduce frictions between South and North by providing an improved, flexible framework for accommodating rapid social change in the South. Although such an order alone will not cure world poverty, it should result in some redistribution in income, wealth, and power from the North, particularly from Northern elites, to the South, particularly to Southern elites. The social history of the industrialized countries indicates that in their internal redistributive battles the poorest segments were typically the last to benefit, yet few would argue that those battles did not, on the whole, mark progressive steps on the road toward social democracy. In the United States, the populist battles late last century did very little to help Mississippi blacks. The exact impact of the New Deal reforms on blacks and Mexican-Americans is also moot.

Discussions as to whether Southern elites are interested in economic gains for their people or in their own wealth and status are singularly fruitless and potentially mischievous unless they are placed in a universal context, recognizing that such a question can be asked about any leadership group. The way it is often discussed in the North is heavy with insinuations about the sincerity and character of Southern elites in contrast with those of the North. This, of course, is an old weapon of status quo forces against those seeking social change. Thus, men like J. Edgar Hoover would ask themselves during the 1950s and 1960s whether Martin Luther King, Jr., and his collaborators were really after economic and political improvements for blacks or simply seeking status and power for themselves. The true motivation of the questioners, of course, is supposed to be above suspicion. The complexity frequently stressed when discussing Northern motivations and systems must also be seen in the South.

It is often said that calls for new international economic rules lead to the necessity to choose between goals of efficiency and redistribution in international markets. The assumption is that present arrangements are as efficient as possible; therefore, changes in them for the sake of achieving redistribution can be purchased only at the expense of efficiency. This essay has argued that present international arrangements are far from efficient; there is plenty of room for restructuring those arrangements so as to make them both more efficient and more equitable. There is a long way to go before hitting the real tradeoff zone. Arthur M. Okun[27] has emphasized how, in the United States, political decisions about fair play can change economic behavior and that it is quite possible that what is good for equality may be good for efficiency. If this is still possible in the largest Northern market economy, surely such opportunities must abound in the international economy, from opportunities for rationalizing the use of the oceans to opportunities for regulating international money, and in many areas in which the international community is now roughly where national economies were at the beginning of the last century.

It may well be that unless the governments of major industrialized nations, particularly the United States, are sincerely committed to a world safe for selectivity, it may be of little use to adopt or sporadically follow international rules intended to bring about such an order. Perhaps only a United States government of a clearly social democratic character, with massive domestic popular support, yet able to resist grass-root protectionist pressures, could be expected to consistently cooperate in building that world. Asymmetrical or occasional application of the principles espoused in this essay could be very pernicious. For example, while the IBRD, the Inter-American Development Bank (IADB), and the United States government restricted the flow of credits to the government of Salvador Allende on thinly disguised political grounds, credits to the Pinochet government are justified by means of arguments that these are sound loans and that politics should be kept separate from economics in those financial flows.

Clearly, Southern countries should not sit around waiting for the arrival of understanding Northern governments and knights

[27] Arthur M. Okun, *Equality and Efficiency: The Big Tradeoff*, The Brookings Institution, Washington, D.C., 1975, particularly chap. 3.

in white armor. Only steady pressure and the buildup of self-reliant Southern bargaining strength appear as sensible strategies. In particular, Southern strategy must have the flexibility to take advantage of favorable world market circumstances if those occur or, if the world economy stagnates and becomes fragmented, to turn to more intensive intra-LDC cooperation and interchange.

Looking beyond the 1980s, one could wonder about the optimum size of nation-states from the viewpoint of securing a peaceful world safe for selectivity. Countries such as the United States and the Soviet Union represent exaggerated concentrations of economic and military power; such concentrations will remain the major threats to world peace in the foreseeable future, contrary to widespread but perverse notions that the major threat is small countries. Very small countries, on the other hand, raise the free-rider problem in the establishment and maintenance of international rules.

Perhaps a world divided into nation-states of about 25 or 30 million inhabitants each would provide the right balance, the framework for competitive markets, plus a true parliament of humanity in which the formula of one nation, one vote would not be in sharp conflict with that of one person, one vote. Citizens of the present superpowers would be relieved of the superhuman burdens that now make a good share of their best and brightest youth oscillate between arrogance and masochistic self-loathing, á la Lawrence of Arabia. The psychic equilibrium of a Stalin or a Nixon would cease to have such terrifying implications for the rest of humanity. (Surely Idi Amin has given humanity less to worry about than these other leaders did.)

Devolution of power from Moscow and Washington to the republics and states forming the two superpowers would eventually be a splendid thing that could then be followed by devolution in other large countries. Such a process would open the way toward the solution of the heavy-rider problem, historically and today more important than that raised by free and easy riders in the world community.

A Selected Bibliography in English on Delinking and Dependency

Amin, Samir: *Accumulation on a World Scale; A Critique of the Theory of Underdevelopment*, Monthly Review Press, New York, 1974.

Arrighi, G., and John S. Saul: *Essays on the Political Economy of Africa*, Monthly Review Press, New York, 1973.

Cardoso, Fernando H.: "Associated-Dependent Development: Theoretical and Political Implications," chap. 5 in A. Stepan (ed.), *Authoritarian Brazil: Origins, Policies and Future*, Yale University Press, New Haven, Conn., 1973.

Cohen, Benjamin J.: *The Question of Imperialism: The Political Economy of Dominance and Dependence*, Basic Books, New York, 1973.

Dos Santos, Theotonio: "The Structure of Dependence," *American Economic Review*, vol. 60, no. 2, May 1970, pp. 231–236.

Emmanuel, Arghiri: *Unequal Exchange: A Study of the Imperialism of Trade*, Monthly Review Press, New York, 1972.

Frank, A. G.: "The Development of Underdevelopment," in R. I. Rhoades (ed.), *Imperialism and Underdevelopment*, Monthly Review Press, New York, 1970.

Galtung, Johan: "A Structural Theory of Imperialism," *Journal of Peace Research*, vol. 8, no. 2, Spring 1971, pp. 81–119.

Girvan, Norman: "The Development of Dependency Economics in the Caribbean and Latin America: Review and Comparison," *Social and Economic Studies*, vol. 22, no. 1, March 1973, pp. 1–33.

Helleiner, Gerald K. (ed.): *A World Divided: The Less Developed Countries in the International Economy*, Cambridge University Press, New York, 1975.

Hymer, S., and Resnick, S.: "International Trade and Uneven Development," in J. Bhagwati et al. (eds.), *Trade, Balance of Payments and Growth*, North-Holland Pub. Co., Amsterdam, 1971.

Lall, Sanjaya: "Is 'Dependence' a Useful Concept in Analysing Underdevelopment?", *World Development*, vol. 3, nos. 11 and 12, 1975, pp. 799–810.

Streeten, Paul (ed.): *Trade Strategies for Development*, Macmillan, London, 1973.

Sunkel, Osvaldo: "The Pattern of Latin American Dependence," chap. 1 in V. L. Urquidi and R. Thorp, *Latin America in the International Economy*, John Wiley and Sons, New York, 1973, pp. 3–25.

Weisskopf, Thomas E.: "Capitalism, Underdevelopment and the Future of the Poor Countries," in J. N. Bhagwati (ed.), *Economics and World Order: From the 1970s to the 1990s*, Macmillan, London, 1972, pp. 43–77.

Equity in the South in the Context of North-South Relations

Richard R. Fagen

ONE

Introduction

This essay departs from the premise that Southern elites will, over the next decade, increasingly win fairer shares of global products and opportunities. This struggle is and will continue to be essentially political. The nature of that struggle and the resources that both North and South bring to it are not, however, the subjects of the following pages—although much deserves to be said on those topics.[1] Rather, in necessarily incomplete form, we are concerned with the equity implications and consequences *in the South* of the struggle for fairer shares that is taking place internationally. Consciously, and not without some sadness, it is suggested that the North-South struggle for fairer shares does not promise an improvement in equity in the South. Thus the pessimism that pervades much of what follows.

Four macroquestions structure the analysis, although they are not necessarily dealt with separately or in order: What is the meaning of increased equity in the South? What are the Southern impediments to increased equity? What are the Northern im-

[1]Among the most recent and useful collections of essays and data dealing with North-South, fair-share, and new-economic-order questions are C. Fred Bergsten and Lawrence B. Krause (eds.), ",World Politics and International Economics," *International Organization*, vol. 29, no. 1 Winter 1975, entire issue; Guy Erb and Valeriana Kallab (eds.), *Beyond Dependency: The Developing World Speaks Out*, Overseas Development Council, Washington, D.C., September 1975; and Roger D. Hansen et al., *The U.S. and World Development: Agenda for Action 1976*, Praeger Publishers, for the Overseas Development Council, New York, 1976.

pediments to increased equity? What is the relationship between the equity issue in the South and a "moderate international order"? The pessimism mentioned above derives from linked hypotheses arguing that (1) normatively defensible equity goals in the South (in the sense of rules for the distribution of increments to national income) will be extremely hard if not impossible to meet given the kind of economic development that characterizes the majority of Southern nations; (2) Southern elites and Northern societies more generally have few enduring incentives (and limited structural potential) for altering the dominant patterns of economic development; (3) the only genre of changes in the South that would enable serious assaults on the equity issue to be made involve socialist forms of economic organization (very possibly involving revolutionary socialism of the Cuban and Chinese variety); (4) from the Northern point of view these have been and are the most difficult kinds of changes to adjust to domestically and internationally; (5) these kinds of changes on a global scale would seriously threaten, both theoretically and in practice, a moderate international order of the sort envisaged by the 1980s Project.

No attempt is made in this essay to explore each of these hypotheses in detail. Only the first two receive more or less full treatment, and the others are only foreshadowed. Nor should these pages be read as a prediction that if the equity issue is not squarely faced in the short run, the poor and the dispossessed will rise up and overthrow "the system." To the contrary, as the above hypotheses suggest, given extant patterns of economic development, class relations, and the instruments of control and repression in the hands of the privileged in both North and South, current patterns of inequity are likely to persist well into the future.

What is to be hoped for, however, is that those elites, both Northern and Southern, that profess a commitment to the poor of the world will increasingly come to realize that this equity commitment is necessarily radical. It goes to the root of questions of class relations, political power, modes of production and distribution, and the structure of the world system, and it implies basic changes in all of them. The age of comfortable assumptions, if not the age of poverty is passing. The *problématique* of equity on a global scale challenges capitalism (both Northern and Southern), the nation-state system, and almost all liberal and neo-classical assumptions about how change does and should take place. If such challenges in turn assault one's sense of "the possible," this only reaffirms the profundity of the problem.

WHAT KIND OF NEW INTERNATIONAL ORDER?

When foreign policy elites in the United States (and elsewhere in the rich countries) discuss the new international economic order, attention is often being directed to the *manner* in which change ought to take place. For example, in a report prepared for the Executive Committee of the Trilateral Commission, a task force emphasized that

the interests of both developed and developing countries will be better served in this historical period by cooperation than by confrontation. . . . It is true that confrontation sometimes brings short-term benefits. But in the longer-run . . . it is bound to stimulate defensive and harmful responses from the governments and peoples of the developed world. The developed countries who have the military, political and economic power can only be persuaded by appeals to mutual interest; emphasis on adversary interests and the abuse of automatic majorities in international agencies is likely to delay the desired adjustments.[2]

Setting aside the implied threat (and the bad grammar), clearly the hope is that "reasonable" leaders on both sides of the North-South bargaining table will recognize the (hypothesized) long-run mutuality of their interests and thus be led to settle their outstanding differences through nonconfrontational methods. The double challenge posed is thus to design or discover regimes (institutions, norms, goals) that can come into being through noncataclysmic scenarios and that once in place will dampen conflict and encourage negotiated settlements and cooperation.

[2]Richard N. Gardner, Saburo Okita, and B. J. Udink, "A Turning Point in North-South Economic Relations," Triangle Paper, no. 3, The Trilateral Commission, New York, June 1974, pp. 19–20.

This procedural perspective on a new international order, emphasizing moderation and cooperation, is—of course—almost always related to a discussion of the substantive goals that should be sought in the context of changed relations. Primary among these goals are increased equity and economic opportunity, generally understood as a "fairer share of the global pie" for Southern societies. Some response to the equity demands of the South is seen as a clear historical necessity. Thus Zbigniew Brzezinski predicted—in words echoed by many others—that

it is to be expected that in the next two or three decades we will witness an intensified crisis in the developing world brought about by the twin impacts of demographic growth and the spread of education. Both will make global inequality even more intolerable at a time when equality is becoming the most powerful moral imperative of our time, thus paralleling the appeal of the concept of liberty during the nineteenth century.[3]

Across a broad band of opinion, the feeling has spread that *some* response to the equity demands welling up from the South must be made.

The need to respond in some fashion to these equity concerns, however, is conventionally understood to be in partial conflict with the "efficient" operation of the ongoing (and, by implication, future) world order. Thus, a summary document prepared for the 1980s Project asks,

To borrow Arthur Okun's phrase, how can we move toward an international system in which "the big tradeoff" between the putative claims for "equity" on the part of the developing countries are balanced against the goals of efficiency in the realization of international economic rules and norms?[4]

Again, this perspective on the goals and problems involved in designing a new international order is widely shared. What thus emerges is a vision of a preferred future that has rather specific

[3]Zbigniew Brzezinski, "U.S. Foreign Policy: The Search for Focus," *Foreign Affairs*, vol. 51, no. 4, July 1973, p. 726.

[4]Roger Hansen, 1980s Project Working Paper, Document 6(5), Council on Foreign Relations, New York, December 1, 1975, p. 4 (unpublished).

substantive as well as procedural content. Stated bluntly, this future is one in which the politically necessary responses to Southern demands for a bigger slice of the pie are made in ways that disturb as little as possible the existing market forces that (purportedly) are conducive to the most efficient allocation of global economic resources. The primary arena of analysis is the international economic system, nations (and national economies) are seen as undifferentiated units, Southern (elite) equity and opportunity demands are seen as potentially erosive of global efficiency, and the "preferred order" is defined as one that would handle the thorny problems that arise from these demands with as little dislocation of existing arrangements as is feasible. (In practice, of course, it would certainly turn out to be the case that the "dislocation" necessary to handle the thorny problems is neither minimal nor insignificant from some Northern perspectives.)[5]

To this point, despite the problems raised by the equity/efficiency tradeoff, there is considerable compatibility between the procedural and substantive elements of the preferred order as presented in the newer, mainstream foreign policy literature. Procedurally, emphasis is given to conflict management and change scenarios that imply the (possibly minimal) nonviolent modification of existing institutions. Substantively, emphasis is given to interstate relations (or intereconomy or international relations as the case may be) and to the preeminence of efficiency criteria (as understood in neoclassical economics) in production and exchange. The equity issue is viewed as a set of Southern-elite claims that—while perhaps normatively defensible—tend to interfere in a number of ways with rational production and exchange on a global scale. But the essentially optimistic premise is that a way can be found to give fairer shares to the South without upsetting the international applecart as currently constructed and in use. In the best of all worlds, the tensions implicit in the equity/efficiency tradeoff would be defused by the South's getting fairer shares in material and opportunity terms, and the North's receiving various concessions

[5] For one view of the potential range of problems see C. Fred Bergsten, "The Response to the Third World," *Foreign Policy*, no. 17, Winter 1974–75, pp. 3–34.

(guaranteed supply, political support, etc.) in return. The perspective is essentially Northern, capitalist, liberal, and state-centric.

If the equity issues were *consistently* presented in this literature as problems of international distribution and opportunities, the predominant compatibility of the procedural and substantive aspects of a changed international order would have a better chance of remaining intact. But such is not the case. At almost every juncture one now encounters expressions of concern for the individuals and groups who are most neglected and impoverished in the South. For example, the Trilateral Commission report quoted earlier emphasizes that

much more must be done to assure that development efforts help the bottom 40 percent of the population in the developing countries. Donor and recipient countries, working together in their mutual interest, should promote development programs that stress not only increases in GNP but also the "qualitative" aspects of development—the eradication of extreme poverty, a better distribution of income and wealth, the improvement of rural welfare, the reduction of unemployment, and broad access to education, health and social services.[6]

Taken seriously, these concerns raise a different set of issues. The search for increased global equity is ineluctably joined to the question of how people live, who gets what and who doesn't get what (and why), and the manner in which lives and patterns of living might and/or ought to be changed. To the international equity issue is joined the question, Will it make any difference for the majority of persons living in the South if fairer shares of global product and opportunities are won by the elites ostensibly speaking in their name?

Equity considered as an *intra*national issue inevitably raises further questions about international order. Conventional—and even some not-so-conventional—discussions of the relationship most frequently focus on the dire consequences that will follow if greater person-oriented equity is not achieved. Admixed with

[6]Gardner et al., "A Turning Point," p. 22. Cf. also the important collection of World Bank studies published as Hollis Chenery et al., *Redistribution with Growth*, Oxford University Press, New York, 1974.

long-standing moral arguments about the rightness of viewing Southern development in these terms (it is wrong that there are so many poor people and such immense disparities in wealth), there is an even stronger "realist" tradition of viewing Northern and even global survival as depending in the long run on the abolition of the most gnawing aspects of misery in the South. Thus, speaking from a national interest perspective, Assistant Secretary of State William Rogers testified to Congress in favor of continued foreign aid to Latin America in the following terms:

It comes down to the proposition that there is poverty of the most extraordinary kinds and dimensions throughout Latin America. Latin America by and large is an underdeveloped or developing area. We can contribute to the process of development. We should do that. Not only because it is in the interest of the poor people of those countries, but it is in our national interest.

Any nation of the world, it seems to me, must conclude that the national interest of the United States is much better served in a community of prosperous, self-confident nations than it is in a community in which large numbers of nations are unable to provide the decencies of life for large numbers of their peoples.[7]

Taking a more global and apocalyptic view, the authors of the Second Report to the Club of Rome close a chapter on North-South relations and the equity question by saying,

If development aid is to lend a truly helping hand to the hungry billions who must find a way out of their poverty, more than investment capital is needed. Unless this lesson is learned in time, there will be a thousand desperadoes terrorizing those who are now "rich", and eventually nuclear blackmail and terror will paralyze further orderly development. . . . Ten or twenty years from today it will probably be too late, and then even a hundred Kissingers, constantly crisscrossing the globe on peace missions, could not prevent the world from falling into the abyss of a nuclear holocaust.[8]

[7]*United States Development Assistance to Latin America, Hearing before a Subcommittee of the Committee on Appropriations*, U.S. Senate, 93rd Cong., 2d Sess., December 13, 1974, p. 38.

[8]Mihajlo Mesarovic and Eduard Pestel, *Mankind at the Turning Point*, New American Library, New York, 1976, p. 69.

With or without the developmental-aid emphasis, these sorts of arguments and predictions are heard on all sides.

But what if the key chains of causality and consequence run in other directions? What if the minimal conditions and actions necessary to make headway on the intranational equity situation imply changes both nationally and internationally that in turn clash with Northern notions of a moderate international order? Whatever the long-run truth embedded in the apocalyptic view of the consequences of failure to achieve greater equity, the second set of questions is actually of more immediate importance. For if in fact there are massive and deeply rooted impediments to intranational equity in the South and if in fact their removal in some sense implies "revolutionary" changes in existing national and international structures, then the contradictions inherent in the idea of achieving global equity in the context of a moderate international order are much more profound than its advocates suspect.

In the remainder of this essay we shall explore these issues by following four interrelated lines of argument: First, we shall attempt to put some order into the discussion of intranational equity. Here the basic question to be addressed is, What are we dealing with when we talk about equity? Second, we shall explore a number of decisional norms for thinking about the equity issue intranationally under the assumption that there already is progress toward increased *inter*national equity—defined as fairer shares for the South. Third, we shall explore some of the Southern impediments to movement toward improved intranational equity. And finally we shall examine some Northern impediments to such movement.

TWO

Equity in
North-South Relations

EQUITY-AS-NONPOVERTY AND EQUITY-AS-DISTRIBUTION

As hinted at in the above discussion, the intranational equity issue tends to be posed in two related but nevertheless separable ways. For some observers its essence is seen in the struggle against poverty, variously understood as the struggle to put acceptable "floors" or minima under standards of life and living. For others the essence of the equity question is to be found in the degree of inequality (usually thought of as economic inequality) to be found in the society and the trends in the reduction (or intensification) of this inequality. Obviously, persons who frame the equity issue in terms of inequality—and thus concern themselves with the relative shares of resources and opportunities received by different groups—are also concerned with the question of poverty. Their hope or expectation is almost always that either through "trickle-down" in an expanding economy or through distributive measures consciously directed toward those who sit on bottom of the economic ladder, poverty can eventually be overcome. Nevertheless, it is important to treat these two approaches separately for the time being. We shall call the first orientation to the equity question "equity-as-nonpoverty" and the second "equity-as-distribution."

173

Equity-As-Nonpoverty

Somewhat belatedly, there has been a marked increase in the production of official Northern statements referring to the poor of the world. Whatever the motives, even those most resistant to "moral" statements in international affairs have now joined the bandwagon of expressed concern. Thus, Secretary of State Kissinger reminded the Paris Conference on International Economic Cooperation at the end of 1975 that

our deliberations here must address the plight of the one-quarter of mankind whose lives are overwhelmed by poverty and hunger and numbed by insecurity and despair. In these regions less than one person in five is literate; one baby in ten dies in childhood, and in some areas closer to one out of two; life expectancy is less than fifty years.[9]

Similarly, for several years officials of the World Bank have been talking about the "forgotten 40 percent" of the world's population, and the phrase has passed into the lexicon of developmentalists of various persuasions.

Whatever the motives of those who now on occasion argue the importance of paying attention to the plight of the world's poor, there is still considerable mystification embodied in the way in which the newly found concern is articulated. At the risk of some oversimplification, I would characterize the mystification as involving definitional issues (What is poverty?) and geographical issues (Where are the poor?).

Despite the bold words of Secretary Kissinger quoted above, the majority of conventional developmentalists think of the forgotten 40 percent in terms of income. The assumption, by no means wholly unrealistic, is that if only they had more money—even small amounts—they would be better off. There are, of

[9]"Energy, Raw Materials, and Development: The Search for Common Ground" (Speech delivered December 16, 1975), Department of State, Bureau of Public Affairs, Washington, D.C., pp. 9–10. There is, of course, substantial irony in Kissinger's reference to "one-quarter of mankind." Had it not been for the Chinese revolution, he would have been forced to refer in his speech to "one-half of mankind."

course, powerful theoretical, methodological, and statistical— not to mention ideological—reasons for thinking of the problem of poverty in income terms. Common sense, however, reminds us that the question of poverty is both more complex than and normatively distinct from the problem of low income. What we are properly concerned with is *that fraction of humankind that lives without minimally acceptable life-sustaining and life-enhancing support systems involving food, shelter, health, work, and culture.* Definitions and standards for "minimally acceptable" levels of accomplishment or support are obviously subject to varying interpretations, particularly as one moves from areas such as nutrition and health, where at least some widely agreed-upon, biologically based standard can be applied, to areas such as work and culture, where socially determined standards predominate. But the general notion that there *are* definable floors or minima to the acceptable human condition is very widely shared.[10]

Although income statistics bear on the problem of poverty conceptualized as substandard conditions of life, the normal usage and interpretation of these statistics tends to understate and underplay the scope of the problem rather dramatically. Latin America provides perhaps the most telling example, for its overall "medium" stage of development gives it some advantages in the comparative statistical game. Let us pursue a few examples.

In a data-rich World Bank essay on income inequality, Montek S. Ahluwalia attempts to join income data to the poverty issue. Somewhat arbitrarily, he takes two different cutoff points for per capita income ($50 and $75) below which it can be assumed that the individual is living in "absolute poverty." He then estimates the percentage of the population actually living below each of these two cutoffs. Table 1 presents his data for Latin America, Asia, and Africa.

---

[10]For more detail, data, and bibliography see the essay by Gunnar Adler-Karlsson, "Eliminating Absolute Poverty," in *Reducing Global Inequities*, the companion to this volume in the 1980s Project series. Adler-Karlsson correctly points out that any serious assault on the poverty issue implies wrestling directly with equity-as-distribution questions.

The first thing to note about the Latin American data (and to some extent this applies to the Asian and African data as well) is that even the $75 cutoff point is arbitrarily low. In none of the Latin American countries listed (and note that for lack of data Guatemala, Nicaragua, and Paraguay are missing) will $75 a year allow one to purchase the necessary food and services needed to subsist at even the minimal levels that almost all observers

TABLE 1
Estimates of Population below Poverty Line in 1969

Country	1969 GNP Per Capita	1969 Population (millions)	Population below $50		Population below $75	
			Millions	Percentage of Total Population	Millions	Percentage of Total Population
Latin America						
Ecuador	264	5.9	2.2	37.0	3.5	58.5
Honduras	265	2.5	0.7	28.0	1.0	38.0
El Salvador	295	3.4	0.5	13.5	0.6	18.4
Dominican Republic	323	4.2	0.5	11.0	0.7	15.9
Colombia	347	20.6	3.2	15.4	5.6	27.0
Brazil	347	90.8	12.7	14.0	18.2	20.0
Jamaica	640	2.0	0.2	10.0	0.3	15.4
Guyana	390	0.7	0.1	9.0	0.1	15.1
Peru	480	13.1	2.5	18.9	3.3	25.5
Costa Rica	512	1.7	. .	2.3	0.1	8.5
Mexico	645	48.9	3.8	7.8	8.7	17.8
Uruguay	649	2.9	0.1	2.5	0.2	5.5
Panama	692	1.4	0.1	3.5	0.2	11.0
Chile	751	9.6	. .	. .	. .	. .
Venezuela	974	10.0	. .	. .	. .	. .
Argentina	1054	24.0	. .	. .	. .	. .
Puerto Rico	1600	2.8	. .	. .	. .	. .
Total	545 (avg.)	244.5	26.6	10.8	42.5	17.4

TABLE 1 (continued)
Estimates of Population below Poverty Line in 1969

Country	1969 GNP Per Capita	1969 Population (millions)	Population below $50		Population below $75	
			Millions	Percentage of Total Population	Millions	Percentage of Total Population
Asia						
Burma	72	27.0	14.5	53.6	19.2	71.0
Sri Lanka	95	12.2	4.0	33.0	7.8	63.5
India	100	537.0	239.0	44.5	359.3	66.9
Pakistan (East and West)	100	111.8	36.3	32.5	64.7	57.9
Thailand	173	34.7	9.3	26.8	15.4	44.3
Korea	224	31.0	1.7	5.5	5.3	17.0
Philippines	233	37.2	4.8	13.0	11.2	30.0
Turkey	290	34.5	4.1	12.0	8.2	23.7
Iraq	316	9.4	2.3	24.0	3.1	33.3
Taiwan	317	13.8	1.5	10.7	2.0	14.3
Malaysia	323	10.6	1.2	11.0	1.6	15.5
Iran	350	27.9	2.3	8.5	4.2	15.0
Lebanon	570	2.9	. .	1.0	0.1	5.0
Total	132 (avg.)	889.7	321.0	36.1	502.1	56.4
Africa						
Chad	75	3.5	1.5	43.1	2.7	77.5
Dahomey	90	2.6	1.1	41.6	2.3	90.1
Tanzania	92	12.8	7.4	57.9	9.3	72.9
Niger	94	3.9	1.3	33.0	2.3	59.9
Madagascar	119	6.7	3.6	53.8	4.7	69.6
Uganda	128	8.3	1.8	21.3	4.1	49.8
Sierra Leone	165	2.5	1.1	43.5	1.5	61.5
Senegal	229	3.8	0.9	22.3	1.3	35.3

TABLE 1 (continued)
Estimates of Population below Poverty Line in 1969

Country	1969 GNP Per Capita	1969 Population (millions)	Population below $50		Population below $75	
			Millions	Percentage of Total Population	Millions	Percentage of Total Population
Ivory Coast	237	4.8	0.3	7.0	1.4	28.5
Tunisia	241	4.9	1.1	22.5	1.6	32.1
Rhodesia	274	5.1	0.9	17.4	1.9	37.4
Zambia	340	4.2	0.3	6.3	0.3	7.5
Gabon	547	0.5	0.1	15.7	0.1	23.0
South Africa	729	20.2	2.4	12.0	3.1	15.5
Total	303 (avg.)	83.8	23.8	28.4	36.6	43.6
Grand Total	228 (avg.)	1,218.0	371.4	30.5	583.2	47.9

NOTE: . . = negligible.

SOURCE: Montek S. Ahluwalia, "Income Inequality: Some Dimensions of the Problem," in Hollis Chenery et al., *Redistribution with Growth,* Oxford University Press, New York, 1974. p. 12.

agree separate the subhuman from the human. To argue that many of the persons classified below the income cutoff (at least in rural areas) have income-in-kind in the form of food or are generally outside the cash economy only blurs the edges of the problem. The powerful secular trend toward the incorporation of even the most isolated rural dwellers into the market nexus is everywhere evident (and almost universally approved of by persons concerned with development). Furthermore, few would wish to argue that those rural isolates who handle very little cash in the course of a year are somehow "protected" from the problem of poverty. Boosting the $75 cutoff point for Latin America to a more realistic, but still artificially low, $100 would in turn raise the Latin American percentage of those below this new "poverty" line to more than 25 percent. Additionally, if Puerto Rico were removed (it is interesting that Ahluwalia and the World Bank seem to have granted it independence!) and the poorer countries of the area included (they are now left out for lack of data), the total percentage of those living below the poverty line would rise even more.

Playing with the income statistics in this fashion, however, does not go to the heart of the problem. Brazil, for example, according to the figures in Table 1, has 20 percent of its population below the $75 income level, yet an estimated 44 percent of its people are in fact malnourished.[11] Similarly, the most casual trip through the slums or countryside of Chile, Venezuela, and Argentina will remind the traveler that there is not "0 percent poverty" no matter how defined, despite the empty cells in the income estimates of Table 1. What exact poverty levels would be found if more appropriate data for Latin America were available is difficult to say. As a rough rule of thumb, however, I would argue that even a $100 income cutoff point underestimates by as much as 100 percent the overall poverty of Latin America. Obviously this higher overall estimate cannot be applied mechanically to any given country. In some cases, for example, Ecuador and the missing nations of Nicaragua, Guatemala, Bolivia, and Paraguay, the poverty levels are by any measure already so high that only fractional adjustments upward would be needed. In other cases, such as the Chilean, Venezuelan, and Argentine examples mentioned above, substantial upward revision would be needed. But overall, Latin American statistics on nutrition, shelter, health, prices, and income suggest that the doubling figure is not an unfair multiplier. At the least, it would

[11]See Raymond F. Hopkins, *Global Food Regimes: Overcoming Hunger and Poverty*, McGraw-Hill, for the Council on Foreign Relations, 1980s Project, New York, forthcoming. Using other income statistics and a somewhat different definition of poverty, Albert Fishlow (conservatively by his own admission) estimated that 31 percent of Brazilian families lived below the poverty line in 1960. Given inflation and the worsening distribution of income in the 1960s, the statistics look no better a decade later. See Albert Fishlow, "Brazilian Size Distribution of Income," *The American Economic Review*, vol. LXII, no. 2, May 1972, pp. 391–402.

seem that 50 percent of the inhabitants of Latin America live in daily violation of the most minimal standards acceptable under Article 25 of the Universal Declaration of Human Rights.

If this line of argument holds for Latin America, it is equally valid, with appropriate variations, for Africa and Asia. Missing data for the poorest nations and similar problems of indexing poverty through income levels make a mockery of the aggregate poverty levels for Africa reported in Table 1. Using the high cutoff point of $75, it should still be clear to any traveler through Africa that more than 43.6 percent of the total population lives in violation of the minimal standards of Article 25. Here and in the Asian case, because the poverty levels as indexed by income are already high, the appropriate multiplier is not 100 percent. Even slight adjustments and the inclusion of the missing cases, however, would push the aggregate number of the impoverished way over the 50 percent level—perhaps to as high as 70 to 75 percent in both instances.

Arguments about the precise statistics and the appropriate indices cannot be settled here; international agencies have been wrestling with these problems for almost three decades now. The point is that those who speak of the equity issue in the South in terms of poverty, hunger, insecurity, and despair should realize that they are talking about *the condition of the majority*. If alliteration is sought, they should talk not of the forgotten 40 but of the majority-in-misery. Furthermore, they should accept the fact that even the "most developed" nations of the South contain large minorities-in-misery and that in some, like Brazil, the number approaches 50 percent. In sum, *the equity issue defined in poverty terms is present in every nation in the South to some degree, and in a majority of those nations it affects a majority of the inhabitants.*[12]

[12]In making this statement it should be reemphasized that by using the criteria of "minimally acceptable life-sustaining and life-enhancing support systems" to draw the poverty line, we are casting the net more widely than is usually the case in World Bank and other international circles. As horrendous as the problem of absolute poverty is, it is joined to and continuous with an equally large (in terms of the numbers affected) problem of "ordinary poverty."

Equity-As-Distribution

The second major way of approaching the intranational equity question is through the examination of the distribution of some valued good—usually income. As a rule, when sufficient data are available the statistical materials are treated in both static and dynamic fashion. Analysts are interested in the shares of income received by various sectors of the population (often, for obvious reasons, attention is focused on the top 5 or 10 percent and the bottom 20 or 40 percent), various measures of overall inequality, and changes over time in the shapes of these distributions as other events (e.g., aggregate growth, industrialization, migration) take place. There can be no denying that the recently constructed data sets on national income distribution are immensely useful and illuminating for a wide variety of purposes— much more so, in fact, when time series are available.[13] For example, the discovery by certain authors that impressive national economic growth performances such as those enjoyed by Mexico and Brazil have been accompanied by *worsening* profiles of income distribution has given pause to many who otherwise or previously celebrated those "miracles" unquestioningly. Similarly, for the construction and modification of certain aspects of developmental theory, distributional arrays of the sort now being constructed are absolutely essential.[14]

Nevertheless, the income distribution approach to equity must be treated with caution for at least two important reasons—in addition to the data and statistical problems normally encountered by persons working in this kind of analysis. First, it is clear that income is only one of the "valued goods" at issue when

[13]The most recent and complete compilation is Shail Jain, *Size Distribution of Income: A Compilation of Data*, International Bank for Reconstruction and Development, Washington, D.C., 1975. Data on 81 countries are included.

[14]See for example Irma Adelman and Cynthia Taft Morris, *Economic Growth and Social Equity in Developing Countries*, Stanford University Press, Stanford, Calif., 1973. Both the promise and the limitations of indexing "social equity" through income statistics are illuminated in the Adelman-Morris analysis.

distribution is being examined. It is not even the same as the more general concept of wealth (ownership of land, etc.), and as the discussion of equity-as-nonpoverty reminds us, the possession of money income does not necessarily translate into nutrition, health, or housing—much less security or culture. In short, there is an overwhelming market bias in the indexing of equity by income distribution alone. For example, Ahluwalia presents data that show that Yugoslavia in 1968 had a lower per capita income than did Spain in 1965, while the two countries had roughly equivalent profiles of income distribution.[15] But on the basis of these statistics alone not even the most rabid defender of market economies would feel entirely comfortable in arguing that the equity profiles of the two countries were therefore similar—or even that Spain was ahead on equity grounds because it was richer in aggregate terms while no worse off in distributional terms! Clearly the scope of Yugoslavian public education and health programs, the state-subsidized housing plans, and the guaranteed price and backup systems operating in rural areas make the lot of the less privileged both more bountiful and more secure in the Yugoslavian case.

The second caution relates to the first. There is some evidence that when distributional statistics are available for other valued goods in a society, Southern profiles show *more* inequality than is evident from the income statistics alone. In all Latin American countries for which data are available, for example, the gini index (a measure of inequality) for the distribution of land is higher than the gini index for the distribution of income.[16] Were com-

[15] Montek S. Ahluwalia, "Income Inequality: Some Dimensions of the Problem," in Chenery et al., *Redistribution with Growth*, pp. 8, 35, and 37. The distributional data are from household surveys in the two countries.

[16] See Bruce M. Russett, "Inequality and Instability: The Relation of Land Tenure to Politics," *World Politics*, vol. XVI, no. 3, April 1964, pp. 442–454, particularly the land tenure data on pp. 450–451. The data support the more general point that income is perhaps the most *equally* distributed index of wealth (or other valued goods) in capitalist societies, and thus the income distribution statistics are *conservative* vis-à-vis the larger issues raised by equity-as-distribution perspectives. For a useful discussion of some of the methodological and statistical problems raised, see Hayward R. Alker, Jr., and Bruce M. Russett, "Indices for Comparing Inequality," in Richard L. Merritt and Stein Rokkan, *Comparing Nations*, Yale University Press, New Haven, Conn., 1966.

parable data available for the distribution of other valued goods, the indices of inequality would also most probably be higher than those generated for income alone.

The conceptual, methodological, statistical, and informational impediments to actually making comparisons of this sort are immense. But as a working hypothesis the notion that profiles of income distribution actually *understate* the degree of inequality in less developed market economies makes a great deal of sense. It is, in crudest terms, functionally necessary that income inequality not approach certain limits lest the economy falter and collapse. But no such functional limits exist in a field such as health, where it is quite imaginable that 20 to 30 percent of the population should enjoy almost 100 percent of the modern health care available in the society. In other words, when we work with income distribution statistics in market economies, we are actually studying the statistical outcroppings of much deeper structures of inequality.[17] Like good geologists, we should value the data generated by these outcroppings but we should also probe for the more basic stratifications that they reflect. And as a working hypothesis, we must assume that the societal bedrock when plumbed will reveal even greater degrees of inequality than are revealed by the income statistics themselves. As unattractive as the income distribution statistics in most of the South are from an equity perspective, we should thus remember that these are essentially *conservative* statistics. When treated as such, they make the equity-as-distribution issues even more dramatic.

EQUITY NORMS AND NORTH-SOUTH RELATIONS

As suggested at the outset, the intranational equity issue is of interest here because a "new" international economic order, allocating increased shares of resources and opportunities to the

---

[17]Note that a reverse relationship between income inequalities and the distribution of other valued goods and services holds in the centrally planned economies. In these economies, the income inequalities (which in any event are not large by world standards) are probably more *extreme* than other inequalities in distribution.

South, is in the making. We want to know the possibilities of and the obstacles to these increased shares touching the equity-as-nonpoverty and the equity-as-distribution questions sketched above.

The first observation to be made is simple but extremely important: we are for the moment excluding from the discussion the revolutionary socialist regimes, such as Cuba and China, that make a direct assault on the equity issue. In such regimes, privilege (understood as the existing structure of distribution) and poverty are attacked head on and simultaneously. Massive redistributions of power and consumption take place. Market mechanisms are interfered with at every turn and at times smashed in near-Luddite fashion. Conventional efficiency criteria in the allocation of resources give way to openly political criteria. All available energies are concentrated on achieving certain minimal levels of living and opportunity for all citizens. This necessarily involves "taking from the rich" in material and opportunity terms and "giving to the poor" with concomitant class struggle, mass mobilization, and political conflict.

It is thus both understandable and even proper—from a certain perspective—that conventional developmentalists remove the revolutionary socialist societies from their calculations and even from consideration when they talk about the South. What gives the concept of "the South" minimal theoretical consistency, in the face of immense and oft-noted empirical variation, is that it comprises market and quasi-market economies. To include those revolutionary socialist regimes that assault poverty and privilege directly—whatever the consequences of that assault for efficiency and short-run "growth"—would only confuse the consistency and problem-homogeneity sought at both the theoretical and the programmatic level. The equity problem as understood here is largely solved or clearly in the process of being solved in the revolutionary socialist countries—whatever other problems exist or are emerging.

A second observation is that outside the logic of the revolutionary socialist experiments it is extremely difficult to elevate the equity-as-nonpoverty issue to the *primary* focus of normative attention. Poverty is so profoundly locked into the structural grain of poorer societies that only the most profound transformations of economics, politics, class structure, and culture enable it to be assaulted directly. Even the wealthier and most people-oriented regimes of the Third World face insurmountable short-term obstacles to delivering poverty-eradicating quantities of goods and services to the marginal sectors of the population. This does not imply that equity-as-nonpoverty must be abandoned as a normative concern. But it does suggest that it will necessarily be relegated to a secondary place—folded back, so to speak, into equity-as-distribution, in the context of aggregate growth. This is a posture with which most conventional developmentalists both North and South will now feel relatively at ease, for as the new neoclassical developmental economics reminds us, the key challenge for nonrevolutionary societies is to ensure that the poor get their fair share (still to be defined) of whatever growth is taking place.[18] If growth takes place and if fair shares continue to be distributed to the poor, then eventually the poverty problem—to this way of thinking—resolves itself. Poverty is not assaulted directly, but rather resolved through sustained concern for the equity-as-distribution problem.

What meaning can be given to the notion of fair shares in this context? To explore this question, a very simple model or representation of income distribution in a mythical country called *Periferica* is useful. Such a representation is presented in Table 2. *Periferica* has 100 citizens (multiply by 100,000 if you need a dash of realism) enjoying a total dollar income of $40,000. Obviously the average income per capita is $400, putting *Periferica* in the middle-upper range of Southern nations in this respect. The income distribution is a bit better than that of Mexico, with the top 5 percent of the income earners receiving 30 percent

[18]This position is best articulated in Chenery et al., *Redistribution with Growth.* It should be noted that this is not conventional trickle-down thinking. The new neoclassical developmentalist belief is that fairer shares can be reform mongered to the poor through complex scenarios primarily involving the public sector, planning and pressure politics. It should also be noted, however, that Chenery and his associates are not talking about *re*distribution in the strict sense of taking from some to distribute to others. They are talking about more equitable patterns of distributing future growth increments—essentially the equity-as-distribution problem as we are treating it here.

TABLE 2
*Income Distribution in Periferica: Now (T) and 10 Years Later (T + 10)
under Two Distributional Rules*

Income Sector (percentile)	Number of Persons	Total Income Share at T (%)	Total Dollar Income at T	Per Capita Income at T	Per Capita Income at T + 10 (proportional)	Per Capita Income at T + 10 (democratic)
95–100	5	30	$12,000	$2,400	$3,000	$2,500
90–95	5	10	4,000	800	1,000	900
80–90	10	15	6,000	600	750	700
60–80	20	20	8,000	400	500	500
40–60	20	15	6,000	300	375	400
20–40	20	6	2,400	120	150	220
0–20	20	4	1,600	80	100	180
	100	100	$40,000			

of all the income. At the other end of the scale, the bottom 20 percent of the income earners receive only 4 percent of the total income. The gini index of this distribution of income is about 0.5, not dissimilar from the typical inequality index for Southern countries with per capita income at this level. The average per capita income of persons in the various sectors is easily arrived at by dividing the total income of each sector by the number of persons in that sector. These annual per capita incomes range from $2,400 for those in the top 5 percent to $80 for those in the bottom 20 percent of the economy. The income ratio of 30 to 1 from top to bottom is again not untypical for societies of this sort.

Now let us imagine that in a long bargaining struggle with the North *Periferica* wins an added $1,000 of income per year because of better prices for exports or some other change in the nature of North-South economic relations. In the first year (*T* + 1) this represents a rather impressive 2.5 percent gain in total income. (As the income base increases each year, the $1,000 will represent a slightly lower percentage increment to income, but in the interests of simplicity we are not here concerned with that fact.) Let us also assume that all of the annual increment of

$1,000 is available to be distributed either directly or indirectly as income to the population of *Periferica*. What is a fair share distributional rule and what consequences for the distribution of income would be noted under this rule after 10 years have passed (at time $T + 10$)?

Few would argue that shares would be distributed fairly if the rich were to get *more* than a proportional share of the increment— for example, if the top 5 percent, who already get 30 percent of the income, were to get 40 percent of the newly won $1,000. This would clearly be *regressive* distribution, and it violates notions of fair shares even though some might argue its necessity in terms of "wise" (efficient) use of income.

Less immediately contrary to common-sense notions of fair shares would be a *proportional* rule. Here the argument would be that proportionality should be maintained in allocating the new income. Under this rule, the top 5 percent would get 30 percent of the new income because they got 30 percent in the past, etc. Using the proportional rule for 10 years, we would arrive at the per capita income distribution shown in the second-to-last column of Table 2. All intersector ratios (including the original 30 to 1 ratio between the highest income earners and the lowest) would of course remain the same as they were at time T.

It is not easy, however, to defend this as a fair-share, equity-as-distribution rule. There is no closing of the gap, the status quo continues, and the extremely low level at which the poorest begin ensures that even after 10 years no marked gain in their power-to-purchase has taken place. The equity-as-nonpoverty component of this distributional rule is for all practical purposes nonexistent: no special distributional consideration is given to those living below the poverty line (however defined).

A more defensible decisional rule for the allocation of shares, and the one preferred here, would say that each individual in the society should get an equal amount of the increment no matter what his or her initial income position. This is clearly a "democratic" allocational rule in two senses: first, it follows the basic democratic norm that all persons in a society should give and receive equally ("one person, one vote," "all equal before the law," etc.). Second, it takes seriously the fact that the increment to be distributed was won at the international bargaining table in the name of "the nation and all its citizens." If, in fact, the new riches "belong to the people" (in the same way that nationalizations are made in the name of all the people rather than in the name of any given class or group), it follows quite naturally that the norm of distribution should at a minimum treat all citizens as equal. Thus, under what we shall here call the "democratic rule," each person in the society, whether rich or poor, receives an additional $10 per year as his or her share of the $1,000 gained by the nation as a whole. At the end of 10 years under this rule, the per capita income distribution will obviously be more equal, with the highest income earners now enjoying only about 14 times the income received by the lowest (see the last column of Table 2). Additionally, since the incomes of those in the poorest fifth of the population have more than doubled in 10 years, it can be assumed that some significant inroads on the poverty problem have been made. Note also that after 10 years under the democratic rule, only the top 20 percent of the society is worse off in income terms than it would have been under the proportional rule. Those in the 60 to 80 percent income sector end up with exactly the same per capita income under the democratic rule ($500), and everyone below the 60 percent line is better off. The rule is thus not only democratic in the equal-shares sense but also majoritarian in the benefits sense.

There are, of course, a huge variety of other, more "radical" distributional rules that could be invented. Some would have true *leveling* potential in the sense that they would cut persons living above a certain level off from *any* share in the distribution of new income, thus allowing those below to catch up if the process went on for enough time. (Note that the democratic rule leads to lessened inequality but *not* to absolute catching up, since the dollar gap between those at the bottom and those at the top stays fixed at $2,320.) Other rules might be *progressive* in the sense of giving larger absolute shares to individuals who sit lower on the income hierarchy. If leveling *and* progressive rules are combined, distribution becomes fully equalitarian. Assuming no compounding of population, $240,000 of total income or $200,000 of additional income would be needed to give each member of the society the $2,400 enjoyed by the wealthiest 5 percent at the present time. Thus, if each year's $1,000 increment were distributed by a leveling-progressive rule that held per capita income to a ceiling of $2,400, in the bicentennial year of our model all citizens would at last be receiving equal income shares. Although more radical rules of this sort have much to recommend them from an ethical point of view, they clearly are even more threatening to the status quo than the basic democratic rule posited. Thus, so as not to load the discussion with anything that might be considered revolutionary assumptions, let us accept this latter rule.

The assumptions of the model are admittedly very "unrealistic." Most obviously, we are dealing with only the distribution of increments gained in the process of North-South negotiations and new international bargains. No increments of growth generated elsewhere are included, and no dynamic processes—of population, investment, productivity, etc.—are considered. But in its very simplicity and lack of realism the model serves to highlight the nature of the normative and political issues we are dealing with.

In any concrete situation, of course, it would be impossible fully to test compliance with this norm. One cannot follow with any precision the uses or the ultimate distribution of an incremental chunk of income once it is mixed into the whole. Thus, it is necessary to consider more generally the factors that condition the distributional patterns currently in place in Southern societies and the possibilities of change in those patterns. In other words, in suggesting impediments to the democratic distributional rule posited above, we must necessarily embed that discussion in a fuller understanding of the larger equity problem in the South.

EQUITY IN THE SOUTH:
THE STATE IN THE SERVICE OF WHOM?

There would be widespread agreement among persons of quite different analytical and political persuasions that the democratic distributive norm is and will continue to be extremely difficult to meet in the majority of Southern nations. Conceptions of why this should be the case, however, and what (if anything) to do about it would differ greatly. This debate cannot be fully joined here. Rather we will limit ourselves to underscoring some basic features of the state in Southern societies. Let us begin, rather indirectly, with a fable.

A visitor from outer space looks at Table 2. It suggests that in *Periferica* after 10 years under the democratic distributional rule, the top 20 percent of the income earners would be worse off than under the proportional rule, the next 20 percent would be the same, and the lower 60 percent would be better off—many quite substantially. He or she, reading the opening sentence of this section, might then wonder why we posit widespread agreement as to the *difficulty* of approaching the democratic distributive norm in the majority of Southern nations. Why should the democratic rule strike earthlings as less probable of implementation than the proportional rule—or one of several quite imaginable (to us) nonproportional or regressive scenarios? Ordinary logic would tell our visitor that since the democratic rule is super-Pareto optimal (no one is worse off after 10 years and in fact everyone is better off), numbers and calculations of personal advantage would carry the day for democracy. Alas, we would have to give our visitor a crash course in power, class, and the marketplace to enable him or her to understand why democratic distribution is so difficult. Even then he or she might remain bewildered as to why the 60 percent who would benefit more under the democratic rule don't simply rise up, seize political power, and dictate terms to the minority 20 percent who clearly gain from proportionality-in-practice (a bewilderment shared at times by earthbound brothers and sisters).

The fable may be vulgar, but the questions raised are not. At issue are conceptions of the nature of class relations in Southern societies; the state as an expression, facilitator, and perpetuator of those class relations; market mechanisms as related to class and distributional inequities; and the manner in which Southern links with the North serve to reinforce existing patterns of power

190

and privilege.[19] We cannot in brief compass hope to illuminate this entire skein of questions, but a few points are essential. Let us begin by examining the bases for the hypothesized underlying pessimism regarding the feasibility of implementing the democratic rule.

One basis for this pessimism is a widely shared understanding that those who control income (or wealth) in Southern societies also to a great extent control or exercise political, social, and cultural power as well. Even persons who reject much of Marxist analysis grudgingly concede that the power resources at the disposal of those who sit at the top of the income-wealth hierarchies in Southern societies are immensely superior to the resources at the disposal of those at middle and lower levels. No matter how those resources are conceptualized (political access, control of the media and the consciousness industry, know-how, allies abroad), the intimate relationship between wealth and power is everywhere manifest. This is not to argue that the top income earners (or the wealthy) necessarily sit in the seats of government or mechanically dictate public policy. Rather it is to stress that the multiple resources which they can assemble, if necessary, in defense of proportionality of distribution (or even regressivity of distribution) are impressive indeed. When the "ordinary" operations of the economy and the polity are not assuring distributional outcomes most favorable to them, they have the capacity to lever the situation back to "normal." In short, we are arguing that class (whether understood in Marxist or more conventional stratification terms) is intimately related to power, and that power, in turn, is used in the service of proportional distribution—or worse. The proposition is hardly new, but it is essential to all that follows.

The second basis for the hypothesized pessimism concerning the future of the democratic norm has to do with the market as an instrument of distribution. Whatever other virtues neoclass-

[19]In what follows, I plead guilty to a Latin American bias. That is, the argument in the remainder of this section has been developed primarily on the basis of my familiarity with that region. I do, however, believe that it is widely applicable to Asia and Africa as well, once certain adjustments are made.

ical analysis assigns to the market, a tendency toward democratic distribution is not one of them. As persuasively argued by even the most liberal neoclassicists, the function of the market is efficiency in the allocation of resources (and rewards), not distributive justice.[20] In fact, it is quite vigorously argued at certain points in neoclassical theory that increments of new income *should* accrue disproportionately to certain sectors of the population (entrepreneurs and/or big consumers) so that savings, investment, demand, and ultimately growth will be maximized. At best, market mechanisms will not shift income shares in a democratic direction except as the structure of production itself changes. Within the existing structure, individuals can of course improve their incomes by moving to a higher niche. But this individual mobility, however widespread, does not contain within itself a dynamic seriously challenging the proportional shares going to various sectors of the society. Thus, in speaking of Southern societies, hardly anyone suggests that "the free play of market forces" will bring in its wake movement toward more equitable distribution however defined.

But if class power and the market both militate against equity in distribution, what—in the words of a famous theorist—is to be done? Everywhere the answer, *grosso modo*, is similar: the *state* must ensure that benefits, opportunities, and wealth are pushed against the grain of social structure and market. From the mildest reformers to the most militant revolutionaries, persons who think about these problems are in agreement that the root of the solution—however that solution is conceptualized—must be sought in a revamped political/administrative process that in some fashion empowers those groups that the existing distribution of wealth and the operation of the market currently leave disadvantaged.

This widespread agreement on the centrality of the state and political processes to the problem of equity-as-distribution, how-

[20]For the noneconomist at least, one of the clearest and most humane expositions of this point of view is to be found in Arthur M. Okun, *Equity and Efficiency: The Big Tradeoff*, The Brookings Institution, Washington, D.C., 1975.

ever, obscures more than it reveals. For revolutionary socialists, the political scenario envisaged includes *within it* coherent solutions to the problems of class and the market. However imperfect the practice may be, the theory is quite clear in stating that a direct assault on class privilege, intended to strip the wealthy of the bases of their status quo–maintaining (and exploitative) power, is to be combined with the substitution (be it more gradual or more accelerated) of central planning for the operation of market forces in production and distribution. For reformers of all stripes, however, the political scenario must necessarily respect to some degree the existing class forces and forms of production and distribution. The equity-oriented reformer thus faces the historically difficult (impossible?) task of discovering those secondary contradictions and possibilities within existing class and economic structures which will allow the state to spearhead a movement of distribution that runs *against* the basic logic of class and market.

It has not been easy for the reformers to admit that facing up to the distributional problem means taking actions that challenge the basic logic of existing class and market arrangements. The realization that cherished institutions of capitalism—not to mention the much celebrated "middle sectors"—are potentially and actually obstacles to more equitable distribution rather than facilitators is a bitter theoretical pill to swallow (a pill still stuck in the gullet of many developmentalists). Nevertheless, something approaching a new consensus is beginning to come into focus. Fairly typical, with the added advantage of being more programmatically detailed than most, are the analyses and recommendations contained in the aforementioned World Bank Studies.[21] There the political scenario advocated is based on "reformist coalitions" able to trade on the fears and realizations of the privileged that they must give something away in the short run in order to survive in the future. That "something" is made concrete in a series of public policies that are seen as conducive to more equitable distribution. The task is seen as delicate, and

[21]Chenery et al., *Redistribution with Growth*, especially chaps. III–VII.

the outcomes are viewed as far from certain. C. L. G. Bell's statement of the problems and possibilities of this scenario is worth quoting at length:

There are a number of regimes for which the strategy proposed in this volume is "out of court." Some are dominated by entrenched elites who will relinquish nothing to the underprivileged except under the duress of armed force. Others have attacked successfully the causes of poverty by means far more direct and radical than those discussed here. Yet that still leaves a considerable range of societies for which the strategy is at least plausible, even though in some of them the likelihood that it will be adopted with any vigor is remote.

In such cases, the key factor is the emergence of a coalition of interests able to grasp power which sees some advantage in implementing a redistributive strategy, despite the fact that some sections of it stand to lose relatively thereby. To survive in the long run in a changing society, elites must make occasional well-timed concessions, and some of them are aware of the fact. Moreover, as the rich do not constitute a class with identical interests, potential disputes among them provide other bases for political alignments, in which the poor may have enough representation to press their cause effectively.

If a workable "reformist" coalition is formed, it will tend to be rather fragile, so the policies chosen to put the strategy into effect, which determine the distributive impact of the transfer of resources, assume critical importance. To be of any use, the impact of redistributive policies must have a measure of permanence. Thus there are two strategic options open to the regime. It can plump for rapid and drastic forms of intervention, whose effects are not easily reversible, either because they change the balance of political power or because of their intrinsic features. . . . The alternative option is less tempestuous and much more likely to be adopted: to nibble away at the problem, maneuvering all the while to stay in power. With small margins of error in maintaining the viability of the coalition, success may come to depend on the quality of political leadership, particularly its ability to inspire confidence and energy.[22]

What is particularly notable—and commendable—about this contemporary reformmonger's guide is that it places politics,

---

[22]C.L.G. Bell in Chenery et al., *Redistribution with Growth*, pp. 71–72.

political conflict, and the question of state power at the center of the equity question.[23] Equally notable—although one might draw quite different tactical and strategic conclusions from the analysis—is the emphasis on the extreme fragility of political coalitions that attempt to reformmonger through distributional changes without first directly assaulting and weakening the class interests that are themselves at the heart of the problem. This said, however, it remains clear that a critical range of problems is left unexamined. Even granting the possibility that reform coalitions of some sort (including military reformers) will come to power in the South and even assuming for a moment that these regimes can survive the assaults of the privileged at home (not to mention the assaults of the privileged abroad—a subject to which we will subsequently return), the situation is not propitious for distributive policies—particularly those as radical as the democratic rule previously advanced.

Why should this be the case? The reasons are legion, many of them well explored in the developmental literature—especially radical critiques of the conventional wisdom. What we wish to emphasize here is the manner in which the reformist regime's possible commitments to equity-as-distribution are limited by the new class forces engendered by economic development and, in particular, the way in which those class forces are interlaced with the international system. Central to this question is the concept of the "autonomy" of the state and its relationship to class and political power.

Everyday understandings of the concept of autonomy emphasize that it refers to "freedom from exterior constraints." Whereas the concept of power emphasizes capacity to accomplish chosen goals in the face of obstacles, autonomy typically refers to the more limited condition of not being controlled by others. The distinction is important, for what reformist elites purport to seek (among other outcomes) is to escape the control of those class forces that would block public policies conducive

---

[23]This emphasis on politics and state action as essential to redress inequities stemming from the operation of class and market is also a central theme of Okun's *Equality and Efficiency* and similar contemporary liberal formulations of neoclassical questions.

to more equitable distribution. The essential question—as Bell and most other modern reformmongers recognize—is the extent to which this is possible.

That reformist elites—and others—are busy strengthening and empowering the state apparatus to intercede and direct the process of economic development in the South is everywhere evident. The bureaucracy expands; expertise is developed; critical planning, fiscal, and administrative responsibilities are assumed; and domestic programs proliferate. Everywhere in the South we are witnessing what has aptly been called the "age of state-centric development." But does the sum of this activity (expanding state power) necessarily signal increased long-run state autonomy from those class forces that are in some sense "antidistributional?"

The answer to this key question depends on the kind of economic development that is taking place. To the extent that the model is essentially growth-oriented, energized by private capital (with or without associated state financing), and dependent to any significant degree on foreign investment, the prospects are very dim.[24] To weave multinational corporations into the development scenario, for example, is to significantly strengthen certain sectors of the domestic class structure while disempowering others. New class alliances with key sectors of the state bureaucracy are formed at home, reflecting the exigencies of attracting and facilitating investment capital. New sociopolitical forces are linked to those sectors of production and distribution that are most fully internationalized (or "modern" in the less pejorative term) and on which aggregate growth depends. The highly tuned and high-technology segments of the domestic economy become ever more susceptible to pressures generated externally but articulated internally by privileged classes and class

[24]Codes of conduct and joint ownership notwithstanding, the antiequity implications of the foreign investment scenario are profound. The scenario affects (negatively as far as improved distribution is concerned in the vast majority of cases) the types of technology that will be used, the kinds of commodities that will be produced, the patterns of consumption that will be encouraged, the way in which labor will be rewarded and allocated (and displaced), and the regions or sectors of the nation that will benefit. Many of the same arguments could also be made for development based on domestic private investment as well, although the critique has more bite when applied to the multinational firms.

fractions. The state itself through the techno-bureaucracy increasingly assumes responsibilities for ensuring the continuation of the political, economic, and social conditions undergirding this web of external-internal relationships. The old, conservative, openly antiequity class sectors recede in political importance as this kind of development takes place. But there is no reason to believe that the class forces that are strengthened, in alliance with the state, are any more favorable to equity measures than were the groups they are replacing. Can it be said under this kind of development that the state is any "freer" from the influence of the privileged than before?[25]

It is this scenario, combining a partially open political process, economic growth, and an *expressed* commitment to improved distribution, that tests the autonomy of the state and thus the limits of equity-enhancing reform. In the worst of cases, the contradictions are excruciating. Is the Mexican state—a long-term articulator of the rhetoric of social justice, a state massively involved in the developmental process, a state that "oversees" an economy profoundly penetrated and multinationalized, with a modernizing industrial sector, export-oriented agriculture, currency no longer tied to the dollar, inflationary pressures and balance-of-payments problems—any more autonomous from domestic, antidistributional class forces today than 40 years ago? Could even the most progressive Mexican regime imaginable consistently decide in favor of impoverished *ejidarios* when the interests of Mexican and international agribusiness are at stake? The answers are obvious for the Mexican case (and well supported by the experiences of the not especially radical Echeverría government), but they would not be much less controversial for any regime, no matter how "progressive" its expressed com-

[25]This is a much compressed version of a modified "dependency" perspective on the questions of class, politics, and development. For a relevant bibliography, see Richard R. Fagen, "Studying Latin American Politics: Some Implications of a *Dependencia* Approach," *Latin American Research Review*, vol. 12, no. 2, Summer 1977. See also Christopher Chase-Dunn, "The Effects of International Economic Dependence on Development and Inequality: A Cross-National Study," *American Sociological Review*, vol. 40, no. 6, December 1975, pp. 720–738, for an attempt to test some relevant hypotheses.

mitments, as long as these kinds of developmental rules and class alliances guided the processes of accumulation and distribution.[26]

If the autonomy of the Southern state from class interests is seen as quite limited and if—in the typical case—these class interests are understood as closely linked to the modern international system of production and distribution, then the behavior of Southern elites—even those with reformist pretensions—who bargain hard for fairer shares internationally while doing little to increase equity at home becomes quite understandable. There is nothing mysterious or even particularly hypocritical about their behavior. These hard-bargaining elites are themselves deeply enmeshed in the very web of exploitative class and market relationships that are at the heart of the distributional problem in the first place. Fairer shares internationally strengthen them, equity at home tends to weaken them—or at least to trigger opposition. Large increments of additional income (imaginable in any case only through oil and perhaps a few other key minerals) may allow them to buy time through a policy of populist handouts—with enough left over in certain cases to buy expensive weapons and even some international goodwill through developmental aid. But a concerted attack on the root causes of the domestic inequity problem undercuts their own essential bases of authority and support.

This is the real dynamic behind the now oft-predicted *embourgeoisement* of much of the South, particularly those regimes that now or in the foreseeable future may be receiving significant new increments of income as new international bargains are struck.[27] What is feared in some circles—and ardently hoped for in others—is that the richer regimes will "go their own way" with their newly won gains, that the Southern bargaining con-

[26]For a useful conceptualization and analysis of the Peruvian regime, generally considered to be the most "progressive" in Latin America outside of Cuba, see Julio Cotler, "The New Mode of Political Domination in Peru," in Abraham Lowenthal (ed.), *The Peruvian Experiment*, Princeton University Press, Princeton, N.J., 1975.

[27]See for example, Roger D. Hansen, "The Political Economy of North-South Relations: How Much Change?" *International Organization*, vol. 29, no. 4, Autumn 1975, particularly p. 939 ff.

sensus will fragment, and that eventually the international equity issue will recede in importance. The prediction has the ring of historical probability about it, but not simply because nationalisms will reassert themselves when the initial gains from Southern solidarity have been harvested and new patterns of international inequality have been established. More central is the fact that the majority of elites speaking in the name of the South *have from the outset* been the spokesmen for, and in some cases even the direct agents of, national and international class interests quite satisfied with the existing world economic system if not with their share of the pie. Under these conditions, we will witness the *embourgeoisiement* of the bourgeoisie—hardly a surprising turn of events.

In sum, the international bargaining process now under way, to the extent that it results in fairer shares for the South, serves to strengthen Southern elites who in the main have little autonomy from antiequity class forces at home. Although some among them may genuinely wish to assault class privilege and maldistribution, they are relentlessly pulled back toward policies that favor the few rather than the many. Windfall increments to income may in some cases serve to alleviate certain impediments to more equitable distribution, but sustained progress in the direction of implementing policies leading toward what was previously called the democratic distributional rule is structurally out of the question. Only profound changes in the developmental strategies currently in use (and most probably the elites currently in power) will significantly alter this situation. Whether alterations this profound can be other than socialist *and* revolutionary remains to be demonstrated historically.

THREE

Perpetuating Inequity:
Northern Responsibilities

Few persons enjoy being told that they are in some sense *responsible* for the misery of others, yet the topic cannot be ignored in an essay of this sort. The word has many meanings, themselves much debated in both abstract and very specific contexts. It is here admittedly used loosely to suggest the manner in which specific Northern policies (and nonpolicies) *and* the economic and political institutions that characterize the North serve to perpetuate Southern inequity. In this spirit, we touch the various domains of Northern responsibilities at three specific points, making no claim to deal with this vast topic in more than very preliminary fashion. The first point of contact is at the macropolicy level. Using the Chilean case for illustrative purposes, we suggest that historically the United States has relentlessly and at times brutally opposed those very Southern political-economic experiments that promised greatest equity gains. The second point of contact relates to the first but is more specific. There we touch on the developmental-aid question and its equity implications. Finally, we step back from specific policy actions and pose a critical although much avoided macroissue of our time in North-South relations: To what extent is the continuation

NOTE: In what follows I deal largely with the United States rather than with all the industrialized capitalist countries because I am most familiar with the United States and the United States is clearly the "leader" (the most responsible) in the trends and activities sketched. As suggested below, "leadership" and "responsibility" should be understood both in structural terms and in the context of specific problems.

of the Northern way of life (advanced, high-consumption industrial capitalism) compatible with significant equity gains in the
South?

In some instances, Northern responsibilities for the perpetua-
tion of inequity in the South are direct, obvious, and tragically
costly in human terms. In the past few decades, the dubious
honor of leading assaults against Southern regimes holding out
the promise of moving aggressively on the equity front has fallen
almost exclusively on the United States. To set the stage for the
most dramatic recent adventure of this kind, it well to recall
C. L. G. Bell's summary of the first and more radical of the two
strategic options open to reform regimes concerned with equity-
in-distribution. The reformers-in-a-hurry, he said,

can plump for rapid and drastic forms of intervention, whose effects
are not easily reversible, either because they change the balance of
political power or because of their intrinsic features; a radical land
reform and nationalization coupled with workers' control are good
examples.

Bell then assesses the risks run by such reformers:

Such moves will probably impose severe strains on the coalition and
alter its support base. Even if the government falls as a result, which
is a distinct possibility, the poor may still be able to defend their gains
in the aftermath.[28]

It would be difficult to find a better brief description of the
reforms and reform strategy attempted by the Allende regime
in Chile than Bell's first statement. Unfortunately for the Popular
Unity government, the "strains" about which Bell writes were
not rooted so much in the coalition itself but rather in the class-
based opposition to the coalition, always supported by and sometimes led by the United States government, which was in turn
urged on and abetted by corporate and banking interests. The
ironies are apparent, for it was none other than Henry Kissinger,

[28]C. L. G. Bell in Chenery et al., *Redistribution with Growth*, pp. 71–72.
Also see above, p. 194.

so recently concerned about the "plight of the one-quarter of mankind whose lives are overwhelmed by poverty and hunger and numbed by insecurity and despair," who was the chief architect of United States involvement in the overthrow of Allende.[29] Furthermore, Bell's hope that the poor might still be able to defend their gains "in the aftermath"—in this case the bloodiest military coup in twentieth-century Latin America—has clearly been made a mockery of by postcoup events. Under the directorship of Jorge Cauas, official "czar" of the Chilean economy under the junta (ironically, until 1974 Cauas was a high official of the World Bank!), distributional policies were and still are consciously the most regressive in the modern history of Chile. The economy is, in the words of its directors, going to be "shocked" back to "health"—with more than a little help from its Northern and international friends.

The Chilean case is illuminative in part because it is, in the statistical sense, somewhat improbable. It is the stuff of historical drama, with characters and actions that clarify and intensify understanding through the crispness and tragic interrelationship of their roles: a democratically elected regime, dedicated to increasing domestic equity and international independence, seeing this as possible only in the context of the construction of socialism, committed to maintaining much of the existing political culture and institutional base, opposed and undercut at home and abroad by the United States and United States–influenced institutions, and ultimately destroyed by a military coup that simultaneously eradicated Chilean constitutionalism (while assassinating thousands of citizens and imprisoning tens of thousands more), bringing into being a regime strongly supported by the United States. It is unlikely that all the elements will ever again be so neatly assembled, the situation so unambiguously "resolved," and the United States so fully exposed (short of armed intervention) as having been directly involved.

[29] In "The United States and Chile: Roots and Branches," *Foreign Affairs*, vol. 53, no. 2, January 1975, pp. 297–313. I have sketched a series of reasons why Kissinger and other high officials viewed the Allende experiment as a massive threat to United States interests. Since that article was written, additional details have come to light.

But the question that the Chile scenario raises—and therefore the importance of the case precisely because of its clarity—is whether or not the United States can and will abandon its historic role as the sworn enemy of reformers-in-a-hurry and/or socialist experimentation in the South. The question is immense in its implications, and the interpretations of why, since World War II, the United States has assumed this rule are multifold and often in conflict with each other. But what is not at issue is that in almost every known instance where United States authorities have had the opportunity to make policy-relevant choices between a Southern regime with socialist implications and some other regime—no matter how repressive and antiequity—the choice has almost always been for the latter. What the Chilean case did was pose the choices and the alternatives most dramatically of all, but the logic employed in making the choices was no different than it would have been had the alternatives been murkier and thus the values in conflict more problematic.

Let me be clear what is at issue here. We are not asking whether the United States can or will in the future consistently give some kind of special advantages and consideration to those Southern regimes, actual or potential, that exhibit serious socialist commitments. Such a policy turnaround for the leading capitalist nation is beyond the political-economic reality of North American society as presently constituted. Rather, what we are asking involves a three-stage question (which in turn deserves to be the topic of a separate paper): First, is it possible, post-Watergate and post-Vietnam, for the United States to deal even-handedly both politically and economically with Southern regimes with Popular Unity-type commitments? In the Chilean case this would have meant treating the Allende regime as if it were the logical inheritor to both the problems and the possibilities of the Frei regime (which it was), rather than as a massive threat to United States interests and thus an enemy to be destroyed. Second, what are the minimal changes in both public and private arenas in the United States which would enable this overall policy shift to come about? Third, how probable are such changes, and what factors external to the United States affect those probabilities?

Thus, the overarching and primary public policy challenge in the North is to enhance the probability that future Southern experiments incorporating important distributive components (which means, in effect, that they will in some degree have a socialist cast) will not be treated in a hostile fashion. In the United States, this implies major movement toward the demilitarization of foreign policy, close public control over intelligence operations, substantial decoupling of business and corporate interests from the conduct of foreign policy, and undoubtedly much more. These are neither short-term nor easy-to-achieve goals.[30]

More modestly, there is also an important equity-related challenge posed by the subordinate issue of development aid. In idealized form, bilateral and even multilateral aid would seem to be an excellent vehicle for Northern influence over Southern patterns of distribution. In this, foreign aid is unlike the fairer shares that are won (or will be won) at the international economic bargaining table or in outright commercial situations. In the latter instance, the logic of the market holds sway. Those who win the fairer shares can in theory do with them as they please. The distribution of the increments to income gained through higher prices, access to new markets, and other trade-related mechanisms is nobody's business but the recipient nation's under current and foreseeable international practice. (A partial exception to this nobody's business norm is the international concern over the recycling of petrodollars. The amounts involved are clearly the crucial factor here, bolstered by widely shared feelings that the newly won shares are not fair.) Developmental aid, however, is different. In theory it goes to those who need it most, not to those who bargain or trade more successfully. It is widely accepted that donor nations or agencies always grant

---

[30]Two clarifications are in order: (1) The "special relationship" with Latin America has historically led to a somewhat special ruthlessness in reacting to socialist-tending experiments in the hemisphere. In other Third World areas, a certain "softness" toward such experiments has at times been evident (sometimes born of a clear strategic/political inability to act decisively). (2) Withdrawal of United States support for repressive regimes is easier to accomplish *without* substantial institutional changes in the United States than are nonhostile postures toward socialist experiments.

or lend money for some specific purpose—it is never wholly without strings. In this loose sense, aid is always interventionist and is recognized to be so by both donor and recipient (although the inherent interventionism is played down for obvious reasons). With aid, the key questions thus become how "need" is defined and what criteria of aid-giving and targeting are to be used.

Although this is not the place to recount the sorry record of the North in general and the United States in particular in the giving and targeting of developmental aid, a brief characterization of that record is helpful. Except for professional apologists, most observers of the United States developmental-aid scene would still find little to quarrel with in C. Fred Bergsten's 1973 critique:

The United States is the least responsive to Third World needs of any industrialized country at this time. U.S. help is small in quantity, and getting smaller. Its quality is declining. It often runs directly counter to the central objectives of the LDC's just outlined. It lags far behind the policies of Europe and Japan.

The United States regards developing countries both large and small (e.g., India and Chile, not to mention Indochina) solely as pawns on the chessboard of global power politics. Rewards go only to the shrinking list of explicit collaborators . . . U.S. development aid, as a percentage of national GNP, is now next-to-last among all industrialized countries.[31]

The equity-related dimensions of the disbursement of aid are actually worse than Bergsten suggests. Again, Chile presents a classic case of the warping of aid criteria and understandings of need. Under Public Law 480 (theoretically among the most need-directed of all aid disbursements), Chile—a nation not on the UN's list of "most seriously affected" (MSA) countries—received 85 percent of all United States food aid for Latin America in 1975. The other 15 percent went to Haiti and Honduras, with neither El Salvador nor Guyana (both UN MSA countries) receiving anything.

[31]C. Fred Bergsten, "The Threat from the Third World," *Foreign Policy*, no. 11, Summer 1973, pp. 102–124, quoted material from pp. 104–105, emphasis in original. Much data relevant to the quantity, sources, and targets of United States developmental aid are presented in Hansen (ed.), *The U.S. and World Development*.

What is really at issue, however, is not this miserable record but whether or not (and how, if at all) it can be turned around. It is in this sense that the aid question is essentially an element of the basic public challenge noted above: the treatment by the North of those regimes incorporating important distributive elements into their developmental scenarios. If developmental aid were (1) conceptualized with equity-enhancing criteria in mind, (2) administered in this spirit, and (3) significantly increased in quantity (the latter making normative sense only if the two former conditions prevail), the United States, other Northern nations, and international organizations would find themselves directing the largest proportion of aid to precisely those Southern regimes that make the most serious commitments to equity-as-distribution activities. The notion of targeting aid to the poor (already much talked about in developmental circles) would give way to the concept of targeting aid to those regimes that are already attacking the root causes of poverty. The two concepts are very different, for the former runs the almost certain risk, now well demonstrated in practice, of passing aid through the hands of elites who for the reasons sketched in the previous section cannot assault privilege—and therefore poverty—without undercutting their own bases of domestic and international support. Overwhelming evidence from the last two decades suggests that *developmental aid cannot overcome what patterns of economic development themselves make improbable.*

Targeting aid to those regimes that are already attacking the root causes of inequality and poverty, however, is far from easy. If they are in fact attacking those root causes, they are also undoubtedly doing many other things that bring them into sharp conflict with the North in general and the United States in particular (nationalizations, etc.). One of the most coherent and precedent-shattering Northern experiments in such targeting to date, the Swedish Development Agency's decision to send its Latin American aid exclusively to the equity-committed Castro and Allende regimes, could hardly be duplicated in the United States. Sweden's internal politics, its marginal role in the cold war, and its lack of basic investments and long-term interests in Latin America made this unusual scenario possible in the early 1970s. The first steps in the United States, if taken at all, will necessarily be much more modest and of a different order. As recent congressional actions tying aid to minimal standards of human rights performance in the recipient nation suggest, the most viable goal in the short run is to get the United States government out of the syndrome of favoring client states, which frequently tend to be repressive regimes, with more aid. These first small steps, although not unimportant, are equity-enhancing only in the negative sense: those regimes most committed to enforcing regressive distribution through repressive practices at home must cease to be the favored recipients of United States aid. But clearly there is a long road to travel before the positive criteria implied in the preferential targeting of aid to equity-committed regimes can be built into programs. It is doubtful, in fact, that changes in United States policy will provide the cutting edge of programmatic shifts in Northern approaches to the question of developmental aid. The domestic obstacles are too great. The lead will have to be taken by international organizations and multilateral aid packages—necessarily supported and partially financed by the United States.

Our final perspective on Northern responsibilities overflows the boundaries of conventional political and economic analysis. At issue is nothing less than the relationship between the Northern way of life (advanced, high-consumption industrial capitalism) and the international equity problem. The range of subjects involved is awesome, and only a few topics will be touched here.

One fairly direct point of entry is that taken by environmentalists who quite persuasively point out that neither known resources nor the ecosystem in general will sustain anything approaching Northern levels of consumption, energy use, and waste for the majority of the world's citizens.[32] The modal pattern of Northern industrial development, and modernization

[32]Recall the oft-quoted statistics about energy consumption: The United States, with 6 percent of the world's population, consumes 30 percent of the total energy. The United States per capita kilowatt consumption (thermal) of energy is two-and-a-half times that of France (hardly a low-energy economy). See Mesarovic and Pestel, *Mankind at the Turning Point*, pp. 135, 139 and passim. Energy consumption of course is only a convenient (but telling) index of other patterns and kinds of production and consumption.

viewed as a replication of this pattern of development, are not viable models for the modernization of the Third World.[33] No matter how vigorously many politicians both North and South attempt to obscure this reality (each group for different reasons), a car in every garage—or even a microwave oven in every kitchen—is not on the global historical agenda. Fantasies that the poor of the world will at some time "catch up" with typical Northern consumption patterns become more difficult to sustain with each day that passes. Fortunately, as the word spreads that past a certain point the quality of life is not directly related to the quantity of goods produced and consumed, a concomitant (although painfully slow) demystification of "more is better" thinking begins to occur in the North.

But if the language of absolute catching up, with its dual implication of achieving the same levels of aggregate production and similar patterns of consumption as those of the North, is not a meaningful idiom in which to discuss global equity issues, the language of relative gap closing still is. As Gunnar Adler-Karlsson points out in his essay in the companion to this volume, the "psychological propensity to catch up" operates at all levels of the system of international stratification.[34] The dominant tendency in a world characterized by rapid communications and the spread of material culture is for persons, groups, classes, nations, and regions to measure their current progress against the situations of those who are immediately above them in the overlapping pyramids of power, income, security, status, and other val-

[33]For useful bibliography and a critique of the developmental literature for its lingering assumptions that "industrialization" in the poorer countries is essentially the same process as that which occurred in the richer countries and is thus a viable vehicle for the same kind of modernization, see Edward J. Woodhouse, "Re-visioning the Future of the Third World: An Ecological Perspective on Development," *World Politics*, vol. XXV, no. 1, October 1972, pp. 1–33.

[34]Gunnar Adler-Karlsson, "Eliminating Absolute Poverty." Analyzing the utilitarian roots of this propensity (closely connected to the industrial revolution and Western materialism), Adler-Karlsson suggests that a less pernicious ethical norm would be to strive to minimize suffering rather than maximize happiness (particularly happiness viewed as consumption—the most common definition of the good life in vulgarizations of utilitarianism).

ued goods. What is quite universally sought is some movement toward the *reduction* of the gaps that separate the self from the proximate reference group located higher on the pyramid. In other words, an ethical norm of *relative* gap closing is powerfully reinforced by the psychological and political realities of contemporary life.

All projections of future North-South gaps, however, whatever the indices of wealth or consumption used and whatever the assumptions made concerning transfers, Southern growth scenarios, etc., suggest that *no gaps will close unless growth and consumption are slowed in the North.*[35] The projected dynamics of the global structure of inequality are strikingly similar to the dynamics of the domestic structure of inequality as set forth in much simplified form in the previously presented model of *Periferica*. Those who are currently most privileged in the global class structure must accept something approaching equal *absolute* shares of increased global product—not proportional shares—if gaps between North and South are going to begin to close. But we have already seen how difficult it is to reform national political and economic systems toward an equal shares rule; globally such a rule would be even more difficult to put into practice. The leading sector of global consumers, the North, is subject to no superordinate authority. What is called for are patterns of institutionalized restraint and resource transfer that

[35] See for example, the analyses in chap. 5 of Mesarovic and Pestel, *Mankind at the Turning Point* and the conclusions of Wassily Leontief, *The Future of the World Economy: A United Nations Study*, Oxford University Press, New York, 1977. It is important to remember that quantitative comparisons and projections of this sort are almost always based on indices of wealth (usually gross national product per capita). More rounded conceptualizations of the quality of life would lead to the use of other indicators that theoretically—and sometimes in practice—vary independently of indices of wealth. Again the examples of the socialist countries are relevant, for vast advances in health, education, and welfare (gap-closing advances) have been made in the absence of concomitant increases in income. It is also worth emphasizing that when one deals in the least "material" indices of the quality of life, gaps not only close but actually reverse direction. For example, in many respects Havana is today a cleaner, safer, and more livable city than New York. The same might be said of certain Eastern European cities in comparison with their Western counterparts.

are unprecedented and very possibly unrealizable in the nation-state system as we know it.

At this point, it should be emphasized that this is not a conventional limits-of-growth argument. We are not claiming that the ecological and system parameters of global resources and productivity are such that future increments of growth are in some sense impossible—whatever truth there obviously is in the overall notion of system limits. What is being claimed is that progress toward global equity, defined as movement toward the closing of gaps between regions, nations, and classes, requires a relative slowing of growth in the North *and/or* resource transfers to the South of a scale and sort that are almost unimaginable given contemporary politics and values.

A host of troublesome questions are raised by formulating the global equity issue in this fashion, for—as an increasing number of authors have pointed out—there is little in the logic of industrial capitalism (or perhaps even in the logic of centrally planned industrial economies of the Soviet sort) that gives hope to the gap closers. The watchword of such industrial systems is *expansion*, nationally and internationally.[36] The search for profits, larger markets, outlets for installed capacity, and security of supply are all central to the health of such systems. As repeatedly emphasized by its defenders and theorists, growth is the key to economic and political viability.

Not surprisingly, these themes have been reiterated with great vigor by official representatives of the North in both national and international forums. For example, the U.S. State Department recently published a flyer on Latin America reminding us that

Latin America's markets are becoming as significant to our continued growth as its raw materials. Our trade surplus with Latin America in 1975 amounted to $1.2 billion. Nearly 1/5th of our total trade now takes

[36]The argument that nonexpanding capitalism is largely a contradiction in terms is well developed by Robert L. Heilbroner, in *An Inquiry into The Human Prospect*, W. W. Norton, New York, 1975, particularly pp. 82–92. Cf. also Richard A. Falk, "Toward a New World Order: Modest Methods and Drastic Visions," in Saul H. Mendlovitz (ed.), *On the Creation of a Just World Order*, The Free Press, New York, 1975.

place with Latin American and Caribbean countries. We look to this area for 34% of the petroleum, 68% of the coffee, 57% of the sugar, 47% of the copper, 35% of the iron ore, and 96% of the bauxite we import. In 1975 we exported more than $17 billion in U.S. goods to the region.[37]

And more generally, the then-Secretary of State informed us, in language that any Marxist economist would find quite congenial until the final phrase, that

the United States cannot be isolated—and never has been isolated—from the international economy. We export 23 percent of our farm output and 8 percent of our manufactures. We import far more raw materials than we export; oil from abroad is critical to our welfare. American enterprise overseas constitutes an economy the size of Japan's. America's prosperity could not continue in a chaotic world economy.

Conversely, what the United States does—or fails to do—has an enormous impact on the rest of the world. With one-third of the output of the non-Communist world, the American economy is still the great engine of world prosperity.[38]

These are rather frank admissions that the "American way of life" is closely tied to the maintenance of certain patterns of resource use and exploitation on a global scale—patterns in which the South is quite important. What cannot so easily be admitted by defenders of this way of life is the idea that these patterns and their continuation are destructive of both international and intranational equity. Yet to the extent that the arguments on the nature of Southern regimes in the previous section of this paper are supported—and there is much more to be said in support of them—it also follows that the continued expansion of Northern capitalism in the historic form that it has taken is antiequity in its implications. The American economy—although it may be "the great engine of world prosperity" to those who are used

[37]"Latin America in the Economic Sphere," *Gist*, Department of State, Bureau of Public Affairs, Washington, D.C., April 1976.

[38]"Strengthening the World Economic Structure," Speech to the Kansas City International Relations Council, May 13, 1975, Department of State, Bureau of Public Affairs, Washington, D.C., p. 1.

to thinking about aggregate growth in a certain fashion—also involves a way of accumulating and using capital that helps to ensure that existing patterns of maldistribution will continue, that gaps will not close, and that many in the South will attempt to emulate the worst of Northern models of production and consumption. The contradiction is obvious: if there truly cannot be "world prosperity" except as the United States and Northern economies continue to expand at roughly the same rates and in roughly the same fashion as they have in the post–World War II period, then there can be no significant movement toward global equity as defined here. Under these circumstances, no relative closing of the gaps between North and South will take place except through direct resource transfers so massive as to be presently unimaginable. One cannot have it both ways.

If Northern capitalism as currently organized is part of the global equity problem, we must ask yet again, What is to be done? For those who live in the North and care about these issues, this is one of the key political questions of the age—one about which those suffering through the contemporary political dialogue have little reason to feel optimistic. Nor is there a medium-term basis for optimism in either Marxist or non-Marxist understandings of class structure and politics in the United States. Almost all who live in this society—even those most wretchedly exploited themselves—are advantaged to some degree from the global division of labor and the United States' preeminent position as the leading capitalist nation. Additionally, having been raised in a culture in which the symbols of nationalism, free enterprise, and individual mobility and consumption are given very high valence, it is by no means easy to accept even a discussion about the values of internationalism, socialism, restrained consumption, and collective responsibility that are implied in all serious approaches to the global equity problem. It is extremely difficult to rally large numbers of persons in the North around anti-imperialist (as opposed to antiwar) banners when those banners contain a critique of capitalism that in turn has direct implications for personal consumption and life-styles. Perhaps environmental problems and questions concerning local control over life and work, the proper allocation of public re-

213

sources, the control of repressive domestic tendencies, and other issues "closer to home" will prove to be more viable avenues to a critique of Northern capitalism in the context of global equity. But in any event, all this is immensely problematic, for what is being asked historically is nothing less than that the North in general and the American people in particular cooperate in the profoundest of transformations of their own economies so that other citizens of the world can eventually live better and so that their own children and grandchildren—if not they themselves—can live more fulfilling and creative although perhaps less materially resplendent lives.

The Political Economy of North-South Relations: An Overview and an Alternative Approach

Roger D. Hansen

ONE

Major Themes and Contrasting Viewpoints

The three preceding essays contribute greatly to an understanding of the highly complex nature of current North-South issues. One senses the potential chasms between normative goals and policies prescribed to reach them and the degree to which some sets of goals are congruent while others are mutually exclusive. The three authors disagree as often as they agree; they all exhibit differing sets of value preferences as they rank-order their goals; and a close reading implicitly (and on occasion quite explicitly) reveals the degree to which North-South issues have much more political and status content than is normally suggested by a purely economic conceptualization of the points of contention between North and South.

While many themes of major importance to the North-South relationship in the 1980s and beyond could be singled out to demonstrate the divergent views of the contributors to this volume, the following four are representative of the more controversial and noteworthy themes emerging from their essays.

1. The "Conservative" Nature of Southern Economic Demands

This theme is sounded most strongly by Fishlow and by Fagen, but with entirely different emphases and from sharply differing perspectives. In Fishlow's view, the New International Economic Order, despite occasional rhetorical excesses, does not necessitate a fundamentally different conception of international economic relationships. Rejecting Marxist contentions of inevitable exploitation, it inherently accepts the mutuality of the benefits from trade and foreign investment. It seeks structural reforms to underwrite a more favorable division of gains to the Third World than the marketplace presently affords. It recognizes the need for a positive sum basis for meaningful negotiation and one in which many developing countries might share.

Based upon his own reading of Southern state demands, Fishlow is convinced that the types of reform that would satisfy them are not only feasible but also desirable. In his words,

A new economic order will not lead to a radically altered global distribution of income, although the South as a whole. . . should benefit. Capitalist institutions will survive, but experimentation to satisfy internal egalitarian objectives could lead to more varied economic models. At best it will be a world in which the North-South division becomes sufficiently blurred to allow for cooperative resolution of pressing universal problems that threaten the prospects for a just and orderly global community of nations.[1]

Fishlow's argument is based on both empirical evidence and personal conjecture. He notes that many so-called Third World countries are increasingly integrated with the international economic system in many functional areas and are benefiting particularly from expanding exports of industrial production. Examining their demands in this light, Fishlow concludes that their real goal is a system that provides them more assured access to Northern markets for a rapidly diversifying list of manufactured exports, increased amounts of capital to help finance rapid growth, and a reformed system of technology transfer that is far less expensive for the developing countries than the present one (most often embodied in foreign direct investment). Since the initiative seized by the developing countries in recent years was "built in good measure on recent evidence of increased economic strength within the context of the old order," Fishlow believes not only that moderate reforms within that order will suffice to ease present North-South tensions, but also that it is reform

[1]See above, p. 14–15.

within a global system, *not* collective self-reliance, which the South really desires.

It is upon this analysis and interpretation of Southern goals and global systemic needs that Fishlow develops his own international economic order prescriptions in the second chapter of his essay. His proposals would allow for the steady expansion of Southern access to Northern product, capital, and technology markets. And a comparison of those goals with the goals Díaz would achieve through a strategy of "selective delinking" reveals the convergent judgments of the two on the types of reforms in market structures—for goods, capital, and technology—that would both satisfy Southern demands for a fairer international system and improve the efficiency with which the international economic system would serve all countries, developed and developing.

These views place Fishlow and Díaz squarely within that element of the economics profession which considers that (1) the present international economic system does contain significant market imperfections; (2) those imperfections are, in the aggregate, biased against the developing countries; and (3) an integrated but nonradical package of reforms can remove much of the anti-Southern bias while improving the global efficiency of the entire system. Neoclassical critics of this view would deny that the present system entails imperfections or anti-Southern biases of a magnitude to warrant such reforms; radical critics would argue that the reforms suggested by Fishlow and Díaz are far too limited to adequately serve the needs of economic development within the countries of Asia, Africa, and Latin America.

Richard Fagen also views the demands presently emanating from Southern countries as essentially conservative once their rhetorical flourishes have been properly discounted. However, Fagen's reasoning on this issue contains a level of analysis not mentioned and perhaps not considered by Fishlow and Díaz. From Fagen's analytical perspective, Southern demands have been articulated in most countries by a governing elite whose perceived views and interests have always been "conservative-reformist" in nature. In his view the majority of elites speaking in the name of the South *have from the outset* been spokesmen for, if not the direct creation of, national and international class interests highly satisfied with the existing world economic system if not with their share of its output. "Under these conditions, we will witness *embourgeoisement* of the bourgeoisie—hardly a surprising turn of events."[2] The premises upon which Fagen's conclusions rest are spelled out in detail in his essay.[3]

If Fagen's conclusion is accurate, the probabilities attached to his following proposition are necessarily substantial:

The international bargaining process now under way, to the extent that it results in fairer shares for the South, serves to strengthen Southern elites who in the main have little autonomy from antiequity class forces at home. Although some among them may genuinely wish to assault class privilege and maldistribution, they are relentlessly pulled back toward policies which favor the few rather than the many.[4]

Thus once again the student of North-South relations and the general reader with an interest in the issues of the 1980s Project are faced with a serious value-ordering dilemma. Assuming for purposes of argument that both Fishlow and Fagen are on defensible analytical and empirical ground, is one pleased or displeased with the conservative nature of Southern demands and the prescriptions proposed by Fishlow? The positive elements include the substantial probabilities of more harmonious and constructive North-South relations at the interstate level, with an added boost to the aggregate development process in the South. The negative elements, on the other hand, include the probability of little or no advance on the absolute poverty problem and the potential risks entailed in failure to address that problem more directly. It is unlikely that any two readers will agree on the normative and policy tradeoffs on this issue; many will undoubtedly reexamine Fishlow's and Fagen's analyses in hopes of discovering a false dilemma.

[2]See above, p. 199.
[3]See above, pp. 163–214.
[4]See above, p. 199.

2. The Differing Goals of First-Order Concern

With apologies to the authors for any unintentional misrepresentation of their positions, let me suggest a plausible reading of their first-order concerns as revealed in the preceding essays. These somewhat artificial distinctions are drawn in order to emphasize the extremely complex mixture of conceptual approaches and empirical observations, of goal selection and policy prescription that come together as one undertakes a "normative/prescriptive" exercise in North-South relations.

Fishlow is the most difficult to characterize, because of both the breadth of issues he covers and the subtlety with which he tackles each issue. This said, let me suggest that his perspective on North-South relations is informed by a mixture of two ideal types: the *global equity* perspective and the *global agenda* perspective. In simplest terms, the global equity perspective arises from questions concerning the present distribution of wealth, income, economic opportunity, and political participation. Some observers choose to focus on these distributional issues at the interstate level; others, on the interpersonal level. The global agenda perspective arises from a growing concern for the need to "manage" such problems as environmental decay, nuclear proliferation, food production, and population growth in a way that elicits the cooperation of most—if not all—nations.

In common with the views of many who adopt the global equity perspective, Fishlow feels that numerous reforms can and should be introduced which will enable Southern countries to increase the pace of their development and the importance of their role in the management of the international economic system. And in common with the global agenda perspective, Fishlow by implication suggests that without a good deal less rancor and a good deal more cooperation between North and South, some of the world's most pressing problems will prove incapable of timely or optimal resolution.

In contrast, Díaz' first-order concern would clearly place more emphasis on *autonomy* at the *national level*. Like Fishlow, Díaz brings many concerns, goals, and prescriptions to his treatment of North-South issues. But his overriding objective would seem to be the development of an international economic system that at the levels of both structure and process creates a maximum amount of tolerance for the exercise of national autonomy and limits as severely as possible the potential for overt and covert intervention by any nation (or the system itself) in the affairs of any other nation.

In contrast to both Fishlow and Díaz, Fagen's first-order concern appears to be a mixture of the global equity perspective and the so-called *absolute poverty* perspective. Unlike Fishlow, Fagen's concern within the global equity perspective focuses on comparisons between *individuals*, not *states*, and his major emphasis is upon the desperate plight of what have variously been called the "forgotten 40 percent," the "low-end poor," or those living in absolute poverty. As Fagen's essay indicates and as all the work being done on this issue also suggests, the definitional problems with the term absolute poverty are monumental. Whatever the empirical referent of the term, the problem of individual poverty is Fagen's major concern, and with it is concern for the ways in which the so-called cycle of poverty can be broken.

The careful reader will have recognized that *each* of the authors shares the concerns of all the others. We are discussing differences in *degrees of concern*. Fishlow, for example, devotes considerable effort in his essay to suggesting ways in which his proposals can crack the cycle of poverty and successfully address the absolute poverty problem. Furthermore, he implicitly criticizes parts of Fagen's analysis when he argues that "deterministic models of dependency give too little weight" to the growing political influence of the low-end poor.[5] And one could hardly miss Fagen's sympathy with Díaz's concerns for developing-country autonomy and the building of a system that places strict limits on intervention in national socioeconomic experimentation. Furthermore, unstated feasibility judgments could further diminish *apparent* differences in first-order concerns.

The point, therefore, is not that the authors do not share similar concerns. It is rather that the ordering of those concerns will suggest different goals, different norms of behavior, and different

[5]See above, p. 44.

policy prescriptions. The briefest explication of the equity issue reveals how crucial seemingly overrefined nuances really are in this area. How do we conceptualize "equity"? In thinking of the concept, are we more concerned with equality of *opportunity* or equality of *result*? Are we concerned primarily with equity as it applies to *states* or to *individuals*? Finally, when we talk about "equality" in the intrasocietal, interpersonal sense, are we really thinking of moving toward less income inequality or toward a *basic human needs* strategy that would attempt to guarantee a floor to standards of living beneath which no person would fall? And can this final dichotomy be viewed instead as a continuum, in the sense that the fulfillment of basic human needs (especially in fields of nutrition, health, and education) will automatically produce greater potential earning power among the bottom deciles of the population?

Current discussions of equity and equality in the North-South context often cloud at least two crucial distinctions: the first between states and individuals, the second between equality of opportunity and equality of result. It is crucial to bear these distinctions in mind, because each of the four possible goals suggests the need for a differing set of policies, and often the policies appropriate to one goal may differ radically from those appropriate to another.

3. The Issue of Feasibility

Both Fishlow and Díaz recognize that the reforms they propose, no matter how congruent they may be with the rhetoric of international economic liberalism in most Northern countries, raise serious issues of feasibility. Both explicitly recognize that powerful Northern interest groups will not welcome more liberal trade or a significant body of enforceable international rules governing the behavior of transnational enterprises and the transfer of technology. Fishlow also notes that the *South* will, at least initially, resist this policy package simply because it does not include large resource transfers from North to South. As he notes, "for the greatest part, the potential increase in foreign exchange earnings relies on expanded trade and credit and thus on a significant developing country contribution as well.''[6] For this very reason Fishlow devotes the final section of his essay to an analysis of the feasibility issue and offers several novel policy proposals to improve the prospects for the building of a domestic consensus in support of his approach.

It is quite probable that despite his recognition of the seriousness of the feasibility issue, Fishlow has *underestimated* existing constraints by not devoting enough consideration to the political milieu within which his economic analysis and prescriptions are cast. With regard to the North, Fishlow considers several major hurdles lightly or not at all. The first hurdle concerns the degree of salience which the "Southern problem" commands within developed-country governments. While Fishlow may be correct that the North-South issue has been "*formally* elevated to at least equal prominence with the global East-West division,''[7] if the word "formally" is deleted, his characterization would seem from all perspectives to be highly misleading. Without the "OPEC connection" the North-South issue would not be much higher on governmental agendas than it was in the late 1960s, which is to say very low indeed.

The second hurdle concerns Northern responses to the Southern problem. If the problem received attention from Northern governments essentially because of the oil issue and the OPEC countries' 1975 decision to link energy negotiations to negotiations covering all developing-country concerns with the "inequity" of the present system, the probability is high that Northern governmental responses to a Fishlow-type set of proposals will be dependent on the oil issue and the OPEC balancing act (internal and external) between North and South. Unless OPEC remains very closely linked to the developing countries and continues to demand a Northern willingness to consider international economic reforms as a price for "reasonable" oil production and pricing policies, one may expect little Northern responsiveness to Southern demands in the short term.

[6]See above, p. 77.

[7]See above, p. 11, emphasis added. The final session of the Conference on International Economic Cooperation (CIEC), held in Paris in late May 1977, demonstrates again the need to distinguish between formal recognition of a problem and the revealed willingness to take serious steps to resolve it.

The third hurdle concerns a far deeper political issue that Fishlow does not analyze at all: the probability that many Northerners will view the Southern challenge as one that is fundamentally political, not economic, in nature.[8] A rapidly developing body of literature and thought within the North equates present Southern demands with the psychic needs of developing-country governing elites and their supporters who gave them access to power and with the more traditional desires for power and status exhibited by all nation-states. Northerners both in and out of government who accept this view of the present North-South conflict often draw the conclusion that any movement to accommodate Southern desires will simply be met by an escalation of demands—a not unreasonable projection if one accepts the eminently plausible conceptual framework through which these observers are analyzing the issue. Such observers would and do advise a course of resistance to almost all Southern demands on the grounds that "accommodation" will simply whet Southern appetites. Related to this is the concern of some Northerners that the serious consideration of Southern demands which Fishlow, Díaz, and others have given them will merely legitimize Southern "bloc tactics" that have served to produce these demands.

And finally, of course, there remain those economic analysts who argue that present market imperfections and biases are not significant enough to warrant reforms of the scope suggested by Díaz and Fishlow. Such analysts note the historically impressive growth performance of the South in the aggregate over the past two decades and the truly outstanding development performances of some individual Southern countries and generally conclude that development problems more often reflect misconceived domestic policies than they do international systemic constraints.

Turning briefly to the South, one need only add that to the extent that concerns of realpolitik, not economic gains, are the real issue for Southern elites, the sooner this interpretation of

[8]See Roger D. Hansen, "Major U.S. Options on North-South Relations: A Letter to President Carter," in John W. Sewell et al., *The United States and World Development: Agenda 1977*, Praeger for The Overseas Development Council, New York, 1977, p. 21–86.

motives is clarified, the greater will be the constraints to Fishlow-Díaz-type proposals, at least in the short to medium term. For if demands do follow each other, set after set, Northern publics and legislative bodies will rapidly develop an intransigent opposition to each and every one of Fishlow's proposals, particularly since each proposal would gore at least one Northern ox; the resulting pleas for redress would be heard with enormous sympathy in Northern legislatures.

In sum, within Fishlow's own essentially economic conceptual framework the constraints on his proposals are serious, and no one recognizes that better than he. But if one adds to the Fishlow analysis a political dimension that, beyond an examination of "commodity power," he did not have the time or space to develop, the constraints loom even larger.[9]

4. Views Concerning a Basic Human Needs Approach

The authors represented in this volume give not the faintest blessing to what has recently but swiftly become a rather fashionable approach to thinking about certain aspects of North-South relations, namely the basic human needs approach. This approach focuses its prescriptions and its resources (if it were to have any) on raising the standard of living of the poorest quarter of the world's population.

"Why not argue for a world-wide war on poverty and oppression?" asks Díaz:

To those familiar with the rise and fall of the Alliance for Progress, the answer is obvious; no Northern government has both the credibility and the resources to launch and lead such a program seriously and globally, not now and not in the 1980s. . . . The sincerity with which some Northern individuals deplore poverty and oppression in the South is to be respected; but it strains the imagination to believe that major Northern governments, particularly those of large countries, could place such concerns at the center of their policies toward the South in

---

[9]See, for example, Robert W. Tucker, *The Inequality of Nations*, Basic Books, New York, 1977 for a detailed and insightful examination of many of the political issues in North-South relations that are relatively unexplored in Fishlow's essay.

any sustainable fashion in the near future. . . . Most people would read the historical record as indicating that very seldom do hegemonic Northern governments let concern for the poor and oppressed in the South determine their major long-run policies toward LDCs; to pretend that they do is far-fetched.[10]

Fagen, for different reasons, shares Díaz's rejection of anything resembling a basic human needs approach. He argues that

Poverty is so profoundly locked into the structural grain of poorer societies that only the most profound transformation of economics, politics, and class structure and culture enable it to be assaulted directly. Even the wealthier and most "people-oriented" regimes of the Third World face insurmountable short-term obstacles to delivering poverty-eradicating quantities of goods and services to marginal sectors of the population.[11]

This line of reasoning leads Fagen to observe that only revolutionary socialist regimes would attempt to mount a serious attack on the absolute poverty problem and to conclude that all other regimes will continue to follow the so-called trickle-down approach to economic development, an approach that, in effect, abjures any specific policy targeting on the problem of the poorest strata of society.

Is the rather short shrift given to the basic human needs approach by Díaz and Fagen entirely warranted in the context of the coming 10 to 15 years? As for Díaz's commentary, one can wholly agree with his characterization of past Northern behavior without letting the issue rest there. For if the most fundamental parameters of international politics are today increasingly being called into question, is the record of past state behavior as constraining as it appears at first glance? Díaz himself allows room for some changes that might trigger a very modest and nonglobal North-South effort in the basic human needs arena. Does a broader consideration of the potential diplomatic—and perhaps normative—constellation of forces in the coming decade allow for more flexibility than Díaz suggests?

[10]See above, pp. 155–156 and 157.
[11]See above, pp. 184–185.

227

In reconsidering Fagen's analysis of the problem, two rays of light pierce the otherwise gloomy atmosphere of his essay. The first concerns the possible overdeterminism of his model. Is absolute poverty so profoundly locked into the structure of Southern societies that the adoption of a basic human needs strategy must await a revolution? If the answer is "not quite," there is some room for maneuver. The second involves a definitional issue in the Fagen essay. He has defined absolute poverty so broadly that he applies the term to well over half of developing-country populations. If we accept his definition, the problems of mounting a strategy to overcome absolute poverty do look overwhelming. But that definition may considerably overstate the magnitude *and* the dynamics of the problem of absolute poverty. Again, if this is the case, there may be more "policy space" than his essay suggests. Of course, *any* definition of a term such as absolute poverty is going to be idiosyncratic until such time as custom dictates an agreed-upon empirical referent. But until it does, the definition chosen may either induce or smother efforts to develop and implement strategies to raise the standards of living of the worlds' poorest people. By broadening his definition to include as many persons as he does, Fagen may well make a basic human needs strategy seem highly unfeasible. A narrower yet defensible definition of the magnitude of the absolute poverty problem may suggest far fewer constraints.

TWO

A Strategy for Meeting
Basic Human Needs

It is clear that none of the other authors in this volume objects in principle to the goal of eliminating absolute poverty, however defined. Their objections are of a different nature, keyed to questions of feasibility, of the potential misuse of the approach for interventionist purposes and, perhaps for Fishlow, of the need for a special approach in the international economic order he envisions. In order to better assess the validity of these objections, a brief examination of the basic human needs problem is necessary.

First, however, it may be useful to sort out some of the terminological confusion that may occur in the discussion to follow concerning "goals" and "strategies," "basic human needs" and "absolute poverty," and "new development strategies." Simply stated, this section views the ending of absolute poverty, as defined in the following pages, as one major goal of a new set of domestic development *strategies*. In later parts of the discussion, *international* programs to support the domestic implementation of such development strategies are also analyzed. The fulfillment of basic human needs, when conceptualized as the elimination of absolute poverty, is more a goal than a strategy. Needless to say, there are in the abstract many different strategies that could conceivably meet this goal. Occasionally, though, we will refer to a basic human needs strategy, especially when equating it with the new development strategies outlined below. These have been selected on the premise that they have the greatest potential for permanently eliminating absolute poverty because of the structural changes—however modest—they would engender in both domestic and international society.[12]

DIMENSIONS OF THE ABSOLUTE POVERTY PROBLEM

Some 0.7 to 1.2 billion people in the world are presently subsisting in extreme poverty, caught in a vicious circle in which their levels of food consumption and nutritional intake lead to high levels of disease and infant mortality and to low levels of life expectancy. (The frequently cited 0.7 billion figure estimates the number of people in the developing countries who are "destitute"; it is also recognized, however, that another 0.5 billion people are surviving not much above this level. Given the short- to medium-term insurmountability of the definitional problems involved—conceptual as well as statistical—both the 0.7 billion and the 1.2 billion figures represent at best rough orders of magnitude.)[13]

Contributing to the syndrome of extreme poverty are inadequate infrastructures for appropriate nutrition, health, sanitation, and education programs. The end result in most cases is early death or, for those who survive, insufficient job opportunities at levels of productivity high enough to break out of this absolute poverty cycle. The most serious problems would seem to be limitations on food and nutrition, health care systems, and educational opportunities. Of course the list can be expanded, together with the definition, to include, for example, shelter, clothing, and drinking water. Yet even this lengthier list is limited to

[12]The suggestions made in the following sections and much of the argument that appears here are also contained, at greater length, in my article, "Major U.S. Options on North-South Relations: A Letter to President Carter," in *The United States and World Development: Agenda 1977*. The other essays in this volume were also drawn on for some of the analysis of viewpoints in that article, as it was written concurrently with my work on the 1980s Project.

[13]The best sources for discussion of both estimates and methodologies can be found in many recent publications of the World Bank and the International Labor Organization.

minimum *physical* needs and does not begin to examine the broader issue of psychological needs.

The one essential need itemized that clearly is more than physical is basic education. It is generally included in the basic human needs approach because it is seen as a critical element in breaking the absolute poverty cycle. The assumption is that a minimum level of literacy will generally be required to enable individuals to take advantage of productive employment opportunities that must also be presented if the problem of extreme poverty is to be overcome.

These employment opportunities must be produced—or at least be *allowed*—by the mix of development strategies chosen in each developing country. While the international system can and often does have a significant impact upon both prospects for and the relative success of *differing* development strategies, let us focus initially on the most fundamental link—that between domestic development strategies and opportunities for those who are living in extreme poverty.

PREVIOUS DEVELOPMENT STRATEGIES

In an effort to capsulize approximately 10 years of academic controversy in a few paragraphs, the following generalizations are offered without further apology for their considerable lack of appropriate qualification.[14]

In most countries of the South, the general development strategies of the 1950s and 1960s emphasized—and therefore place their incentives on—limiting consumption, raising savings and investment rates as rapidly as possible, investing heavily in the protected modern industrial sector of the economy, and con-

---

[14]Those interested in more detailed analyses of the issues raised so briefly here are advised to consult the following works and the literature cited therein: H. Chenery et al., *Redistribution with Growth*, Oxford University Press for the World Bank, New York, 1974; Irma Adelman and Cynthia Morris, *Economic Growth and Social Equity in Developing Countries*, Stanford University Press, Stanford, Calif., 1973; and John W. Mellor, *The New Economics of Growth*, Cornell University Press, Ithaca, N.Y., 1976.

centrating government expenditures on "economic" rather than "social" overhead projects such as education, health, housing, and sanitation. They did so on the assumption that this approach to development would ensure rapid economic growth, the benefits of which would in turn "trickle down" to the entire population in the form of growing per capita income. The costs to the poorest 40 percent of the population in many countries that followed this general pattern of development strategies have now become fairly clear. In a very significant number of countries, not only have the *relative* incomes and standards of living of this group decreased, sometimes markedly, but considerable evidence suggests that the *absolute* incomes of the bottom 10 to 20 percent have fallen in a sizable number of countries.

The reason that the trickle-down strategy has produced such distributional results in cases where it has also achieved commendable aggregate growth rates—for example, in Mexico, where the average annual growth rate has exceeded 6 percent in real terms for over 30 years—can be partially understood when one identifies the constituents of the forgotten 40 percent. The overwhelming majority of this large poverty group is rural in origin, composed of landless rural laborers or subsistence farm families. In the developing world as a whole, these rural groups constitute over 70 percent of the poverty population. Obviously, a strategy of economic development that concentrates tax structures, commercial policies, and public expenditures on the development of a modern, capital-intensive industrial sector does nothing of a *direct* nature to increase the development prospect for the rural poor. Trickle-down policies will affect such groups only as increased employment in the modern industrial sector absorbs surplus labor (thus creating a situation in which rural wages may be expected to rise) and increases the urban demand for agricultural production. (The latter may also have the effect of raising rural wages and employment *unless* capital-intensive modes of agricultural production limit the use of rural labor and increase the concentration of landholding to the detriment of the country's smallest agricultural producers.) Much evidence suggests that in developing countries following the trickle-down strategy, agriculture has become both larger in scale and more capital-intensive, contributing directly to the falling relative incomes and rising unemployment of the rural poverty groups. Demographic trends, of course, have added substantially to the magnitude of the problem.

The impact of the standard trickle-down strategy has produced similarly equivocal, if not detrimental, results for urban poverty groups—the unemployed, the underemployed, and the self-employed in the service sector and in the traditional labor-intensive manufacturing sector. The concentrated rewards to both capital and labor in the protected capital-intensive industrial sector— resulting from limited competition, skewed prices of the factors of production favoring capital-intensive modes of production (despite average unemployment and underemployment rates of more than 30 percent), and the development of a "labor aristocracy" within modern industries—have prevented the anticipated rapid absorption of the urban unemployed and the drawing down of excess labor reserves from the rural areas. These outcomes have thus severely limited the capacity of the modern industrial sector to perform the function required for trickle-down to benefit an entire population.

In sum, the standard development strategy of the past two decades emphasized rapidly increased investment and employment in the modern capital-intensive sector of industry financed by the savings from that sector's newly generated income and often by net flows from the agricultural sector. Agricultural concerns were generally limited to the production of commercial crops to feed urban populations and earn foreign exchange. The explicit or implicit premise of this general approach to development was that it would produce significantly higher rates of savings and investment than any alternative mix of strategies and that the growth of the modern manufacturing sector would eventually ease whatever unemployment problems were developing in rural areas and traditional urban sectors as a result of the concentration of incentives in the modern industrial sector.

Even in countries where this policy approach has succeeded in aggregate growth terms, it has more often than not failed by most equity measures for several reasons. First, and in many ways foremost, with only a few exceptions, rates of growth in employment in the modern industrial sector have been very disappointing. In some countries they have exceeded population growth rates, but not by enough to limit rising rates of urban and rural unemployment. In many other countries, labor absorption in the modern sector has hardly done more than keep pace with population growth.

A second reason, intimately related to the first, is that living conditions in rural areas have often deteriorated for landless laborers and subsistence farmers. A policy that concentrated rewards almost exclusively in the modern industrial sector (and, to a degree, in commercial agriculture), without producing high rates of labor absorption in that sector, tended to contribute to a steady deterioration of living standards for these two rural groups. Only a fairly comprehensive strategy of rural development—as in the case of Taiwan, for example—would have been likely to produce different results. Without such a strategy, conditions for the poorest segments in rural areas were bound to deteriorate, if only because rural population growth rates in the developing countries have averaged close to 2.5 percent annually.

A third indicator of failure is that the urban poor—the unemployed and major segments of the service and traditional manufacturing sectors—have benefited little from the trickle-down approach. In simplified terms, the major reason has been that while output per worker has grown faster in the modern than in the traditional sector, employment in the modern sector has not grown significantly as a proportion of the total labor force. Contributing to this phenomenon have been the emerging political power of unionized labor and the resort to capital-intensive technology in the modern industrial sector, and inappropriate government policies (e.g., subsidized credit, overvalued exchange rates for capital-goods imports, and high degrees of protection) that encouraged such development. Thus the traditional manufacturing and service sectors have also paid a price, in terms of relative deprivation, for the standard trickle-down strategy.[15]

[15] See Mellor, *New Economics of Growth*, for evidence on this point.

THE EMERGENCE OF NEW DEVELOPMENT STRATEGIES

The overall results of this general trickle-down approach to development have led a growing number of governments, economists, and aid practitioners to examine alternative policies in the past several years. While it would certainly be an exaggeration to suggest that anything approaching unanimity exists concerning the major ingredients of a new approach, it is possible to suggest that a consensus seems to be emerging on several issues that might well alter the conceptual as well as the operational content of development policies.

In highly simplified terms, one can say that the newly emerging approach—which attempts to maximize productive employment as well as growth—comprises four major ingredients: (1) a strategy for rural development, (2) a strategy for industrial development, (3) a "human resource" strategy for training and education, and (4) a strategy for population stabilization.

A strategy for rural development designed to meet the goals of increased employment, reduction of extreme poverty, and greater equity in income distribution would ideally entail (a) significant changes in land tenure, (b) greater access to agricultural production inputs in addition to land, (c) increased expenditures on rural public works projects, (d) assistance to rural-based, labor-intensive manufacturing, and (e) increasing rural access to health and educational facilities. In many countries, land reform is both the key to the success of new rural development strategies and their most formidable political obstacle.[16]

Like its rural counterpart, refined strategies for industrial development would attempt to achieve two related goals: to overcome some of the past deficiencies of excessively rewarding growth in the modern industrial sector, and to undertake a new set of policies to increase employment in the traditional urban

[16]Country by country, the less opportunity for land reform exists, the more attention must be focused on labor-intensive manufacturing activity. For a description of the twin focus on increased employment and production in both agriculture and labor-intensive manufacturing in rural areas, see Mellor, *New Economics of Growth*.

sectors and gradually transfer some assets to the poor in order to improve their longer-term life chances. It now seems generally agreed that in all but the most exceptional developing countries, continued reliance on a capital-intensive expansion of the modern industrial sector to solve the urban poverty problem will produce disappointing results. Skepticism concerning the capacity of the modern sector to absorb the already excessive urban labor force is based on present rapid rates of urbanization, the small share of the modern industrial sector in total urban employment, and the generally limited opportunities for job creation through modern-sector growth.

A good deal of thinking is now being devoted to the general question of human resource development. The emphasis is on the provision of adequate levels of education (formal, informal, on-the-job training, and so forth), nutrition, and health care to enable entire populations—both men and women—to contribute to economic development within a policy framework that is geared to providing increasing numbers of productive job opportunities. The rural and urban strategies noted previously are essentially designed to expand employment opportunities; both sets of strategies imply increased access by the poor in all areas of the country to primary education and health facilities, with greater emphasis on preventive medicine, postnatal care, and nutrition. The provision of such facilities creates jobs in the initial construction phase. Moreover, the completed facilities themselves are part of the asset-transfer process whereby the poor develop an enhanced capacity to increase their standard of living by their own efforts and rise above extreme poverty levels. It is worth underscoring this point by noting the conclusion of a recent World Bank study:

The design of a poverty-oriented strategy requires the selection of a mix of policy instruments that can reach the target groups that have been identified. While we advocate maximum use of instruments that operate through factor and product markets, often they will not be sufficient for this purpose. We have therefore given particular attention to a range of direct measures, such as land reform, the distribution of education, and other public services, and measures to redistribute assets toward the poverty groups. Without such a redistribution of at least the increments of capital formation, other distributive measures are not likely to have a lasting impact on the poverty problem.[17]

The reason for including efforts to achieve population stabilization in the new development perspective goes well beyond the demonstrated demand for birth control facilities. Some proponents are primarily concerned about the ecological capacity of the globe to absorb population increases, which at present rates double the world's population every 35 years (or, more dramatically stated, lead to a sevenfold increase over a century). Others are more specifically concerned with the effect of high population growth rates on the poorest strata of the population in the developing world; a labor force growing faster than employment opportunities in most developing countries leads to lower wages, increasing unemployment, greater fragmentation of minuscule agricultural landholdings, increasing numbers of landless rural laborers, and lower social expenditure (on a per capita basis) for basic health and educational facilities for the poor. Finally, there are those who emphasize a more subtle argument: that high birthrates in developing countries are a *reflection* of poverty and exaggerated income inequality and that birthrates will fall as a consequence of the successful implementation of the other development strategies sketched above.

Thus the four major elements in these alternative strategies of economic development close the circle. Proponents of these strategies believe that a new mix of policies and policy priorities can produce much greater productive employment and thus attack the absolute poverty problem with much more success than was achieved in the 1950s and 1960s—but with little sacrifice in rates of economic growth. From this analysis flow logical policy prescriptions for coping with the problems of rural and urban poverty and unemployment (though with significant allowance for specific problems in different countries). Inherent in such prescriptions are efforts to slowly redistribute incremental assets to the poorest strata of society, providing them with access to long-term benefits from continued economic growth. Among such proposed assets transfers are health and

[17]Chenery et al., *Redistribution with Growth*, p. xvii.

educational infrastructure expenditures to bring to the poor those forms of health and nutritional care, family planning services, and education most relevant to their needs; in most cases these are the least expensive forms, for example, preventive medicine via paramedics and primary rather than secondary and college education. Finally, the creation of more jobs, rising levels of literacy, and health standards that lower infant mortality rates are perceived to lead to changing views on optimal family size and to gradually lowering fertility rates among the target groups of the new strategy.

BASIC HUMAN NEEDS AS A
SPECIFIC DEVELOPMENT GOAL

Not all the thinking and research about new development strategies (or altered mixes of strategies, e.g., emphasis on labor-intensive forms of agricultural and industrial production, on production for domestic markets and for foreign markets, etc.) has incorporated an explicit basic human needs goal. But most of it does so either indirectly in attempting to alleviate the unemployment/underemployment problem in developing countries, or more directly in attempting to reduce present inqualities in the distribution income and wealth. Within the past two years, however, an increasing amount of work has focused specifically upon the problem of designing and implementing a basic human needs (BHN) approach with the goal of eliminating absolute poverty within the next quarter-century. In this sense a basic human needs strategy—for example, the approach being examined and developed by the World Bank—is not so much an alternative to employment-oriented strategies or redistribution-with-growth strategies as an extension or variant of the same genre of development economics. Only if the objective of meeting basic human needs becomes the *exclusive* short-term goal of a country would a conflict necessarily develop between a BHN strategy on the one hand and the other new developmental approaches focusing on a more equitable mix of employment, income distribution, and economic growth.

Serious work on the BHN approach undertaken thus far suggests that many conceptual and operational hurdles must be cleared before it can be presented with the necessary degree of concreteness in any single country, let alone the very large and divergent group of countries generally labeled "developing." Assuming that the *concept* of basic human needs can be defined—e.g., what are they, and who isn't receiving them—many crucial operational issues remain. Among the most important are the following:

1. Designing public services so that they actually benefit the target populations—i.e., the absolute-poverty groups

2. Directing social change and establishing institutions to ensure the poor a place and voice in maintaining the services they need (agricultural extension and infrastructure facilities, health and educational facilities)

3. Producing the domestic and external resources required for the financing of a BHN program in any country

The first problem is the economist's classic "leakage" problem. How can one design a rural development program that assures that the benefits of new technologies and other agricultural inputs (fertilizers, water, pesticides, etc.) actually reach the target populations? Experience throughout the world suggests that the best designed programs can and will be subverted by regional and local sociopolitical systems and power structures that drain the benefits from such programs for middle- and upper-income landowners and merchants, accomplishing little if anything for the poorest strata of society.

Thus the second operational problem noted above: Can systems of social change be adopted as part of a BHN program that would involve the poor and minimize the leakage problem?

Finally, there remains the strictly financial problem. If all the other conceptual and operational hurdles to the acceptance of major ingredients of a BHN strategy could be overcome in any number of countries, can the financial hurdle also be overcome? The strictly financial cost to a country of implementing such a strategy will depend upon many variables: the percentage of its population that is below the absolute-poverty line; the extent of the reforms necessary to achieve set targets (how much land reform, change in factor pricing, new infrastructure); the room for maneuver allowed by contesting interest groups, etc. These and many other factors will determine the speed and degree with which any individual government can move toward the adoption of a BHN strategy. And all will have a financial as well as a sociopolitical aspect. The less the apparent cost to middle- and upper-income and status groups is, the easier the introduction of a BHN approach will be.

What might be the cost run for achieving the basic human needs goals outlined above? One sentence will be allowed for numbers, since the present state of research on the topic merits no more. Let it simply be stated that two estimates resulting from different approaches and (possibly questionable) methodologies suggest that absolute poverty could be virtually ended within 10 to 15 years at a cost of $125 billion (in 1973 dollars) and that an asset-transfer policy to assure the forgotten 40 percent of a firm floor above that poverty level in the future might cost approximately $250 billion.[18] Assuming, for the purpose of argument, that a consensus could be reached on the operational characteristics of a program to eliminate absolute poverty along the lines of the new development strategies outlined above, one crucial political question becomes, Who pays the piper—the developing countries themselves, the Northern countries concerned (if only normatively) with the problem, or some combination of the two? *If* there were an absolute minimum of leakage and *if* the available estimates are at all meaningful, we are talking about an annual cost of $10 billion to $13 billion per year (in constant dollars) for the next 15 to 25 years, depending on the actual goals set. A glance at the latest figure of $13.6 billion for the annual flow of official development assistance from the member states of OECD's Development Assistance Committee (DAC) shows

[18]See Mahbub ul Haq, *The Poverty Curtain*, Columbia University Press, New York, 1976, and Chenery et al., *Redistribution with Growth*.

that such assistance alone could more than cover the cost of implementing the basic human needs approach described if the great portion of it were devoted to this objective and if the above conditions were met. This is a very big if, considering that over 50 percent of official development assistance (ODA) is presently being allocated to middle-income countries and for programs unrelated to the goals of the basic human needs approach.

It is also obvious that the same achievements theoretically could be financed from within the developing countries without any North-South transfer whatsoever. The World Bank has estimated that a 2 percent annual transfer from the upper classes to the bottom 40 percent of the populations of the developing countries could successfully finance both the short-term and the long-term goals of the strategy over a 25-year period.

Two percent of annual developing-country GNP today approximates $10 billion. Stated this way, the annual transfer sounds manageable. It sounds less manageable when one considers that 2 percent of GNP is equal to 10 to 20 percent of total government revenues in most developing countries. In order to transfer that 2 percent to the poor via new investment programs, either taxes (or other forms of government revenue) would have to be significantly raised or major cutbacks would have to be made in present government programs. The adoption of either course would guarantee dissent of varying proportions from those domestic groups currently favored by tax profiles and government-expenditure programs.

The *domestic* asset-transfer strategy seems even less practicable in the case of the poorest countries. In these countries, where per capita incomes average about $150 (at official exchange-rate terms, which produce misleadingly low dollar figures), the changes in tax and expenditure programs needed to eliminate absolute poverty within 25 years would be far greater than those implied in the preceding discussion of aggregate developing-country averages.

Thus the basic human needs approach inevitably arrives at the political constraint that confronts any ambitious attack on poverty. In this context, it is worth quoting the reaction of an authority on India's development problems and policies to the proposed strategy mix in the World Bank-sponsored study noted above:

The problems of poverty in India remain intractable, not because redistribution objectives were inadequately considered in the planning models, nor because the general policies of the kind prescribed in this volume were not attempted. . . . The major constraint is rooted in the power realities of a political system dominated by a complex constellation of forces representing rich farmers, big business, and the so-called petite bourgeoisie, including the unionized workers of the organized sector. In such a context, it is touchingly naive not to anticipate the failure of asset distribution policies or the appropriation by the rich of a disproportionate share of the benefits of public investment.[19]

One rather obvious conclusion following from the above considerations is that the likelihood of a major movement within a large number of developing countries toward the comprehensive development strategy outlined earlier may depend *very significantly* upon the degree to which the world's developed countries share the costs, thereby easing the political constraints on such an approach. Is it realistic to expect such cost sharing to be forthcoming in the foreseeable future?

Other major feasibility issues must also be considered as one weighs the advantages against the disadvantages of proposing the adoption of a basic human needs strategy. In addition to the question of financing, the following major obstacles are posed: (1) the potential opposition of most Southern elite groups (for reasons so compellingly analyzed by Fagen), (2) the potential opposition by many Northern elite groups (also considered in passing by Fagen), (3) the intervention issue—the strong Southern opposition to "guidance" and "oversight" of their development programs and performances by Northern donor governments or international organizations (an issue touched on at several points in Díaz's essay), and (4) the "human rights" issue. Finally, it should be remembered that the *capacity* to actually put into operation a basic human needs strategy of development of the type analyzed above, which has been assumed for the

[19] Pranab K. Bardhan, in Chenery et al., *Redistribution with Growth*, p. 261.

purpose of exploring various aspects of the approach, has itself been subject to question. There is considerable concern about whether the institutions, values, and human resources needed to make an attack on absolute poverty succeed, exist in many of the developing countries.[20] One might, for example, conclude that Fishlow believes that more can be accomplished to ease the basic human needs problem of the world's poorest billion within his own more familiar and tested policy framework than through the introduction of a complex and generally untested set of policies targeted specifically on the low-end poor.

While space precludes a detailed examination of each of these feasibility constraints, a very brief examination of them may serve to suggest that given the changing parameters of international politics in the present decade, the probabilities against the successful launching of a basic human needs strategy within many developing countries are not as overwhelming as is sometimes suggested. It may also serve to indicate that Díaz's and Fagen's concerns about the inability or unwillingness of the North to participate actively in such a strategy (*without* hidden motives of limiting Southern autonomy) may be overstated.

Is the approach feasible financially? If the admittedly "back of the envelope" calculations that have been undertaken to date are at least suggestive of orders of magnitude (although one must admit that the methodologies employed are not very encouraging), a program to provide all the world's people with minimum standards of nutrition, health care, and education might be purchased within 15 to 25 years at a cost of $10 billion to $13 billion per year. As noted above, official development assistance from DAC countries already exceeds this figure. How much of present assistance could be switched to the financing of an internationally accepted basic human needs strategy? Surely many countries, including the United States, would continue to spend some of these funds on other programs of aid to countries in which they

[20]However, critics often ignore the fact that one aspect of a basic human needs strategy would be the development of the human skills necessary to organize and administer such a program. After all, we *are* examining a strategy that, given a 15 to 20-year life span, is as much a *process* as a *goal achievement* exercise.

had other than basic human needs interests. Let us then assume that the North is to pay most of the bill and that half of the present ODA funds could be allocated to a basic human needs program. The *additional cost* might then come to $7 billion to $10 billion per year for 15 to 25 years. Are amounts of that magnitude feasible? Four points suggest that if other pieces of the North-South puzzle were to fall into place, this figure would not be impossible to reach. First, that additional amount would already be available if the DAC countries alone were allocating to foreign assistance the 0.7 percent of GNP figure accepted by most of them as part of the international strategy for the Second UN Development Decade. Second, if agreement were reached internationally on such a strategy, one could expect an additional contribution from some of the OPEC countries with adequate financial liquidity. Third, the strategy is one that is most likely to continue to draw support from Northern legislative bodies. Increasingly over the past decade, those legislatures have attempted to target aid funds to programs and projects that had an immediate impact upon the poorer segments of developing-country populations. A basic human needs strategy—if properly devised and implemented—would be fully consonant with those expressed wishes of developed-country legislatures. And finally, support for such an approach among a still small but influential segment of Northern elites has grown sharply within the past five years. The briefest look at the outpouring of writings from such groups as the Club of Rome, the Aspen Institute, the Dag Hammarskjold Foundation, the World Bank, and even the International Labour Organisation should convince the most skeptical observer that a changing perception of development problems, international equity, and—to use a favored phrase of the day—the *global problématique* has rapidly developed within many Northern elite groups, all supportive of a global basic human needs approach.

Many skeptics would argue that the greatest hurdle to the adoption of basic human needs strategies within most developing countries is not the financial question and the potential role of Northern financial contributions but rather the unwillingness of developing-country elite groups to accept and implement such a strategy regardless of where the financial support might come from. Will these elites ever accept and implement a set of policies which, in the medium to long term, may reduce their socioeconomic status, political power, and relative economic position— even if these reductions are slow and incremental? Many observers have strong doubts. The *dependencia* school of analysis would deny the possibility, as would many Northern and Southern observers of different persuasions. One distinguished Southern analyst, Mahbub ul Haq, makes the point emphatically:

Fundamental institutional reforms are, in fact, the essence of new development strategies. At the heart of these reforms is a change in the existing control over the means of production and access to key services. Normally, the rich exercise enormous economic power within these systems because they control most of the means of production in the society, such as land and capital. That is why land reforms and public ownership of major industries have become the key elements in any institutional reforms. But these reforms can easily become a whitewash, and have, in many societies. Unless there is the necessary political will, it is impossible to change the established relationship between the owners of the means of production and those who have been perpetually denied these resources. What normally happens in many societies is that the governments nationalize a number of industries, banks, and some key services, like education and health, and they place these industries and public services in the hands of the bureaucrats or the same interest groups as before. It is not surprising, therefore, that these reforms amount to mere tokenism and not any real restructuring of society. This is really what has happened in a good part of South Asia, where the bureaucracy or the landlords or the industrialists have readily and enthusiastically embraced all the symbols and slogans of socialism.[21]

Haq adds the obvious point that it may take entirely new political alliances to implement basic human needs strategies in these countries, and ends by noting that the restructuring of economic and political power needed to implement the policy at the local level "cannot happen without a mass movement or a popular revolution." Even if Haq's analysis of the requirements

[21]ul Haq, *The Poverty Curtain*, p. 67.

may be overstated, the problem he poses cannot be dismissed without risking a global charade at the expense of the poorest people in the South and the taxpayers in the North, and feeding growing domestic and international cynicism about all economic assistance programs negotiated by governing elites, North *and* South.

Yet when one examines the Southern elite problem carefully, one again finds more room to maneuver than might have been the case as recently as 1970. First, there is a growing awareness within most developing countries of the magnitude and the seriousness of the absolute poverty problem. Until the past five years the eventual capacity of the trickle-down approach to overcome absolute poverty conditions was seldom questioned. Southern governing elites were for the most part following models suggested by good neoclassical economists. Second, as the magnitude of the problem grows, so do the potential sociopolitical dangers to many Southern elite groups of failing to respond directly to it—not with oppressive political tactics but with positive economic programs. With population growth rates in developing countries averaging close to 3 percent per year, with open and disguised unemployment rates running from 25 percent upward, with increasing international constraints on rapid growth, and with governing institutions exhibiting serious weaknesses in many developing countries, the prospects increase that governing elites and their allies may well reconsider former opposition to policies that would direct more benefits to the low-end poor.

How would an "average" developing country respond to a major OECD initiative that included significant new funding? Fourth World governments—i.e., the very poor nations—unless they have chosen extreme self-reliance, could not help being interested in the prospects of access to a very significant increase in desperately needed foreign exchange and resources on a scale well above what would be available to them through domestic tax reforms. Unless the performance criteria and the degree of intervention tied to the use of these funds were so ethnocentrically and ostentatiously Northern as to be unbearable, negotiations might begin rather quickly.

As for Third World countries, consider the following case. An elite group has presided over 40 years of steady growth in a country that, among developing countries, is highly industrialized. The elite group's politics are highly institutionalized, and it faces no serious organized political opposition. Yet despite the country's growth performance, the forgotten 40 percent of its population living in poverty is relatively, if not absolutely, worse off than four decades ago. Birthrates are close to 3 percent, unemployment exceeds 25 percent, and for the first time in decades, the political system shows signs of fragility. How would the governing elite of this developing country react to the possibility of a significant new source of foreign exchange to help finance programs it has been promising to its constituents and gradually attempting to implement?

Reviewing Fagen's essay, one is tempted to suggest—though with at least a modest amount of doubt—the following dichotomy: if an elite feels itself to be in firm control and is unconcerned about potential sociopolitical disruptions from the bottom deciles of the society, then a basic human needs approach would face a serious Southern elite problem. Such an elite is unlikely to adopt programs deliberately aimed at fostering the welfare of the poorer members of its society. But what if the elite (itself increasingly disparate because of the very process of development) is feeling less and less certain of its position and sees that a restructuring of some significant government spending programs and fiscal incentives might provide access to substantial international funding (and, not incidentally, an extended lease on its own privileged position)? In the latter case, the Southern elite problem *may* prove to be less of a constraint on the adoption of a global basic human needs strategy than many observers have suggested.

There are reasons to believe that in the time frame of the 1980s Project, the Northern elite problem may also be somewhat overestimated. Let us assume that many Northern business groups will prefer (highly profitable) "business as usual" policies vis-à-vis the South and will shy away from any global "poverty program" for both ideological and self-interested reasons. What seems to be changing are the views of many other segments of Northern elite groups. These include not only members of the

247

organizations, noted above, who support the basic human needs approach (the Club of Rome, the Aspen Institute, etc.) and appear to give the highest priority to their own versions of the global equity issue; they also include non-equity-oriented segments of Northern elites, whose major concerns focus on such practical issues as population control, environmental problems, and potential resource scarcities. To cite but one example, George Ball's support for what comes close to a basic human needs strategy is rooted in his feeling that only such an approach can effectively begin to slow global population growth rates.[22] What I am suggesting is that a growing segment of a heterogeneous Northern elite group, for many different reasons and from many different value perspectives, may converge on the proposition that a global basic human needs strategy is congruent with their goals for a moderate international order in the next 10 to 20 years. And whatever their concerns, they will not be of the cold war security type that produced support among similar groups for the Alliance for Progress. To this extent, at least, Díaz's analogy to the Alliance is overdrawn.

The intervention issue may remain one of the major obstacles that the basic human needs strategy will have to overcome. If such a strategy is not administered in a way that *assures* that the target populations do in fact receive the benefits promised, the program (like many domestic poverty programs) will fail. Most of the financial assistance will be skimmed off by those (ranging from major political figures to petty local bureaucrats and landlords) who control the political, economic, and social points of leverage in developing countries. On the other hand, *if* an administrative scheme or organization is devised which is truly capable of monitoring program performance, most developing countries are at least initially likely to refuse to allow the degree of intervention in domestic affairs necessary to carry out a valid monitoring function. Is there any way to avoid choosing between the serious leakage effects that would accompany an unmonitored program on the one hand—thus preventing per-

[22]George W. Ball, *Diplomacy for a Crowded World: An American Foreign Policy*, Little, Brown, Boston, 1976.

manent structural improvement in the position of the absolute poverty population—and the opposition of Southern states to a professional monitoring program on the other?

The resolution of the intervention issue most probably would necessitate the disbursement of funds and performance monitoring by some (new?) international institution, perhaps with links to the technical and administrative capabilities of the World Bank. If a North-South negotiation on the other quid pro quos—many noted in Fishlow's and Díaz's essays—were to succeed, the need for a highly qualified, specialized, and neutral agency still would seem essential to any basic human needs bargain. The psychological importance of such an agency can hardly be overestimated. For if the developing countries were to allow some of their sovereignty to be diluted by international monitoring procedures, it would be important for the North to make the same type of concession by giving up the unilateral right to make the allocation decisions. Could this Northern concession of sovereignty be achieved? During the course of several years of planning and negotiation, I certainly do not find the idea beyond the realm of the possible. The issue would, quite probably, be decided by the tenor and outcome of an entire set of North-South negotiations rather than on the basis of the proclaimed merits of the basic human needs issue alone.

Finally, there is the human rights issue which is bound to be linked to the development and implementation of any basic human needs strategy. The strategy is nothing if not one that focuses on the basic socioeconomic needs of individuals. In this sense it is non-state-centric in the extreme; its entire raison d'être is permanently to elevate the living conditions and life chances of the poorest segments of all developing-country populations. With its emphasis on asset transfers or asset accumulation in the form of educational, health, and other production-specific benefits for the poorest, it is a policy that, without ever saying so, begins to put some flesh on the skeleton of the second half of the UN's Universal Declaration of Human Rights. It is in this latter section that the socioeconomic human rights insisted on by the less developed countries found their way into the Universal Declaration. It is in this section that one finds the following types of concepts: the right to a standard of living adequate for the health and well-being of individuals and families; the right to security in the event of unemployment, sickness, or disability; and the access to economic, social, and cultural rights indispensable for dignity and the free development of personality.

If the North were willing to extend substantial financial support at the global level for an effort of this kind, might not that very strategy offer an opportunity to bridge the widening chasm between developed and developing countries on the issue of human rights in its broadest sense? At the present time the North (and especially the United States since the advent of the Carter administration) has pressed vigorously for universal recognition of those human rights found in the first half of the Universal Declaration: political, legal, and civil rights that are rooted in the evolution of Western civilization. But this concentration on one segment of human rights, no matter how important, may prove to be counterproductive even in the narrowest sense of expanding the acceptance of those cherished Western values and norms.

If, on the other hand, Northern countries were jointly to advocate and make a substantial financial contribution to those *economic* human rights (needs) of the poorest in the developing countries, they would then be in a far better position to draw those countries into a serious discussion of *political* human rights, which seem to be of greatest importance to the developed countries. For the first time since the signing of the Universal Declaration, progress might be made at the global level specifically *because* Northern and Southern human rights concepts would be linked both programmatically and conceptually.

Doubtless, those who warn that the raising of the human rights issue will exacerbate North-South tensions in the short to medium term are correct. But if a basic human needs strategy should be forthcoming, that issue may prove to be not only less exacerbating than anticipated but also a potential building block for a new and more truly global set of universal norms—shaky as they may seem at first. In a normative exercise like the 1980s Project, the probabilities of such an outcome, even if fairly modest, cannot be overlooked. This is especially the case if one feels that the human rights issue cannot be exorcised from North-

South relations in any case. For then one's choice is reduced to making the best of, and not avoiding, a difficult situation. Present United States governmental leadership, a sizable contingent within Congress, and major segments of Northern elites appear to feel increasingly committed to affirmative actions on the issue of human rights. The choice then may be slowly narrowed to two courses of action: (1) push Western concepts of human rights to the point of alienating many developing-country regimes, while eventually being forced to make "security" exceptions for needed "allies" or (2) attempt to strike a wider bargain on the human rights questions by redefining the concept itself to include both halves of the Universal Declarations of Human Rights. In the latter instance it would be far easier for many developing-country governments to enter into serious discussions on new international norms of behavior because what they tend to view as "Western cultural imperialism" would have been substantially vitiated by the broadened definition of human rights and by a set of proposals to address the issue of basic human needs.[23]

[23]Further discussion of the human rights issue can be found in a forthcoming 1980s Project volume by Jorge Domínguez et al., to be published for the Council on Foreign Relations by McGraw-Hill, New York. The author wishes to express his appreciation to Professor Domínguez for several stimulating conversations on this general set of issues.

THREE

Conclusion

My personal opinion is that if the OECD countries *were* to act as a group and *were* by 1980 prepared to pledge a figure anywhere near $20 billion per year to a basic human needs program, one could anticipate the beginnings of a very serious negotiation. All the analytical, definitional, and operational problems would remain to be resolved, as would such matters as the nature of the international agency chosen to disburse the funds and measure performance. But serious negotiation would have begun—and with it, one hopes, a joint effort to establish a delicate balance between domestic sovereignty and international oversight.

Were Fishlow, Díaz, or Fagen evaluating this basic human needs strategy, they would undoubtedly find many reasons— analytical, empirical, and normative—for skepticism with regard to the implications for policy prescriptions. Fishlow might suggest that too little empirical or analytical work has been done to merit putting much faith (or many resources) into a basic human needs strategy. He would also undoubtedly argue that if his own prescriptions were implemented in both North and South, the problems of the low-end poor would soon disappear as global comparative advantage began to open productive employment opportunities for today's absolute poverty groups.

Díaz would undoubtedly remain equally concerned about the potential slips—intentional or otherwise—between a "noble" idea and the policy process that is likely to end by betraying it given the forces at work in the international political economy.

His value preference would most probably still rest on a system "safe for selectivity" and freed from the interventionist possibilities of a basic human needs strategy.

And Fagen would probably doubt seriously that Fishlow's proposals will ever be implemented in a way that satisfactorily addressed the internal equity question; that, indeed, is the major theme of his entire essay. But surely Fagen would also be skeptical of the view that the North would ever agree with the South on a global scheme for addressing the absolute poverty problem in a serious manner. Bandaids maybe; serious surgery no.

I could end this essay with the disclaimer that I included the discussion of a basic human needs strategy simply to acquaint the reader with a theme of more than a little topical interest at the present moment in North-South relations. This would be disingenuous. I have included this analysis because it reveals my own idiosyncratic ordering of value preferences. In simplest terms, I would like to see such work on basic human needs become a major addition to Fishlow's set of reforms. I do not view this effort as conflicting with his proposals at all; to the contrary, I believe it is wholly congruent with them in the longer term if properly put into operation.

Whether adding this baggage to Fishlow's suggested reforms is likely to doom both packages or increase the probabilities that both are accepted is a difficult question to answer. A priori, I find little reason to believe that the coupling of the two approaches weakens the attractiveness or the feasibility of either, and I suspect that in the 1980s Project's time frame, the linking may actually *enhance* the probabilities of the acceptance of Fishlow's proposals within the North. Whether it will have the same effect in the South will probably depend on the gradual shaping of North-South relations in the coming years.

Selected Bibliography

Amin, Samir, *Accumulation on a World Scale; A Critique of the Theory of Underdevelopment,* Monthly Review Press, New York and London, 1974.

Bergsten, C. Fred, "The Threat from the Third World," *Foreign Policy,* no. 11, Summer 1973, pp. 102-124.

_____, "The Response to the Third World," *Foreign Policy,* no. 17, Winter 1974-75, pp. 2–34.

Bhagwati, J. (ed.), *Proposals for a New International Economic Order,* M.I.T. Press, Cambridge, Mass., forthcoming.

Cardoso, Fernando H., "Associated-Dependent Development: Theoretical and Political Implications," chap. 5 in A. Stepan (ed.), *Authoritarian Brazil: Origins, Policies and Future,* Yale University Press, New Haven, Conn., 1973.

Chenery, H., et al., *Redistribution with Growth,* Oxford University Press, New York, 1974.

Cohen, Benjamin J., *The Question of Imperialism: The Political Economy of Dominance and Dependence,* Basic Books, New York, 1973.

Dos Santos, Theotonio, "The Structure of Dependence," *American Economic Review,* vol. 60, no. 2, May 1970, pp. 231-236.

Erb, Guy, and Kalleb, Valeriana (eds.), *Beyond Dependency,* Praeger Publishers, Inc., New York, 1975.

Hansen, Roger D., "The Political Economy of North-South Relations: How Much Change?" *International Organization,* vol. 29, no. 4, Autumn 1975.

_____, et al., *The U.S. and World Development: Agenda for Action, 1976,* Praeger Publishers, Inc., New York, 1976.

Haq, Mahbub ul, *The Poverty Curtain,* Columbia University Press, New York, 1976.

Helleiner, Gerald K. (ed.), *A World Divided: The Less Developed Countries in the International Economy,* Cambridge University Press, New York, 1975.

Hymer, S., and Resnick, S., "International Trade and Uneven Development," in J. Bhagwati et al. (eds.), *Trade, Balance of Payments and Growth,* North Holland Publishing Co., Amsterdam, 1971.

International Labor Organization, *Employment, Growth and Basic Needs: A One-World Problem*, Praeger for the International Labor Organization, New York, 1977.

Johnson, D. Gale, *World Food Problems and Prospects*, Foreign Affairs Study 20, American Enterprise Institute, Washington, D.C., 1974.

Leff, Nathaniel, "The New Economic Order—Bad Economics, Worse Politics," *Foreign Policy*, no. 24, Fall 1976, pp. 216-217.

Schachter, Oscar, *Sharing the World's Resources*, Columbia University Press, New York, 1977.

Tucker, Robert W., *The Inequality of Nations*, Basic Books, New York, 1977.

Wriggins, W. Howard, and Adler-Karlsson, Gunnar, *Reducing Global Inequities*, McGraw-Hill for the Council on Foreign Relations, New York, 1978.

Index

257

About the Authors

ALBERT FISHLOW is professor of economics at the University of California, Berkeley. He received his Ph.D. in economics from Harvard in 1963 and is the author of numerous articles and two books on American economic history and Latin American economic development, especially concerning Brazil. These contributions to the field of economics have earned him professional awards. In 1972–1973 Mr. Fishlow received a Guggenheim award and was visiting fellow at All Souls College, Oxford. More recently he has turned his attention to foreign economic policy, serving as Deputy Assistant Secretary of State for Inter-American Affairs in 1975–1976 and currently as a member of the editorial board of *Foreign Policy*. He is a member of the Council on Foreign Relations.

CARLOS F. DÍAZ-ALEJANDRO is professor of economics at Yale University. He was born in Havana, Cuba, in July 1937 and has been living in the United States since 1953. Since obtaining his Ph.D. from MIT in 1961, he has taught at the University of Minnesota and Yale. His publications include books and articles on international trade and the economic development of Latin American countries.

RICHARD R. FAGEN is professor of political science at Stanford University. He has also taught in Mexico and Chile. He has been a fellow at the Center for Advanced Study in the Behavioral Sciences as well as the recipient of research awards from the Ford, Rockefeller, and National Science foundations. During 1975 he served as president of the Latin American Studies Association, and he is the author or co-author of seven books and many articles.

ROGER D. HANSEN is the Jacob Blaustein Professor of International Organization at the Johns Hopkins School of Advanced International Studies. He was formerly a senior fellow of the 1980s Project at the Council on Foreign Relations. He has also been a senior staff member of the National Security Council and a senior fellow of the Overseas Development Council. His publications include books on Mexican and Central American economic development and numerous articles on global distribution of income, North-South relations, and relations between the United States and Latin America.